Upper Apartment for Rent, Cheap

My Journey to Freedom and Ultralight Backpacking

By Carol "Brawny" Wellman

Edited by David "Rainmaker" Mauldin

May all your trails be light
- Carol "Brawny" Wellman

ISBN 0-9728154-0-6

Library of Congress Control Number 2003090087

Dedication

I dedicate this work to women everywhere, in every land, who, like me have struggled, are struggling now, and will continue to struggle for self-determination and respect. And to David "Rainmaker" Mauldin, for his confidence in my journey, and through all my faltering, instilling the courage to press forward.

Acknowledgments

To the many friends who have requested a compilation of what I have done, and what I know about ultralight techniques, I extend my sincere gratitude.

To the leadership of the fundamentalist church I attended in Illinois, who abandoned me at the onset of this journey, my sincere appreciation for their rejection, thus kindling the spirit of defiance and resolve.

And above all, I wish to thank David Mauldin for his extensive support in all my endeavors, particularly this manuscript. My deepest respect, and admiration for all the skills he possesses, and patiently taught me.

Disclaimer

Everything printed herein is true, although many of the names have been changed to protect the guilty. Techniques described are based solely upon my experiences and observations, and no responsibility for their results or the failure thereof are suggested, implied, or accepted. Each person who leaves home, especially venturing into the backcountry, takes their health and well being into their own hands.

These three subjects normally are placed on separate pages. In the true ultralight spirit, they have been grouped here to save weight.

Chapter One

The First Time/ River to River Trail

It started to rain during the night, a steady drizzle on the tarp. I figured they would be okay, the two of them in a dome tent. Drifting in and out of sleep, I finally became aware of the storm brewing. We had to get packed up soon, and off this bluff before the thunder and lightning rolled. It's amazing what kids can do when they think their lives are in danger. And besides, this was an Adventure, an adventure for all of us. It was our first time ever backpacking.

I'll take the blame for all the gear choices. Two years ago, standing at a gas station in Stanley, Idaho I saw this older guy come walking in. Shirtless, tanned to a fine bronze, long and lean, he had a very confident, secure look in those piercing eyes. And he had strength, that aura of personal strength. He came down out of those mountains, alone. I guess he was dirty. Was he? All I can remember is the awe that a man might come down out of those mountains. Alone. He seemed unaware of us Tourists. I was hooked.

"Get everything in your packs before you come out of your tent, okay guys?" I called over.

Nothing. "Hey, are you guys awake? We need to get down off this bluff before the thunder rolls."

Rumbling in the skies, stirring in that cheap K-mart tent. "Where's the door? Hey, Mom, where's the door?" Josh cried sleepily.

Kids! I crawled out of the bug screen from under my tiny tarp. Wearing a rain poncho, I came to investigate. During the night, between the two of them, they had rolled, tossed and turned, until the dome, not staked down, had worked itself over on its side. Now, they lay on the zippered door. Laughing, I encouraged them both to move over; they inched to one side. I reached under the tent and started to unzip it. They took over. Extracting themselves, we finally got packed up. Breakfast was whatever they could find in their food bag, while the rain dripped down our ponchos that dreary morning.

Josh led the way. All we had to do was follow the blue rectangular blazes on the River-to-River trail. We headed east, towards Garden of the Gods. It was late March and there were no bugs. That was the reason for coming down from Chicago-land so soon. There was water, and plenty of it. Christine followed her brother. I could see them ahead, as we wound our way through those trees just barely starting to bud. I wanted them to enjoy this. They were the reason I could come at all. It was our home-school field trip. Suffocating in a church where women had no power, I learned to work the system. Manipulation. I hated that word, but it was the honest truth. If I could convince my husband something was for the kid's sake, and they wanted to do it, then I had a chance.

I had two cross-country ski poles for hiking sticks. My hands were getting wet and cold, quite cold. The water started running down my long sleeve thermal underwear top, eventually becoming wet up to my shoulders. I didn't feel too warm. I looked ahead. They still hiked. Something in their forms scared me though. They seemed to shrink into their ponchos. Those ponchos! It covered their heads with a hood. The back came over their small homemade packs and stopped just above where their sleeping bags were cinched on. They kept their arms tucked inside, but the side vents allowed water to get in, anyway. Every step following them, racking my brain for a solution, fearing the dreaded hypothermia we hear so much about, I wondered just what the outcome would be. What book knowledge would help me now?

As we crossed streams, I looked into their eyes. They weren't talking much. Weird. Just plodding onward, eastward. As we approached Garden of the Gods, overhanging rock appeared. "Hey, let's stop and get out of the rain awhile, get a snack, okay, guys?"

"Yeah…" that's all. Yeah. Finding some rocks, we perched and watched the drenching rain continue to fall. Josh did some exploring, but basically we sat and ate one candy bar apiece. Don't eat them all! Boredom began to creep in, and they were getting colder.

"So," I suggested, "let's hike some more, that should warm us up."

Their clothes were damp, their long sleeves wet and their packs soaking up water where it dripped off those ponchos. I can't believe we took ponchos. That's what everyone said to take. Everyone I chatted with online in the hiking chat room. Ponchos and hiking poles. Never again.

We hiked a couple more hours. Finally, we skirted a deep cave with wood piled in the back of it. God bless whoever thought of that. "Hey, lunch time. Time to stop." We made a roaring white-man's fire. As the area warmed, we took off layers of clothing, hung them on sticks over the fire and dried out everything. We cooked soup, then ramen noodles and ventured out just long enough to haul in replacement wood. They started laughing, talking. What a relief, the signs of hypothermia were gone.

The rest of the trip was an adventure, but to this day, that's the key phrase "Remember the time we found that cave and had a huge fire?"

It takes a measure of misery to make memories.

During those three nights and four days, we saw more deer than humans. Hawks and falcons soared overhead. Cries of wild animals filled the night, while raccoons threatened to rob us of our food. We trudged through trenches of mud and clay, while rivers of water ran down the deeply eroded trail. Horses, we learned, were the cause of that. I loved it all, and wanted more.

The Sawtooth Mountains of Idaho

I realized then he meant it. There would be no more backpacking, no mountains or alpine lakes. No challenging terrains and adrenalin rushes. I must return to the façade of mindless Christian contentment. Our marriage had been crumbling for many years. We preserved the family name with charades and endless posturing. To survive emotionally, I had learned the fine art of withdrawal and avoidance.

After the trip to southern Illinois with two children, backpacking on the River-to-River Trail, all I could think of was another chance to hike into the backcountry. My husband finally agreed to a short backpacking trip in the Sawtooth Mountains of Idaho.

Although I knew it was part of his pacification strategy towards me, I was elated. This time I would do better. Our gear would be more protective from the elements. The itinerary called for parking at the trailhead, hiking 26 miles to Red Fish Resort, then meeting my married daughter and her husband. They would bring their mule, loaded for the journey back along the same trail. This would not be redundant. Coming from the Midwest, all mountains were spectacular, and the alpine reaches a marvel.

That bright morning the two of us headed out. The flowers were blooming and a cool breeze softened the summer sun's rays. A sign at the trailhead warned of a mother black bear and her cubs ahead. I had never seen a bear in the wild. This was scary. They kill people, don't they? We hiked along, not talking much. He apparently was not enjoying it, out of shape and not appreciating the climbs. Somehow, it seemed a weight dragged on my heart. We camped in a lovely spot that night, getting water out of a lake, cooking a simple meal. A recurring thought plagued me, that although not alone, there was no companionship.

The next day we arrived at the resort and camped along the gravel road. That evening I washed clothes, took a shower, and discarded everything I didn't use those first two days. My pack still weighed over 30 pounds, with only 2 days of food. My half of the tent was nearly 3 pounds. My sleeping bag was another 3. The cooking system was an archaic system of paraffin and wick, melted together in an empty tuna fish can.

My husband surprised me by saying that the next day he would load the mule with everything he had been carrying except the camera. If the mule could not take his load or he had to carry anything else besides the camera, he would not hike. Instead, he would just drive our son-in-law's

7

truck around to the pick-up point to meet the rest of us. That confirmed my gut feeling and dread.

My daughter Charity and her husband Paul arrived as planned the next day with my teenage son, John. He was packed and ready to carry most of his own gear. The mule was loaded with about 70 pounds of various things. We headed out. Paul, bringing the mule, was delayed and took a wrong side trail. My husband's, Charity's and Paul's gear were on the mule. I carried only half a tent. John had half his tent and his gear, but no water bottles. His water bottles were on the mule, too. My husband rode the ferry 5 miles across the lake to shorten his journey. He had the camera and met us. The four of us stood there on the trail, realizing two couldn't hike further because they had no gear. I softly suggested, "Can John and I continue to the pick-up point, and you all catch up if the mule arrives? If the mule doesn't get here, you have to return to the resort, right? You could meet us tomorrow by driving the truck around to the trailhead."

Reluctantly, permission was granted, and John and I set off. Wow, what freedom! What luxury. I was the master of my experience. Then, the sobering realization that I must take care of my son, there, in bear country, enhanced the thrill of adventure. It was up to me to find acceptable water, navigate, and call a halt for the evening. I had half a tent. He had a part of a smaller tent; the other part was on the mule. Together we would rig something for both of us. Marvelous. I love these challenges.

Paul realized his error, backtracked and finally caught up to the others. The three of them caught up to us at a mountain lake where John and I had stopped to camp for the night. I retrieved the other half of my tent, and set it up properly. Somehow, in some minute way, a fierce determination crept in. Never again would I carry only half a tent. I would never allow myself to depend on anyone again. And, a feeling grew, later to be defined as the disgust at self-imposed weakness.

We hiked out the next day. Never did see a bear. And then he told me. Not any more. No wife of his was going tramping all over the countryside. He didn't like to do it, so that was settled. What self-respecting husband would put up with that, he demanded.

You can't make anyone like backpacking. But what if you love it? The chasm grew wider in an already unspanable void, two people growing in opposite directions.

A Lot to Learn

Those two trips showed me that I had a lot to learn. I was carrying car camping gear on backpacking trips. It was heavy and not really effective nor efficient. I had a small flashlight, changes of clothes, a big freestanding tent, and an inexpensive, heavy sleeping bag. The cooking system mimicked a campfire. It was sooty, messy, heavy, and time consuming. I carried extra paraphernalia that was never even touched. I loved thinking about the self-sufficiency; power and adventure of trail life. Sadly the realization struck; I was going nowhere. All the gear I created and sewed would do me no good. My life was caged in by the doctrine of a male dominated, fundamentalist church, locked in by a loveless marriage to a man demanding I give up my interests. If you give up your interests and passions, then you give up your identity.

His decision was final, no more backpacking for me. Obey, or be thrown out. I thought that the cage holding me was only physical. If I quit attending that church and the lock of marriage was broken, the door would open and I could go free. But the cage had been built for 25 years, bar by bar, firmly cemented into a foundation of fear and guilt. It would take over 5,000 trail miles and three years to break down most of them.

Transition

My husband issued a list of ultimatums, limiting my freedom and personal choices even more. He planned to sell the car he had given me, and keep the money himself. All the clothes that I wore and all videos I wanted to see would be subject to his approval. I must quit the job I had just found, and have no personal money. I could not go on existing like this. The will to live had drained away, just as my identity had. When I wouldn't agree to his terms, the line was drawn, and he coerced me to leave the family home "for the children's sake". He felt I was corrupting our children. I blame the church leadership for much of this heartache. The rejection, lies, and isolation they encouraged from my friends and children will never be forgotten.

Several months after my divorce, I moved to the mountains of Georgia. I was hired immediately by a hospital as a full time cook. Rainmaker and I had met in a hiking-oriented Internet chat room previously. When he extended the invitation to accompany him for his second year's hike on the Pacific Crest Trail in 2000, I accepted without hesitation. The previous year, 1999, he hiked from the Mexican border, just south of Campo, California, to Sonora Pass, California. He would resume at Sonora Pass in the High Sierra in July, and reach Crater Lake by mid September. Here was the opportunity of a lifetime. Rainmaker was incredibly experienced, and I expected to learn a great deal. I got much more than I bargained for.

Chapter Two

Pacific Crest Trail 2000

David "Rainmaker" Mauldin thru-hiked the Appalachian Trail in 1992. His journey was 2,162 miles, and lasted seven and a half months. One evening he suggested, "You should write down why you want to do this. Some people think it's all about fun. Then, when it quits being fun, they go home."

At first I resisted, thinking, "I have no clue. Why does there have to be a reason? Why does it need an explanation?" But, because of my great respect for him, I took a lot of time to think it over, pondering the purpose while earning enough money cooking at a hospital. Finally, in February 2000, I wrote this:

Wondering

Modern life seems so soft, in a physical sense.
A person could live their whole existence on this earth
Without ever breaking into a sweat,
Without ever needing to use every inch and fiber of their being.
Without ever tasting a physical struggle, defeat, or conquest.
Or ever making a conscious decision to live.

I guess that's what my purpose in pursuing these trails is,
to use and explore every inch and fiber
of myself, of my world.
Pressing to the outer limits of my abilities,
and when I have been there, to press further.
Wondering if what I am will serve.

Hoping to realize that what I am has served.

There is a line in the movie Ben Hur.
In the hull of the slave galley,
where the men are chained to their oars,
the captain of the ship warns them,
"You are here to serve this ship. Row well, and live."
That line always runs through my mind when I think of my body.
It is here to serve my purposes.
I feed it, and allow it rest,
but I chain it to my will.

Some athletes have that sort of attitude.
The record setters.
Not content with what has been done.
Looking to push the limits.
Asking their body for more.

Survival, in extreme conditions has always fascinated me.
It takes an indomitable spirit.
Willingness to do whatever it takes, and never say die.
There are stories of men and women eating ants,
bark, cadavers, and sled teams.
Reports of coming back from nowhere,
when given up weeks earlier as dead.

People improvising shelters and clothing, living and surviving.
Forcing their bodies on,
though in pain and agony.
It's not fun.
It's not a good time.
It's life with the minimum of resources.
But I think it then becomes
the ultimate experience.

So I am wondering.

Wondering what every mountaintop will feel like.
Wondering what each valley will hold.
Wondering what it will be like to ask my whole being
to surrender to the primitiveness of self-reliance.
I am not going alone this time,
but it is my responsibility to hike the miles, and survive.
I am not afraid.
It takes a measure of misery to make memories.

I think I will love it all.

Until then I will be wondering.

It took a lot of emotional energy to write those lines. They come back to me unexpectedly during difficult times on the trail. Pressing the outer limits of my abilities, and when I have done that, to press further. It amazes me what inner strength can be summoned, and I am forced to wonder, are there really any limits?

As I started assembling my gear for this two-month journey I soon realized Rainmaker would have to be asked for his advice. He never boasts or brags and his wealth of knowledge is not revealed unless requested. He has hiked the European Alps solo, forced to stay in his tent for three days while stranded by a snowstorm, reading by candlelight, listening to the avalanches nearby. He has cooked supper in Denali Park, Alaska, while watching a pair of grizzlies playing and roughhousing just a hundred and fifty yards away. All over Europe and the United States, Rainmaker has gathered a wealth of knowledge. He will share it willingly, but only if I asked.

My gear for this first long journey finally assembled, included: A North Face synthetic, youth sleeping bag, rated for 20 degrees which weighed 2 pounds, and a Z-rest sleeping pad, cut to a length of 36 inches, weighed 8 ounces.

Rainmaker showed me his esbit stove, and I bought one just like it. It uses solid fuel tablets, and is the size of a stack of playing cards. Twenty-four hexamine tablets, a lighter, some matches, a 20-ounce capacity aluminum pot with lid (found at a garage sale), aluminum foil windscreen, plastic cup and spoon together weighed in at 16 ounces. That was my cooking system.

To carry water I used four 32-ounce capacity plastic soda bottles (6 ounces) and one 20-ounce capacity plastic sports bottle (1 ounce).

My external backpack weighed 2 pounds, 14 ounces and my silnylon pack cover weighed 2 ounces.

The Murphy bag (basically a repair kit), and medical bag were 8 ounces. It included a pack pin and ring, safety pins, electrical tape, needle and thread, a couple rubber bands, Imodium (anti-diarrhea tablets), sunscreen, Ibuprofen, Neosporin, a one ounce bottle of rubbing alcohol, and cotton balls.

My personal hygiene kit with toothbrush, toothpaste, dental floss, lotion, comb, toilet paper and trowel weighed 6 ounces.

Tyvek ground cloth, and aluminum stakes together weighed 17 ounces. The tyvek was my part of the shelter that we brought. The new, two-person tent I made, the Lakota, weighed 2 pounds, 2 ounces. Rainmaker carried it.

The Lakota tent Rainmaker and I designed together. It has a 5x7 foot floor, a front and rear vestibule, and Velcro closures. There is over 30 feet of Velcro on this ultralight tent. It was our home for 9 weeks.

The clothes I brought included a pair of full-length Lycra pants, and some nylon shorts for town weighing 11 ounces (for both). I had two pairs of 100% nylon socks, a pair of heavy socks, undergarments, and nylon scarf all weighing only 6 ounces total. I carried three shirts, a 100% silk long sleeve shirt for 3 ounces, another 100% polyester sports-shirt that also weighed 3 ounces, and a pullover sweater (30% wool, 70% acrylic) that weighed 8 ounces. I felt well prepared.

Some kid size, knit, stretch gloves; a pair of waterproof gloves used for kitchen work, a balaclava, and small fleece mittens weighed about 5 ounces. My sandals were a whopping 7 ounces. I made some silnylon gaiters that registered 1 ounce on the scale. I had a blue rain jacket, black rain pants, and a mosquito head net. Combined weight was 11 ounces.

I started the hike wearing tights, 100% nylon shorts, nylon socks, and Jordache long sleeve shirt totaling 14 ounces. My broad brimmed cap weighed 2 ounces. I left Sonora Pass carrying a fanny pack, with a compass, mosquito repellent, and a disposable camera. That weighed 8 ounces. Some anti-bacterial towelettes and a bandana were 8 more ounces. Then, my hiking poles were 18 ounces, and my ice ax, a gift from Rainmaker, another 18 ounces. The Photon light, a spring-loaded utility knife and cord were the last ounce. Total weight for all of this was 17 pounds, 10 ounces.

I was very proud of this pack weight at the time. Everything listed seemed essential. I give Rainmaker much credit for allowing me to learn gently, without forcing any of his ways on me. He taught by example and never by sermons.

Sonora Pass to Sierra City/ Getting the Hang of It

On July 6, 2000 Rainmaker and I began our drive to Sonora Pass, California. We drove 27 hours straight, taking turns at the wheel. Finally leaving Kansas, we stopped the following morning in Limon, Colorado. We looked forward to twenty-three hours of rest in a motel. There was no use wearing ourselves out on the road driving, when we had an 800-mile hike ahead of us.

The beautiful panorama of Colorado was breathtaking. All across the western horizon, distant snowcapped mountains loomed. That fantastic scenery along the highway would soon be our daily bread. We spent Saturday night at a motel in Salina, Utah, and arrived at my sister's house around 8 p.m. Sunday. We visited a couple days there, then along with her family, drove to Sonora Pass and camped Thursday night. After an extremely windy night, Rainmaker and I packed up, kissed my sister and nieces goodbye, shook hands with my dear brother-in-law and headed out at 7:00 a.m. It was scary. Did I have everything I would need for the next week? There were no towns to use as bail out points before we reached Echo Lake, seventy-six trail miles away. Did I know Rainmaker well enough to hike with him, alone, into the wilderness? This first morning he looked quite fearsome, with a quiet, determined demeanor. He reminded me of that man I saw hike down alone from the mountains in Idaho, so strong, so self-sufficient. He didn't need me to survive, but I sure needed him.

Sonora Pass northward in July is the most beautiful flower garden, with every color, size, and shape clustered in artistic arrangements. With a backdrop of 10,000 ft. mountains we crossed two snowy sections of trail. If necessary, we would use our ice axes. I had so much to look at, and think about, it was totally incredible. I felt like a country girl visiting New York City for the first time.

There was abundant water, many runoffs from snowmelt, a couple rivers and a lake. In some places, the trail went straight up a snowfield or crossed a river. I finally concluded that it was not necessary to carry 2-3 quarts of water at all times. The scenery exceeded my greatest expectations. I was hooked. Words couldn't describe the splendor, photography can't capture it, and a video camera would fail miserably. I marveled at the extremes, a huge mountain, and yet a skinny narrow treadway winding up and over it. The incongruity of massive snowfields and acres of delicate flowers thriving nearby. The incredibly wild and unpredictable environment, yet the wonderful ambience of being home.

Just before stopping one day, we worked our way down some treacherous trail. The PCT is nothing to play around with. A misstep could be fatal. I saw Rainmaker ahead of me, and thought, what a paradox. Here we were in a wild, unforgiving place, with wind, heat, snow, narrow loose trail, and enormous blowdowns. Then, here was a man, prepared to meet it all with just what's on his back, and he's comfortable with this. Astounding. That evening, David found a campsite nestled just above a wide stream, swollen with snowmelt. He taught me that in the evenings, when you cross water, you will generally find a camp site that has been used previously, if you look hard enough. Someone before us had this same need, and if we looked diligently, we might avail ourselves of their labor.

We generally slept with our food in our tent, prepared to defend it, reasoning that the bears here were wild and unaccustomed to people. Hunting in season was permitted, keeping the wildlife skittish. We averaged 14 miles a day. Later that first week, though, a sudden thunderstorm kept us pinned down under the shelter of a stand of tall pines for a couple hours. We hiked a modest 13 miles, but were satisfied just to be alive.

I learned so much. Rainmaker would give lessons periodically on maps and navigation: how to decipher topography maps, coordinate them with the guide book, and then take readings with the compass set with the proper declination. The ability to match the blue contour lines in the book with the mountains surrounding us on the trail seemed to be a magical gift. One day, I hoped to possess it.

Another day we hiked for over an hour on a narrow, loose, rocky ledge along a mountain ridge 1000 feet above Blue Lake. The gale force winds made it very difficult to breath, much less make progress. We both managed to keep our hats, which were tightly cinched with chin cords sewn on before leaving home.

Let nobody tell you it's summer there. I wore all the clothes I brought just about every night. I slept in a 20-degree synthetic bag. Rainmaker wore thermal underwear, a balaclava, fleece hat, and rain parka. We sat in our sleeping bags while cooking outside.

Each morning we woke about 6 a.m. and cooked our breakfasts, each on our own stove. By 7:30 we were packed and on the trail. After a couple hours hiking we took a snack break. Then, around noon we would stop for an hour lunch break. Three hours after resuming, we would take an afternoon snack break. By 5 pm we were looking for a campsite large enough for our tent, preferably with water close by. The Lakota was light, but it required a lengthy tent site. It measured, with its vestibules on either end, 12 feet long and 5 feet wide. We could sit up in it, and enter and exit without climbing over each other. Rainmaker had a tent zipper fail in the High Sierra the previous year, so he requested that for this new tent we use Velcro closures. The amount of Velcro on that first tent I made was incredible. There was over 30 feet of both hook and loop strips. It was my first experience sewing with silnylon, and a bigger project than I anticipated. Both front and back screen doors, and front and back silnylon storm doors had Velcro on the vertical sides. If the hook strips would contact the screen, it was very difficult to remove without ripping the screen. If a portion of the front Velcro became attached to some portion of the back door Velcro, once stuffed into its storage sack, it became a bundle of confusion. The entire tent was gray, which made it was very hard to tell the floor from the canopy when the Velcro was all tangled. To rectify this technical problem I learned that when taking it down in the mornings, all of the Velcro had to be completely matched in its proper position in order to identify its parts when pulling it from its stuff sack in the evenings.

The first week nearly over, our food bags almost empty, we happily hiked into Echo Lake Resort. From there we hitched into South Lake Tahoe. This would be my first resupply ever. I had no idea then how unusual it was to have such a large town for our convenience. Resupplying for 106 miles is quite an endeavor. We estimated it would take 8 days on the trail. Cooking separately was much easier for us than trying to negotiate what to have for meals and snacks. This section I opted for SUGAR! Last section I had mixed nuts, granola, and beef jerky, all high fat, but low sugar. All the things the books say you need. This time I gave into complex and simple carbohydrates. It seemed that's what my body craved.

The following directions I wrote in my journal on how to resupply food:
1. Find a decent grocery store and/or a Big K.
2. Buy everything you're craving, think you might crave, looks good and is cheap.
3. Carry it "home".
4. Dump onto your bed all food leftover from last week's section.
5. Dump all the food you just bought onto the bed.
6. Groan, grimace and swear!
7. Remove all excess packing, piling into, covering and burying what is commonly referred to as a "waste basket".
8. Condense various foodstuffs into plastic zip lock bags, placing them into stuff sacks. Nibbles are allowed.
9. Shuffle backpack contents over and over till this mass fits and is reasonably stable for carrying through the Wilderness.

We mailed home our ice axes, my gaiters, a pair of socks, journal pages and a few other non-essential things. I was anxious to get back to the peace and solitude of the mountains. Rainmaker, pleased that I chose to resupply and get back on the trail, admitted he'd had some doubt about whether I would commit to another section. It seemed I was starting to get the hang of this. We were really weighed down with food for the 106 miles to Sierra City, making the inevitable climb out of town into the mountains laborious. Not knowing what new adventures lay ahead was incredible. Thankfully, I no longer felt so bewildered by the data book.

This section offered opportunities to cool off in ice-cold lakes during lunch breaks. We met a lot of weekenders, Forest Service workers and thru-hikers. My opinion of long distance hikers had grown. All those I met (up to that point) were intelligent, articulate, and very kind. I suppose I officially joined their ranks, having resupplied and recommitted myself to this wonderful wilderness experience.

We each had our aches and pains, but that is the nature of a long hike. It became normal to wake up stiff, hobble around for a while, and then pack up. Once hiking, the stiffness dissipated, but injuries would flare up. Rainmaker and I have concurred that on the trail; "What don't kill you, hurts like hell!"

It was great how quickly we lost track of the days and numbers on a calendar. Concerning dates, the only difference it made to us was the possibility of seeing a lot of weekenders or if we would get to the post office in time to pick up our much needed drop/bounce boxes. Besides our hexamine (fuel) tablets, they held various medicines, vitamins, laundry powder, guide pages, writing paper, aluminum foil for new windscreens, zip lock bags, sun block, spare gloves, tent stakes, postal tape, bandanas and most importantly, instant coffee.

Standards changed. It used to bother me if anything was in my drinking or cooking water. Now I just thought in terms of parts per million. However, I refused to drink anything looking at me from inside my water bottle. Hiking clothes were washed in streams whenever possible. In the extreme heat of the day, I would strip my shirt off, rinse it in the cold stream, and redress, right on trail. Obviously, the wildness of a long distance hiker was seeping into me, and the contrivances of civilization were falling away.

My first live wild bear encounter happened during our lunch break at a wooden bridge spanning a creek. We had left our packs leaning against a nearby tree, washed in the water without soap and ate while sitting on the bridge. I heard a loud crash in the woods but said nothing, thinking, like a city girl would, that kids were tearing around out there. After lunch we went to get our packs and heard more crashing. Rainmaker looked at me and said, "I think it's a bear." Craning my head around the trail to see, not 50 ft. from us, a bear was doing the same. It was startling to see this cinnamon colored creature; he appeared comical with his curiosity and reminded me of a Disney character. Rainmaker had put his pack on already and commanded, "Carol, get your pack on." Then we stood watching the bear. Suddenly, he started walking down the trail towards us. Rainmaker calmly moved off to the left and I followed close behind him, frightened at the bear's direct approach. He picked up some rocks, so I grabbed a big one, too. The bear swerved to the left, then Rainmaker moved back on the trail. We watched as the bear ambled off into the woods, then Rainmaker told me, "I think he's been cut loose from his mother recently and he's not doing well. He is looking for something to eat." I remembered the trout we saw swimming in our lunchtime creek and hoped he would catch some.

We hiked into the little town of Sierra City, population 228. There we ate supper at a nice restaurant and reserved 2 nights in Sierra Buttes Hotel, reputedly a brothel in the old days. This town's only store proved a more challenging resupply, with its tiny deli and shelf selection. I bought candy, pop tarts, bagels, and ramen. A hiker box sat on a bench outside the store; Rainmaker told me I could take anything out of it I wanted. It had stuff other hikers left for that purpose, either not wanting to carry it, or being superfluous drop box items. Rather than throwing supplies away, a small cardboard box was found and labeled for the benefit of other hikers. This was right up my alley. I rummaged through the contents and from the box selected a jar of peanut butter for my bagels, and some powdered drink mix.

Rainmaker used a long plastic toolbox for his "bounce box". It started out weighing about 19 pounds. He shipped it parcel post, insured. I used a "drop box", a small cardboard box, shipped only once and containing supplies I anticipated needing at that point. There were 2 more bounce boxes sent to me by my sister farther up the trail. My first box weighed around 3 ½ pounds, and was uninsured. Rainmaker was able to shift through his entire inventory, choosing what he needed and bounce the rest ahead. I had to buy stuff here, like a spray can of insect repellent, 20% Deet, that I wouldn't normally choose. Not thinking I would need another bottle of 100% Deet until farther up the trail, I put one in my next drop box! Rainmaker paid $1 more in postage than I did and saved money in these small towns. Next year I will definitely opt for a bounce box.

We found interesting things on the trail. The list included: several apples in various places (which we split and ate), a valid credit card (Keith, where are you??), $.49 (in various locations), Aloe lip sun block, rated SPF 30 and perfectly good, a wrapped piece of root beer barrel candy, and a large man's left tennis shoe next to the trail, with this note firmly attached: "For sale or rent. For more information, see One-Shoe-Pete at Switchback 95." Then later on, a nearly new, rolled up tent laying on top a rock next to the trail. We lifted the package, evaluated the situation, and decided that no way would we haul it the remaining 35 miles to Old Station to mail it home.

Crossing a stream in Lassen Park I found my magic trail spoon. It's best not to turn down gifts from the trail gods, or they will quit giving stuff to you. That same metal spoon has been with me on all my hikes. It is my only eating utensil.

In northern California, the trail changed so that lack of water became a daily issue. We hiked and camped through water alert zones, which meant trail with no water for at least 12.5 miles. Our eyes and ears become attuned to the gurgling sound of water, which I found is surprisingly similar to the sound of wind rustling leaves. The heat compounded the situation. I followed Rainmaker's example and carried my full capacity of 148 ounces of water. I also learned how to "tank up" by taking breaks at water sources, drinking as much as possible over the course of half an hour, and not leaving until I could hear my stomach sloshing. He taught me how ration water to the next sure source, and his method of dry camping. At times, trail angels left water caches. Many large caches have a notebook, or register where hikers write thank you notes, give advice, or say hello to friends. Some registers have a written note by the angel, stating how often they replenish the water. Trail etiquette teaches to take only two quarts, but at times the trail angel will encourage hikers to take more. One register, 11 miles into the Hat Creek Rim walk, had this observation, "No matter what you think about pickles, they are the only thing you can do with cucumbers." Another memorable statement, which has become a personal motto, said, "In the end, no one wins, and you find the race was only with yourself."

Rainmaker had a cut-down milk jug hanging from the back of his pack, having scavenged the milk jug from a trash receptacle in South Lake Tahoe. He used it to sponge bathe at night, weather and water supply permitting. I stubbornly adopted my own method of pouring liquid soap onto my camp towel, applying a couple tablespoons of water and dry cleaning myself. Both methods required very little water.

Our gear and clothes were forest green, brown, gray and black. Those colors are nearly undetectable, especially in shady areas. A study by researchers has shown that bright colors attract bears. They also infringe on the perceived solitude of others, and hinder stealth camping. The term "stealth camping" evokes all sorts of images. It simply means finding an unused spot, and being as close to invisible as possible. It has virtually no impact, visually, audibly, or physically. Stealth camping doesn't necessarily mean illegal camping. Sometimes it is done in the interest of safety, for instance if a person must camp near a road. Other times, it is to insure some privacy, or to get away from an obnoxious person.

As we approached northern California, there was a very strong cat urine odor, which reminded me of the lion's house at the zoo. We saw fresh Mountain Lion tracks, large prints and long strides. Several bears had come in close contact with us, including a mother and cub, a camp robber, and a night roamer. Bear and cat sign do not seem to cross one another's territories. This is also cattle country, and bovine odor and sign is very common, and not welcome.

That summer I wrote:

You know you've been on trail too long when things start eating their way out of your food bags instead of into them. Or when you classify plants according to how well they work as toilet paper. Or when you feel safer walking unarmed through lion country, than walking unarmed through small town (pop. 228) America. Or when stealth camping means hiding from people instead of bears. Or when you hear a car and can't identify its sound.

Important sources of information for the trail ahead are the various tracks and "sign", otherwise known as feces. From the first day we were hiking, I memorized Rainmaker's shoe prints (an enormous size 13, figure 8 with herringbone tread). Another hiker, who was just ahead of us, had a waffle pattern, "Well, it looks like Waffle Foot has taken this route. He must be deciphering this mess the same way we are." Sometimes close to the road, there'd be several interesting, well-traveled trails, and at the trail intersection all kinds of footprints, going around in circles probably saying like us, "Where in the hell is the PCT?" The Pacific Crest Trail is seldom labeled in the Sierra. Some sure signs you're on the PCT are: thru-hikers tread (memorized from past encounters), water bars, rock ducks, bike tracks (illegal), and plenty of horseshit. We noted bear sign, big cat sign, dog sign, dog-just-drank-sign, and Llama-dragging-its-traces sign. It is possible to tell which direction they're headed, what they've just eaten, and how big they are. This information can tell you if you're likely to meet them, how hungry they might be, and how likely you are to be eaten.

First priority upon reaching our nightly campsite was to clear a suitable spot for the Lakota tent. Rainmaker at the head end with both his hiking poles, I at the foot end with both of my hiking poles, would jointly set up our home for the night. It required both sets of hiking poles for the frame. Then, after the tent was done, we would go about our nightly preparations differently. Usually, I began heating water for coffee immediately. Rainmaker cleaned up and changed into his lounging clothes first. He made his coffee after dinner to enjoy with dessert. I ate dessert before and sometimes after dinner. The hard part was not to eat two or three day's worth of snacks while supper was cooking.

We both had mummy bags designed to fit persons one inch shorter than our actual heights. They're very narrow and lightweight. They are thought of as a garment, fitting snugly, rather than a bag that one might have room to roll around and change clothes in. Rainmaker climbed into his, and began stretching, shuffling, thrashing. Finally he pulled the hood up and zippered it shut. A sigh. The battle won this evening. I handled mine a little differently. I got in, bent my knees, pulled up the hood and zippered it shut. Then I stretched out, my feet pushing the limits to make room.

In the morning, I placed all my gear and food on my Z-rest, pulled it out sled style and found some random place to sit. Rainmaker would take 2-3 items at a time; place them neatly and methodically in place at the exact same tree he lounged at the night before. While I sat and sorted my chaos, my coffee was ready and steaming. Rainmaker calmly contemplated his organized assortment while his water came to a boil. We had most of the freedoms of solo hikers, and all the benefits of a partnership. Watching each other was a great source of entertainment. Although Rainmaker is so methodical, and I am so impulsive, both of us still achieved the same goals: fed, watered, bathed, rested, and ready to hike the next morning.

A sunrise is a gentle thing. Some say the color "explodes", but I find it requires patience to experience all the changes. There always is a magnificent sense of peace and privilege, of expectation and wonder, for no two sunrises are the same. As I contemplated the glorious skies from our crest site, I realized my life had changed just as spectacularly. I was learning to navigate, read the trail guide, and figure out the differences between a saddle, a crest, a north-facing-west-rising slope and a promontory knob. In order to finish the Pacific Crest Trail in Manning Park, Canada with Rainmaker next year I needed to hike those first 1,013 miles (that he'd hiked in 1999). Pondering the desert section, and the possibility of going alone, it was evident I could never have considered this previously. Lack of skills, financial dependency, reasonable and unreasonable fears and no personal freedom would have prevented it. But, just as I watched the rising sun in the eastern sky affect the entire western sky, I watched this journey affect my entire being. My life was unfolding like the colors before us. That thought was as beautiful as the sunrise, but a bit daunting as well, because it meant the whole day lay before me. What would I do with it?

Improvising becomes a fine art on a long hike. The better one becomes at this, the lighter the pack can be. September arrived and I was using all my clothes to stay warm at night. What was there for a pillow now?

My Journey to Freedom and Ultralight Backpacking

Ramen noodles, my journal, "powders bag" (coffee, powdered milk, hot cocoa, etc), stuff sack for tent, and empty zip lock bags placed in my clothes bag served quite well. It was easy to fall asleep after a full day of hiking. If the dry ramen was broken into bits, it wasn't too lumpy. During those cold nights I regretted cutting down my Z-rest. The insulation under my feet would have been quite welcome. When my hexamine fuel tablets ran low, I supplemented them with small bits of paper trash and cotton balls, which had been soaked in rubbing alcohol and used for hygienic purposes. I quit burning plastic candy wrappers, however, at Rainmaker's request.

Waking up before daylight, preparing breakfast and getting dressed in the cold had its drawbacks. As the days grew shorter and colder, we began looking forward to light fixtures, a furnace, coffee pot, our refrigerator stocked with delectable food, hot running water and soft things, like couches, carpeting and super-size cotton bath towels.

Rainmaker said he lost one bandana and a green Coolmax t-shirt, and if that was all, he was satisfied. I pondered this statement and concluded that all I lost were some illusions: The illusion I could do these 18- mile days without feeling it, the illusion that the nightmares from my past life would cease on the trail, and the illusion that I could ever "return" to a peopled and motorized society and be the same person I'd been.

Rainmaker and I finished our season's hike at Crater Lake, on September 15, 2000. During those two months we received trail magic, kindness from total strangers, cards and gifts sent to our post office drops. E-mails commending our progress came to my Yahoo account, which I read when I could get to a computer in trail towns. These tokens, which may seem small in everyday life, were so precious.

I came home planning to return to the Pacific Crest Trail the next spring.

Chapter Three

Pacific Crest Trail 2001/New Designs, Soloing

I had to wait seven months before resuming my journey on the Pacific Crest Trail. The first 1,013 miles would be solo. I had never done anything quite this extraordinary before. The actuality of it seemed so remote that plans were made with little fear or panic. That would set in later, as the time of departure drew near.

My tent, the Cherokee, weighed 19 ounces

My gear list from last year had to change. What I needed most was a lightweight solo tent. Everything that I learned when making and testing the Lakota was incorporated into a smaller tent, the Cherokee. Made of silnylon, and no-see-um mesh, it weighed an official 1 pound, 3.2 ounces on post office scales, and required 6 stakes. I used my hiking poles for the front frame, and a café curtain rod for the back pole. Velcro was used for the closures, but this time barely 4 yards of it. The tent was only 6 feet long, and 32 inches wide. I could sit up in it. With a small vestibule in the front, and a window in the back, I was quite proud of my new tent.

I built a "packless" system. Using the same backpack from last year, I removed the pack from the external frame. Then, specially made stuff sacks were strapped securely onto the frame. At first, it was very confusing as to what ditty bags went where. However, the system performed quite well once I became better organized during the actual hike. One of the features was a variable capacity. The pack system had sufficient space so I could carry enough food for 192 miles: Kennedy Meadows, up Mount Whitney and back, then over to Vermillion Valley. It took 10 days. When I entered the Sierra, the extra clothing and ice ax fit as well.

I started out with four silnylon sacks, but found that three larger ones were easier to manage. It was important to have the load evenly distributed horizontally. Each stuff sack had loops in the bottom and side seams. Because silnylon is so slippery, care had to be taken when cinching the bags tightly. If the gear inside slipped to the middle of the sack, the result would be a cinch strap working its way off the end, and not doing its job.

The first sack to be placed on the frame was the middle one. A closed cell pad was rolled up and placed horizontally in it, giving it a firm shape. Into this horizontal cylinder was placed a large black garbage bag, into which the sleeping bag was then stuffed. In the mouth of that sack was the Murphy kit, for repairs. This middle bag had fabric loops that fit over the vertical bars of the pack frame.

The top stuff sack was placed on the frame next, and cinched to the middle one. I usually kept my food in this stuff sack. In the mouth of the sack was my cook set, giving me easy access for cooking any time of the day. The bottom stuff sack was cinched through the loops, around the frame and to the middle sack. This bottom sack contained my clothes, hygiene kit, and tent. All sacks had draw cords that were clipped together to secure them, preventing their loss. Each of four water bottles had different carrying bags, cinched to the frame itself, one at each corner. This allowed me to carry five liters (using two 1.5 liter bottles, and two 1 liter bottles) of water comfortably in the desert. Some water was used from every bottle, on a rotation basis, to keep the load balanced.

The blue rain jacket from last year's hike was replaced by a more stealth appropriate gray silnylon rain/wind jacket. Instead of the cream colored polyester shirt, I took a black silk shirt. I used a bounce box, instead of drop boxes, which allowed me greater access and flexibility in changing gear and resupplying. The bounce box, a yellow plastic toolbox, was long enough to accommodate my ice ax, which had to be shipped to Kennedy Meadows, and then returned at Echo Lake.

I added a ¾ length, closed cell pad, because at that time I thought a good night's sleep on the trail was worth the 7 ounces. I kept my Z- rest from last year until I reached Sonora Pass. For a while, it was strapped on behind my back, using it for the back portion of a hip belt. The Z-rest became so flat and compressed that it was useless. At Sonora Pass, I placed it in a trash receptacle.

For the first 1,013 miles, I was solely responsible for arriving in one piece, which was a sobering concept. I carried the Pacific Crest Trail

Guide, the data book, and a new compass. The guidebook for California is over 400 pages long, so it was cut into sections, placed in the bounce box, and each section retrieved as needed. I burned all used guide pages as I hiked. At first, I also brought five bright blue ribbons, to mark any trail to an offsite camp. Because I am so directionally challenged, it seemed wise to mark a path back to the PCT from any campsite I used. In my heart, I carried all the knowledge Rainmaker taught me last year about navigation.

Gear List Before and After

I brought the same North Face 20 degree youth sleeping bag that weighted 2 pounds, with a Z-rest, cut to 36 inches (8 ounces) and a closed cell pad 48 inches long that weighed 7 ounces.

My single wall one-person tent, the Cherokee, with 8 stakes and guy lines weighed 1 pounds, 7 ounces.

The external pack (frame only) was 1 pound, 14 ounces. Its special stuff sacks and cinch straps added another 6 ounces, and I had a silnylon pack cover weighing 2 ounces.

At Kennedy Meadows, 697 miles from the Mexican Border, I bought an army blanket from the proprietor for two dollars. My sleeping bag just wasn't keeping me warm at high elevations. Heading north into the High Sierra in early June, my sleep system had to be supplemented. There on the deck of the Kennedy Meadows Store, I measured the blanket to the smallest size I could tolerate, cut it with my razor knife and sewed it with dental floss. That army wool bag liner weighed 2 pounds, 3 ounces. I mailed it home from Tuolumne Meadows as a keepsake. At end of the trail the sleeping bag was still with me, although I had Rainmaker bring my fleece liner for the last 800 miles. Some suggested that because it was a youth bag, it was of poorer quality than a full sized bag would have been.

I ditched the Z- rest, which had been abused to near uselessness. I sent the Cherokee tent home from Echo Lake Resort when Rainmaker arrived to meet me. We shared a Coleman Cobra tent that weighed 3 pounds, 10 ounces. We did not use a ground cloth, but shared the weight of the tent and accessories. I swapped out my packless frame system for a Nike day-and-a-half pack, in Bend Oregon, made some modifications and it weighed 21ounces. I then needed only two silnylon stuff sacks, which weighed a total of two ounces. The pack cover made the entire trail. It is still in good enough condition for another few thousand miles of hiking.

Clothing

I packed one pair of 100% nylon socks, one pair of fleece socks, one set of undergarments (for town use), and a nylon scarf, totaling 6 ounces.

A 100% silk long sleeve shirt with silk bottoms was 5 ounces, another 100% silk long sleeved button down shirt was 3 ounces.

For my warm layer, I brought an expedition weight Thermax top and midweight bottoms weighing 15 ounces, some knit stretch gloves, fleece mittens, and a balaclava adding another 4 ounces.

My silnylon rain jacket with mitts attached, silnylon rain pants, and mosquito head net came to 7 ounces.

After Rainmaker joined me and we hiked in Oregon, the climate changed to rainy and cold much of the time. I ended up with one pair of smart wool socks to sleep in, kept the silk set of long underwear and expedition set of long underwear. I ditched the button-down silk shirt in exchange for a fleece turtleneck and light bottoms to sleep in. I switched from fleece mittens to Thinsulate gloves. All this extra clothing increased my pack weight by over a pound and a half, but many cold days hiking and rainy nights sleeping I was thankful for every last stitch. The silnylon rain clothes and head net were kept to the end. Surprisingly, I needed the head net even into September.

I started the trail in my hiking clothes, a pair of 100% nylon shorts, nylon socks, and a sports top that weighed 7 ounces. My broad rimmed felt hat was 3 ounces. The Faded Glory Trail runners weighed 24 ounces. I always hike with telescoping hiking poles.

I wore the same pair of shorts the entire trip, as well as my sports top. I changed to Smart Wool socks and also needed new shoes in Mohave. I bought high tops, which finished out the last 1,400 miles. I also added a two-ounce pair of shower flip-flops, for wearing in town.

My Komperdell hiking poles with snow baskets weighed 18 ounces. They served as the frame for my tent. The Grivel Mont Blanc ice ax (shipped in my bounce box) was another 18 ounces. It has a safety leash, which is a specially made nylon leash, 3 feet long, for slipping the wrist through, and cinching tight. Should one go on a slide, the ax cannot be yanked from the hand because the leash firmly anchors the person to it. Also, my ax has a rubber head shield, to prevent injury if I fall on it while it is strapped to my pack. Of course, the shield is removed when the ax is needed. I sent the ice ax home, as well as the snow baskets at Echo Lake.

I carried two Photon LED lights, a red and a white. My round, spring-loaded utility knife, which I found in an office supply shop, weighed only 5 grams once the metal key ring was removed. I added a G.I.-style can opener and a whistle and threaded these items all on a cord. My watchband had broken in the desert, so I threaded the remaining leather strap and watch face onto the cord. This "tool kit" weighed just 1.5 ounces. I cut my camp towel down so it only was 3 ounces.

I kept all these tools for the duration of the hike, cut the camp towel down further, and used it as a bandana as well. I ditched the regular bandana.

Murphy Bag, a repair kit for what can go wrong, will, had electrical tape (wound around water bottles), a small spool of black thread and a needle, pin and ring (clevis pins) for the external frame pack, safety pins, and wire.

Once I bought my Nike pack in Bend Oregon, I no longer needed clevis pins or wire for pack repair. I stopped carrying thread and used dental floss instead, which is stronger.

Personal Hygiene Kit included a toothbrush, traveler's size toothpaste, floss, cotton balls, rubbing alcohol, Vaseline, tweezers, razor, mirror, and comb. I carried these items in a mesh ditty bag to keep my toothbrush fresher, and dry. All of this was 8 ounces and I kept it until the end of my hike.

First Aid / Chemicals Kit consisted of: Imodium, Ibuprofen, multi-vitamins, a small tube of Neosporin (antibacterial ointment), some mole skin, and chlorine carried for water treatment in a 2 ounce bottle. The weight varied, depending on how much was left. I got rid of the moleskin, used up the Neosporin and didn't bother to replenish, took all the vitamins and figured they weighed too much to bother with. However, I continued to use chlorine.

The Fanny Pack was for my disposable camera, current maps, compass, sunscreen, insect repellent, and lip balm. This weighed over a pound.

Later, the fanny pack was replaced with a tiny ditty bag hung from the hip belt. It was big enough for my camera, sunscreen, Deet and lip balm. Current maps went in my shorts pocket. Future maps were kept with my journal. I burned my old maps daily as supplemental cooking fuel.

I took the original outfit to the post office. The postal employee set it on her scale and it registered 12 pounds, 15.5 ounces. This was an improvement over last year's weight, and I was satisfied with it at the time. This was without the hiking poles, my shoes or ice ax. The ice ax was carried for only 390 miles.

I really don't know what my final base weight was. I was heavy on clothes and sleeping system, but had to work with it because I am a very cold sleeper and hate shivering. One thing I learned about sleeping bags, though. Never take an old worn out one on a long hike. Had I just paid the money and bought a better bag, I would have saved several pounds of weight, and slept warmer.

Bounce Box
The following contents were mailed General Delivery, to predetermined post offices. Things were added or removed on a regular basis, about every 250 miles, which included trail guide and data sheets for upcoming sections, socks, gloves, spare sunglasses, extra sunscreen, lip balm, 100% Deet (bug repellent), traveler's size toothpaste, petroleum jelly, liquid soap, vitamins, Imodium, Ibuprofen, instant coffee, pot scrubbers, gallon zip lock bags, aluminum foil for backup windscreens, hexamine tablets (solid fuel) razors, 4 ounces laundry soap, stamps, envelopes, journal paper, toilet paper, cotton balls, ice axe, and postal wrapping tape.

Departure and Reality
As the flight date of April 26, 2001 drew near, panic set in. Rainmaker called it "fantasy running headlong into reality." He told me it was normal, and that there was nothing out there I hadn't gone through before. Last year's hike had included high mountains, desert conditions, lost trail, wild animals and seclusion. There was nothing new, just more of it.

I didn't realize then how much of my gear was homemade. As a friend later remarked, "People on the trail compete just the same, but with less. You don't buy into that. I admire you." Never thought of it before. It takes a brave person to head out for five months on the trail with homemade gear as your lifeline. Brave enough to trust your designs and workmanship to the elements, brave enough to stand the skepticism of other hikers, brave enough to shun the ridicule of people still tethered to mainstream America. Looking back, I guess I was brave. At the time, it was my desire to have the lightest gear possible, which meant taking my small stature into consideration, and creating all the gear myself. Finances were an issue as well. I worked 6 months at my old cooking job to support this hike, and to continue a minimalist lifestyle.

Mexican Border to Kennedy Meadows
I kissed Rainmaker good-bye and boarded the plane for San Diego. Looking at him for the last time as I walked away, I felt totally numb and unable to comprehend the enormous adventure ahead. My tent, rain gear, and clothes, all irreplaceable, were carried on the plane in

silnylon stuff sacks. The pack frame and water bottles, zipped in a garment bag, were checked as baggage. A good friend picked me up at the airport in San Diego; I slept on his couch that night. At 5 a.m. he made breakfast for me, and we headed for the Mexican border.

We drove past several manned Border Patrol cars on the dusty road near the sleepy town of Campo. My friend Charlie drove right up to the monument. We got out of his sports vehicle, and walked up to the southern terminus of the Pacific Crest Trail. There was a formidable barbed wire fence, a barren stretch of land and a woman starting out on horseback. Photos were taken, good-bye hugs exchanged, and I started hiking north. It was twenty miles to Lake Morena. That was my first goal. I had never done a twenty-mile day, not with a full pack. Not ever. I hiked alone, and became confused as the trail skirted Campo. Read the guide pages, use the compass. Think, look around. Finally, I backtracked a couple hundred yards to where it bypasses the town westward. The scenery was beautiful, better than I had imagined. Who would have thought the desert could support so many varieties of flowers. The huge white lilies were especially amazing. Where were they getting enough moisture to put on such a display?

That first day I struggled with directions and self-image, wondering aloud, "Who the hell do you think you are, out here alone, trying to get to Sonora Pass?" Calm down, eat some jellybeans. They were my entire food supply until Lake Morena. One pound of candy and 4 quarts of water, being rationed at one quart per five miles.

Crossing what the guidebook termed an "unreliable" stream I took a break, drank more water, and squatted in what I would later learn was poison oak. There was no one to be seen, not north, not south, as I scanned the hills and valleys. I guess there were other hikers on the trail. Every so often there would be a shirt, piece of plastic sheeting, or a pair of pants, signs of illegal immigrants crossing our southern border, looking for the American Dream.

Finally at Hauser Creek, 15 miles by one o'clock, I sat down to rest before the last 5 hard miles. A likely place near a dried out stream was full of horse droppings and the stench was nearly unbearable. I would much rather make the steep climb and then a descent into Lake Morena than camp here, anyway. I met Jeff who came to rest beside me, and gave him some water. The creek was a hopeless horse dump, and neither of us would dredge water out of it. We exchanged pleasantries, and then I pressed on.

I made those 20 miles by suppertime on Friday evening. There was a cookout, and people arrived continuously. The third Annual Zero Day

My Journey to Freedom and Ultralight Backpacking

Pacific Crest Trail Kick Off Party officially began on Saturday, and the entire day was spent meeting hikers and trail angels, creating an ultralight cup with new found friends, learning how to make various stoves from soda cans, watching a territorial dog fight, attending a water cache review and competing in a gear contest. I won a prize for my silnylon rain suit, labeled by judges as "the best innovative gear item on the trail in 2001." My jacket had the mittens attached, which had never been seen or done before, to the best of anyone's knowledge.

Sunday, a complete breakfast of eggs, bagels, muffins, oatmeal, fruit and steaming hot coffee was offered at sunrise. Hikers packed and headed for the trail. Everyone, it seemed, was all spread out. I hiked alone, passing a few guys resting on the side of the trail. We chatted a bit, but some insecurity kept me hiking solo. I felt they would invite me to accompany them if they so wished. I started doing huge miles, and earned a reputation as a strong hiker. This was unplanned and unintended. My miles were unpreventable. I find that the same compulsions we have in our regular lives, we bring with us to the trail.

My biggest problem was missing Rainmaker. Evenings were the worst, from about 5:00 p.m. until I went to sleep. I missed his reassurance and our nightly camping rituals. To cope with this homesickness, I hiked until nearly dark each day. Once, I almost had a disaster looking for a campsite along a ridge walk. One spot was big enough, but if I ventured out after dark, I could have easily fallen off a cliff. That night I kept hiking until a small ledge just above the trail appeared. Squeezing in beneath some manzanita bushes, I set up my tent on a fairly level spot, ate raw ramen noodles and drank Kool-Aid. Camping directly on trail is always an option, but because it is also an animal highway, I would rather camp somewhere aside.

I felt very strong physically and met lots of good people on the trail. Weather was perfect, the scenery outstanding. All the senses become finely tuned. I felt totally alive. This is a true desert environment. If there is a rhythm to be found hiking the PCT, it is to be found with one word: Water. Where is the next water, and can I get there today? It may mean a 21-mile day. It may mean 26. I learned to cook at water sources, sometimes in the afternoon. With the pot washed, and teeth brushed, the need for camp water is very minimal. Still, in the desert I filled all my water bottles and would hike until evening. Perhaps there would be water when I camped, perhaps not. I hated to carry water; I learned to walk to the next source, however long that might be. By rising early, and being on trail by daylight, many miles can be covered before the heat becomes unbearable. Less water is needed in those early hours, too.

Solo is wonderful and the independence is great. However, it can be lonely at night and a bit frightening to be so totally on your own. Sometimes, in desperation, I would sit on the side of the trail with my topography maps, compass and trail guide until I could figure out where I was. The greatest fear was missing the only water in 30 miles. I never camped until I was sure of my location. Most days I hiked alone, but passing and being passed by others, sometimes referred to as leap-frogging. Often a few of us would camp together.

Trail runner shoes rule here. The few with leather boots have swapped out, cut them into submission, or left the trail. The type of socks seems to vary, some with smart wool, others with Thorlos, many with just some nylon blend. Nylon shorts proved very comfortable, drying easily after rinsing in rare creeks. The sewn-in pockets have eliminated the need for a fanny pack. I went back to my Esbit stove; having to use metal stakes for a cooking pot support with my other stove doesn't cut it in this rocky terrain. At night, I was just too tired to fool with pounding in stakes, leveling them, and hoping my pot wouldn't tip over.

One guy lost his hat in the wind. Thankfully, I remembered to add elastic cord and a cord lock to cinch my hat tight when it was windy. Many types of sombreros or hats are worn in the desert. An uncovered head or simple bandana would be dangerous with such strong sunrays. One hiker was sunburned so badly the first day out, her peeling shoulders were a warning to all. Sun block is not a luxury here. I learned to carry the best available.

One day I was uncertain of the predetermined "grassy spot" friends were to meet me at to camp. Holding the guidebook in one hand, reading while I hiked, I set my left foot down and suddenly heard a tremendous rattle. I glanced down while jumping ahead, and saw a large rattlesnake about ten inches from my foot. The snake crawled off, still rattling its tail in warning. I just about stepped on him, and he was mad! I learned many lessons, among them don't walk and read at the same time, stay focused. There is no such thing as being too alert.

The Pacific Crest Trail joined the Tahquitz Valley Trail just before Idyllwild. Three trails were mentioned in the guide, and in good times would be easy to follow. However, in May, with snow still covering large sections, I became concerned. Footprints seemed to be going in all directions, and I lost the footprints of thru-hikers I'd been following. Reading that I had to climb to 8,500 ft, and then descend again, I started up a peak. There were water bars, a good sign. There were footprints, but going in all directions. My compass said I was heading north, but that isn't always an indicator of correctness. Finally, a PCT post appeared, I stooped, put my hand on it, and kissed it. I had one meal of corn mush left in my pack, and the evening dusk was settling in. Finally back on track, I hiked to Saddle Junction, where no camping is permitted. I went down the Devil's Slide Trail toward Idyllwild about ¼ mile and put up my tent, very relieved to at last I know where I was.

I spent several weeks leap-frogging with a woman name Becky. She was a young soloist, a great conversationalist, independent and wild. I called her Trail Animal, a name that didn't stick but delighted her immensely. She reminded me of my daughters, sharing a female bond. I went through a week of mother-worry when she disappeared from the trail, not leaving word, nor being seen by any thru-hikers. She had hitch hiked into town, returned to the trail to hike a few more miles, and then backtracked to the same town she'd left.

I watched the ants on the trail. They were quite amazing. Some larger black ones tried to stuff a leaf down their hole, a joint effort that reminded me of kids putting a huge quilt down a laundry chute. Tiny ants formed four lanes, 2 coming and 2 going, across the trail. Amazingly co-coordinated endeavor in this heat! Red ones swarmed over my shoes and socks while I sat barefoot in a last scrap of shade at 9:00 a.m. The mountain itself provided some shade before the sun rose higher. Some other ants hauled an enormous, lifeless stinkbug across the sand. I could imagine their mom saying, "I would like to know where you plan to put THAT!"

Hikers congregated in the shade of Joshua Trees or a rare creek, waiting out the noontime heat, talking strategy, planning resupply points, reading maps, and discussing topography. This was not your average group. Everyone was self-sufficient and strong. As soloists, we knew no one was going to take care of us, no one owed us anything. But, bonds were built as we went through the same things together. Suffering builds unity faster than fun.

The towns are spaced far apart on the PCT, each one an oasis of relief and pleasure. Food, shade, water, medicine, clean clothes, some human faces, no bears or snakes in the near vicinity, what more could we want? One hundred miles between resupply points was not uncommon.

The trail has been full of "almosts". One day I almost slid off the ledge while crossing a snowy section. My foot slid down the mushy last step and I found myself sitting in the snow bank, hiking poles pinning me, holding me to the ledge. I couldn't get up until I unsnapped my pack belt and let go of one pole. Sure wished I had my snow baskets for my poles, but they were in a box bound for Kennedy Meadows.

I learned to forget the "almosts". I almost got lost; I almost missed my last water source. I almost stepped on a rattlesnake; I almost had to sleep right on the trail. I almost ran out of food. If one would dwell on that, they would get pretty scared. Somehow, each day should start out fresh with no worries or fears, so I learned from my "almosts" and kept hiking.

"The man who follows the crowd will usually get no further than the crowd. The man who walks alone is likely to find himself in places no one has ever been."—Alan Ashley-Pitt

The fear of the desert was a curious thing. At the town of Agua Dulce, so much fear generated by the endless worry over waterless stretches and heat caused entire groups to road walk (cutting off 30 miles of desert) or slack pack large sections. I was glad I opted for neither. We'd already done desert hiking in the previous section. I did not want this portion, the Mojave Desert, to beat me before I even tried. The desert is not a thing to fear, neither to be attacked by nor to flee from. It is something to be experienced, and respected. Found two beautiful feathers; a confirmation of trail gifts to come.

Anyone who has done PCT switchbacks knows the agony of endlessly winding mile after mile to descend just ten feet in elevation. There is a good side, though. One benefit was if you suddenly realized that a great photo opportunity was missed. But, not to worry. An hour later, another chance, perhaps closer, perhaps not, presented itself. The view of that same marvelous rock, that curious tree, of Interstate 15, was nearly identical. The drawback of such routing or "over engineering" was the tendency for some hikers to cut, or bypass, the switchbacks. I was burned on that once, and learned my lesson well. By taking a shortcut down to what appeared to be a switchback, I got on a side trail, temporarily losing the PCT that was heading around the canyon, instead of down into the canyon.

Seeing all these poor plants uprooted when hikers crossed downhill made me ponder the struggle of life. Most little plants start the same way, all created equal. A seed fell. Ten years later, having finally soaked up enough moisture, it germinated. In ten more years it grew big enough to have stickers, thus reaching its full potential. But life throws a curve, and places one in a favorable location, another in a bad. Those out on their own, with no big brother to shelter them, get run over in life. And it's not their fault. Sad to see such tenacity rewarded thus.

One instant food I enjoyed a lot was the "4-cheese" mashed potatoes. I was surprised how light it was. A box came with two packages containing 4 servings each and together weighed only 7 ounces. That made 2 suppers for me. A beef stick, or some salami broken into pieces and added to cornmeal, cooked over low heat was amazingly filling as well. To avoid lumps, I brought the water to a low boil, then while stirring slowly, sprinkled in the cornmeal until the consistency was thick. Ramen noodles, broken into bits and placed in a peanut butter jar, can be solar cooked. By filling the jar with water, screwing on the plastic lid, and placing it in the sunshine, within half an hour, the noodles will be softened and satisfyingly warm. Sprinkle in the flavor packet, if desired. Ramen noodles can be eaten raw, like pretzels, so I always considered them a good investment in the food bag.

After only five weeks on the trail, civilization meant little. It didn't matter whether we slept in our clothes, brushed our hair, said our bedtime prayers, had all four-food groups, or wore things inside out. Personal strength and tenaciousness were the intangible values now. It's not what we wore but what we did that earned respect. Long distance hiking culture has a way of developing its own jargon. Some of my terms are defined below:

Trail Animal - A long distance hiker who is thoroughly comfortable being dirty, smelly, stealth camping and hiking mega miles (20+) every day. Usually has a wild gleam in the eyes, prone to laughter without reason, especially when hiking solo. Happily eats ramen and oatmeal, but will cause a stampede for pizza, beer or the use of a telephone.

Trail Maintenance - Originally meant to signify a pee break, but further elaboration includes removing stones from shoes, changing clothes, stopping for a drink or other things designed to make the miles less miserable.

Stampede - Term for the onset and completion of a mad rush to a goal, initiated by a trail animal who has pizza on his or her brain, and knows where he or she can get some an ungodly distance away. The proposed mileage is initially deemed to be impossible by other hikers, but the idea is implanted and the stampede is on. From that point, breaks are limited to a quick pee and a chug of water, lasting no more than 2 minutes. In 6 weeks, I have been in 4 stampedes. They usually involved 5 – 6 hikers.

Treadmill - This happens when trying in vain to gain elevation on a four-foot wide, sandy, undulating trail. Using hiking poles like mad and climbing, one suddenly looks over to the trail's edge and realizes they've been hiking by that same damn rock for 15 minutes.

Undulation - The vertical or horizontal waves of trail tread. The vertical ones caused by illegal mountain bikers are especially maddening because they are totally uncalled for and preventable. Thru-hikers have verbally expressed bodily harm intended for such offending bikers, solely in the interest of such prevention. No hard feelings. The horizontal ones caused by canyons are just there because they have to be, or else this trail wouldn't be 2,659 miles long.

We celebrated upon reaching Kennedy Meadows. It meant the end of the desert; now there would be plenty of water. It meant we had come 697 miles. For most of us, it meant reunion with our cherished bounce boxes. There was access to a newly installed pay phone, the enormous hiker box and a wonderful little store with quaint showers, soap and laundry facilities. We showered, washed clothes, stuffed ourselves with hot food and kept that phone busy for hours. In preparation for elevations above 10,000 feet, I bought an old army blanket for $2, trimmed it down, and sewed it with dental floss. I used it to supplement my sleeping bag. This added two extra pounds of pack weight, but I couldn't have done the High Sierra without it. The price for starting this trail with a worn-out sleeping bag would now be paid.

Kennedy Meadows to Tuolumne Meadows/John Muir Trail
From Kennedy Meadows to Tuolumne Meadows, in Yosemite National Park, hikers do not cross a single paved road for over 235 miles. I packed food and supplies for 192 miles, which included a 15-mile round trip day hike to the summit of Mount Whitney, then over to Vermillion Valley Resort. With ten days of food, my ice ax and blanket liner, my pack now weighed twenty-eight pounds on their scale. In the desert, I used my Cherokee tent every night, but sometimes just as a "bivy bag", spreading it out on the ground, and crawling in. The condensation was tolerable in such a dry climate. Once we entered the High Sierra, in early June, I used my tent properly every night.
Ascending from an elevation of 6,120 ft. to 10,540 ft., we noted plenty of water and every creek was swarming with thousands of

hungry mosquitoes. Upon reaching a suitable campsite, I would immediately set up my tent, and then throw everything, including myself, inside. Those with bivy sacks were very limited. Friends intending to hike straight through to Vermillion Valley Resort, but lacking strong bug repellent, decided to hike the two miles down to a parking lot on a side trail, hitch into Lone Pine and buy something, anything. The bugs were making them nuts. Becky told us the natural herbal stuff that she carried didn't work at all.

The Gorp Bag

This is a phenomenon I have noticed among many long distance hikers. A gallon size zip lock bag is filled with a decent recipe of Gorp. This name originated when good old raisins and peanuts were mixed together for trail food. Nowadays, there are more elaborate recipes. For instance, the one with equal amounts of peanut M&Ms, walnuts, raisins, and yogurt covered dates. It is an enormous amount of food, and sometimes cannot be finished before the next resupply.

At the next town, perhaps a 13-ounce bag of pretzels, or a hiker box find of sesame sticks and sunflower seeds is thrown into The Gorp Bag. Better to carry one large snack bag than several tads of food.

In the following town we find leftover Chex breakfast cereal joining The Bag. Or some "Does anyone want these?" apricots gets dumped in, along with some indecently moist raisins, or questionable dried apples.

One renowned Bag made it all the way from Idyllwild to Kennedy Meadows, 423 trail miles, where its owner committed said Gorp bag in disgust to a hiker box. Within 2 hours another hiker claimed it. Thankfully, that hiker finished it by Vermillion Valley.

No way could recipes ever be written for a 300 Mile Bag. It may be the most awesome of trail gorps, including shredded coconut, freeze dried strawberries, corn and peas. Included, but not limited to, may be Captain Crunch, Kandy Korn, peanuts, bacon crackers, and corn nuts. It is not a matter of imagination. It is a matter of not enough zip locks. Well, that and convenience. At snack time, one just hauls out The Bag and munches. If holes develop, as in even the best of Bags, a duct tape patch is used. If the zip refuses to lock, a hiker may chose to double bag. Crumbs are not thrown away, but eaten, regardless of salt or sugar concentration. A note of caution however, eating from zip lock bags containing food of such origin is like playing Russian roulette with your stomach.

From Kennedy Meadows to Crab Tree Meadows it is 63 trail miles. There, many PCT hikers camp, hike 7.5 miles on a side trail to summit Mt. Whitney the next day and return to camp that night. There are bear boxes (metal food storage lockers), which are fully utilized. Hikers stash anything they don't need for their hikes to Mt. Whitney, with an elevation of 14,492 feet, the highest mountain in the contiguous United States. At a campsite so remote from roads, there was no fear of theft. Only long distance hikers use such a place and the honesty among our peers was a given. Someone was more likely to leave something behind than to steal anything.

On June 10th, I cooked breakfast, and was on the trail at 7 a.m. with Ben. It was quite overcast, with a line of blue to the west. We planned to summit, if at all possible. Mt. Whitney is the southern terminus of the John Muir Trail. The Pacific Crest Trail joins the JMT for nearly 170 miles, then they split at Tuolumne Meadows. Without a summit of Whitney, there would be no point in finishing the JMT in Yosemite Valley. We stripped our packs down to essentials, placing gear and extra food in the bear box. My external frame, now equipped with just one stuff sack, carried clothes, snacks, one full water bottle, ice ax and rain gear. It weighed about 5 pounds total and felt like nothing. This was my first taste of a seriously ultralight pack weight.

There was ice on the log when we forded Rock Creek. An hour later, we came to Guitar Lake. The dark clouds moving eastward gave us hope the weather would clear. Snowfields began to appear. Key rocks used for climbing were covered with thick ice. "Just follow the footsteps, don't worry about the trail," Ben called back to me as I approached a set of 3 switchbacks. He waited at the top of that section, and cautioned me not to touch the icy rocks. On hands and knees, I pulled myself up and over the snow bank. We gained 4,500 ft. of elevation in 7.5 miles. It was mentally exhausting watching for ice, snow and loose tread with every footstep so near the edge and just inches away from eternity.

Since it was Sunday, many day hikers appeared on the Whitney Portal Trail, which joined ours just 1.7 miles from the summit. Some carried crampons, ice axes and packs. They seemed winded, theirs being a longer and steeper trail. Near the summit, ice mounds taller than me covered the trail, requiring axing-in and pulling myself over and onto a narrow ledge. Picking our way to the top, much of the trail obscured with snow or boulders, we gained the summit at 12:15 and stayed until 2:00 p.m. Going down was easier because the snow became soft and mushy. There was dangerous post holing, where one breaks though the snow crust and becomes lodged up to the groin. Climbing out of such a hole, hopefully on solid snow near by, took extra time. I learned to watch for the bluish tint just beneath the snow's surface that warned of such danger.

Near Guitar Lake there was so much snowmelt that I lost the trail and bushwhacked straight down, seeing the PCT/JMT winding around the lake below. Ben had gone ahead and I took a little extra time.

I had just a few problems with the altitude. During the night, I would fall asleep just fine, then I'd wake feeling breathless. Once I adopted a No Fear attitude, slight headaches and mild nausea disappeared. If everyone around you says they feel sick, it can affect you. Ben and I decided we felt fine. The high top trail runner shoes were a good choice for this section, keeping out loose stones and some snow. For the first time I tried some Smart Wool socks. My feet stayed warm and comfortable, even though they were sopping wet by day's end.

The next day, Becky rejoined us. We forded streams barefooted, pressed on to Forester Pass, highest point on the PCT at 13,200 ft., all the while anticipating the snowy climb. We needed to get there before it refroze in the evening. These areas are dangerous in early season because the approach to the pass is often snow covered, and hikers may find themselves traversing a snowfield undercut by water. The first clue is the sound of a rushing river, while it remains unseen. At that point, one gets to higher ground, avoiding the sunspots, or low melted areas, with that same bluish tint.

Forester Pass, highest point on the PCT/ Ben, Becky, Brawny

After the pass, the northbound trail below was totally snow covered with footprints diagonally traversing the slope. We three had cross-country skied before, so with that same gliding motion we descended the slope. When at last we were back on a small piece of dirt footpath, we celebrated by placing clean snow in our empty peanut butter jars, stirring in some packages of cocoa mix, and making Ice Cream Slushies. We spent the rest of that day hunting the trail, which was covered in snow, ice and water.

Things You'd Rather Not Hear:

"It's all down hill from here." - Somehow those words always precede the worst of sections, but draw one into an insanely huge mileage day. Be careful who tells you that. They may just be trying to get rid of you.
"The prices there are pretty reasonable for California." - Means outrageous to normal folks.
"So, are you having fun?" – Excuse me? You mean I'm supposed to?
"There's a horse camp upstream." - This just after you've drunk a quart of untreated water from this lovely creek.
"Don't worry, he's waiting for you, Honey."-From a weekender, especially disturbing when you've been hiking alone for days. Who could be waiting?

Pinchot Pass, Mather Pass, and Muir Pass, are all noteworthy. South bounders were questioned on the snow cover and depth. Sometimes I found myself frustrated by lack of calories while slogging through miles of snow. The last hour before each pass was usually spent searching for footprints, avoiding sunspots and under washed snowfields. The PCT / JMT doesn't always summit at the low spot of the pass. We followed footprints, guessed at the meaning of obscure guidebook passages, took compass readings, and checked maps to find our way. Often I caught up to Ben. Two sets of eyes are good at times like this. He was a man of few words, and the few were to the point. One day while climbing at over 10,000 feet, he turned and stated, "I feel like shit." I burst out laughing. I knew he wasn't asking for help, just stating an observation.

Finally, with Vermillion Valley Resort only 27 miles away I could enjoy the last bites of my food, and save a breakfast for tomorrow. My ramen had been supplemented with wild onions for 9 ½ days. At night I dreamed of candy bars and woke up disappointed. At this point, anything was good and money seemed unimportant. Clean clothes and hair (without every last strand coated in dust), became worth whatever the cost in dollars and cents. The day before reaching our resupply, we met a young man who was filled with fears, who talked about all the bad things that might happen to people. He even skipped a section because he feared tainted water. Fear is a very negative force; deadly to dreams. I have been very afraid many times. Hate to let it beat me without a fight, though. I just get up everyday and hike, trying to not to worry about tomorrow's trail until tomorrow.

There are two choices for getting to Vermillion Valley Resort. Either take a boat ride across the lake, $15 for the round trip, or hike 6 miles one way. I chose the boat. There, tent cabins, a small store, laundry and shower facilities were built on the dusty shore. We spent one night, feasting and laughing. The only outside contact is via cell phone, at $2 a minute. I hauled lots of goodies out of Vermillion Valley and ate like crazy: cookies, gorp, gourmet coffee, and red licorice. This was my reward for last week's hunger.

People dream of hiking the John Muir Trail. It's an incredible place; plenty of water and lush meadows, high passes, innumerable waterfalls and cascades, wildlife and flowers. There are also beautiful clear skies and ice covered turquoise lakes surrounded with snow-covered ridges. Words or photos can never convey the quality of the unfolding panorama. All five senses marvel at the birds singing, marmots whistling, water and wind rushing, soaring eagles, circling ravens, and dark clouds threatening. There were these magnificent, sculpted cedars, tender shoots and delicate flowers clinging to a 12,000 ft. cliff, the earthy smells of damp earth and bodies, the taste of clear ice water and wild onions. This was no postcard trip; it was the total surround of an Omni-max theater. I planned to finish the JMT by day hiking to Yosemite Valley from Tuolumne Meadows, getting a ride back to Tuolumne Meadows, then picking up the PCT where I left it, and continuing north.

Hikers on a budget learn to get the most luxury for their buck. At Red's Meadow, just one day from Tuolumne, I bought a 24 oz. loaf of wheat bread, 18 oz. jar of peanut butter, 13 oz. bag of Nacho Cheese Doritos, 8 oz. jar of cheese salsa, 4 king-size candy bars and 11 black liquorish sticks. There were free hot showers near the campground, thanks to thermal springs nearby. Each of the showers had a private "room" with cement tub. I placed the jar of cheese salsa on the ledge of this enormous cement tank inside the little room that was mine. Opening the chips, I basically ate while showering and washing trail clothes. My shower lasted an hour. I finished the salsa, threw away the jar, and was ready to hike.

Generally speaking, we are not into possession of things, but possession of experience. The few things we have with us are well worn with daily use and their respective weight in ounces quoted upon request, or even in defiance, as in "Yeah, well, this 4 pound camera is taking pictures that will last me a lifetime!" I have seen several Pocket Mails, cell phones, guitars, and tiny radios. Each person perhaps has one "luxury" item. One JMT hiker summed it up "Seems like the longer your hike is, the less you carry."

Fording A Creek

I've learned a lot about fording creeks since I started in Campo. First, let me describe and define a PCT "creek". Out here anything with water flowing is either a spring, streamlet, lake outlet, or a creek. Back home, some of these would be classified as Class 4 rivers.

Just to name a few, there's Evolution Creek, Bear Creek (there must be at least 5 Bear Creeks out here), Kerrick Canyon Creek, Stubblefield Canyon Creek, and Kennedy Canyon Creek. The trail will parallel, from a ridge, one of these "creeks" as it roars down canyon. In the back of your mind runs the thought, "How on earth am I going to ford that thing?"

But, thankfully, it crosses at a fairly benign place where it has widened and slowed and most boulders are not in motion, at least not now. Usually the trail resumes directly across the creek and the objective is clear. A simple rock hop is possible in many streamlet crossings, the rocks having been placed a long-legged man's stride apart. Cobweb had this magnificent way of ricocheting himself, rock-to-rock, zig-zagging across. Momentum is the key word here. One must not stop to consider.

Early one morning, I had already committed myself to such a hop. Seeing the next one an impossible 5 feet away, I stopped. This necessity was the mother of the invention I called the "Sacrifice the Queen" maneuver. In chess, the dumbest move apparently is to lose one's queen, the most powerful piece. However, it may save the whole game. That's the term I used for putting my foot on a slightly submerged rock, allowing that shoe to momentarily taste water, and then using it to complete the ford. It appeared unskillful, but to any sneer of laughter, I lifted my head with haughty eyes and simply stated, "I sacrificed the queen." That usually shut them up with a look of complete confusion.

41

Sometimes a creek crossing looks like a barefoot necessity. Nothing immediate presents itself. Then running up and downstream to find an easier place ensues, perhaps a partial log, met by a boulder, a point peeking out. That's all one needs.

Ice may be present. The logs may be unstable. Hiking poles definitely help for balancing, touching points on either side of logs, and for checking water depth. When all else fails, off come shoes and perhaps socks. Laces are tied in a knot and shoes slung around the neck. A crossing is slowly made diagonally, wading down stream, allowing the current to bring you and the thousand feasting mosquitoes ashore. No grimace or groaning is permitted for a Classy Crossing. This barefoot crossing has the benefit of some thorough cleansing action for feet as well as socks.

And always, of paramount concern is the pack. Sleeping bag and food must not fall in. Feet and legs may need to suffer to insure such, with slow, sure steps in icy cold water.

The whole procedure is an art form.

Tuolumne Meadows has a post office, café and store, joined together in one long building. Outside there are many picnic tables and two pay phones. The tourist crowds were not easy to maneuver around, and we long distance hikers stood out like wild animals. I didn't spend any time in Yosemite Valley, but simply hiked down in a day, completing the JMT, and was back in time to stealth camp. Most hikers sent their ice axes, surplus supplies and winter gear home. I sent my Army blanket bag liner home but elected to keep my ax until I got to Echo Lake out of respect for Rainmaker's and Cindy Ross' near death experiences at Sonora Pass. And, too, in defiance of a local weekender who told me to mail it home. I might have been the only hiker that year to carry an ice ax through this section, but it had a dual purpose. It was a good weapon.

The trail has been great, and challenging, but the time had come to shift gears. I had to slow down because my rendezvous with Rainmaker in Reno, Nevada was still over two weeks away. I would miss seeing my thru-hiking friends, especially Ben and Becky. Those behind me would catch up and pass. Trail friendships are just that, and seldom continue into the other world. We love what we have when we have it; we let go of what we must when it's time.

Tuolumne to Echo Lake

These last 156 miles of my solo adventure, I planned to hike slowly. Nearly three weeks remained before Rainmaker flew in to join me. I carried an estimated eleven days of food, in two stuff sacks. Only the campsite at Glen Aulin had a bear box. It also had some bears known to harass hikers in their tents. So, that first night out I continued another 12 miles to McCabe Lake Trail junction, buried my food under rocks between large boulders and gathered some smaller rocks to place in the vestibule for ammunition, should the need arise. No sign of a human camp nearby, no fire rings, no human footprints or trash. This was definitely a stealth campsite. To maintain a low profile, all my gear was kept inside my gray Cherokee tent.

Many hikers spent extra time in Yosemite Valley visiting relatives, climbing cliffs and just relaxing. Others had hiked quickly ahead to avoid the 4th of July-No-Post-Office at Echo Lake on this long weekend. It seemed that all the thru-hikers had disappeared. So, all alone, and trying to relax, I slept late, cooked oatmeal for breakfast, and piddled around to my heart's content. However, I still was on the trail by 7:30. That inner drive that plagues me fought this slower pace. The next day, I only hiked about 10 miles and buried my food again. That was a big job since my food filled two stuff sacks.

I forded several wide streams that were very low for this time of year. The climb up Benson Pass was ambiguous. If it hadn't been for the rock ducks (ingeniously piled rocks, used as trail markers), I don't think I could have found the way. One important note; don't ever cut switchbacks in a multi-use area, you could very easily end up on a spur trail, and not realize it for several miles.

Later, I crossed Kerrick Canyon Creek and cooked supper. Maybe it was the appetizer of double hot chocolate or the black liquorish sticks, but somehow the Ramen and Cheese delight didn't go down very well. Or perhaps it was the dried apricots? Anyway, I felt ill. I didn't want to camp where I'd cooked, but my stomach hurt. Slowly I stood up and contemplated the situation. It was already after 5:00 with a 900-foot climb ahead and a steep descent on the other side. Suddenly, off to my left walked a beautiful black bear. I don't believe he saw me, or perhaps he was just being nonchalant. Decision made; guess I can hike some more tonight. I put on my pack while watching the bushes where the bear had disappeared and saw him cross the creek using rocks like a human would do, and then dash off. Either he had caught my scent or saw me at that point. I hiked another 3 miles and camped among some boulders, forgetting to pick up water at the last mosquito infested stream crossing. A dry camp, indeed. That was a 19-mile day.

On June 27th, the next day, I did an unbelievable 25 miles. It was windy, cloudy and cold, and not a soul to be seen all day. Very lonely for a face; I just would have liked to see another human being. Finally, in the distance, two people were fishing at Dorothy Lake. They watched me the entire time I skirted the east side of the lake. Greeting them when I drew near, they completely ignored me. A bit later, I met a park ranger on horseback, and talked to him for a while, begging him to check my permit, Whitney stamp and all. He finally relented, while reminding me we could have snow that night, any night, in the Sierras.

The last 13 miles to Sonora Pass are narrow, very windy, and at times snow covered. I stopped, put on my silnylon rain suit and later negotiated an ice slope using my ax. If one ever intends to slide down an ice slope, or glissade, it is not recommendable when wearing only shorts. From experience, I found it is quite rough on the skin, and can shred the only pair of shorts you have. My silnylon rain pants were very useful at these times. Rainmaker later told me he used a large garbage bag for his slides.

Early that afternoon, I reached Sonora Pass, and ate lunch. To my delight, Becky hiked in. We stealth camped in the same spot Rainmaker spent his last night, camped in 1999, and the exact spot he and I camped together our first night last year in 2000. It was time for connection. A special reverence for this place made me defy the perceived threat of a stranger who lurked, binoculars focused on the tables where we had supper. Becky had met him earlier when getting water, he with the duct-taped vest, who asked too many questions and refused to look her in the face. But, didn't I carry my ice ax? Just let him come and threaten us. It's a fool who tries to move a wild animal from its lair.

I had lightened my pack by throwing out some food and the Z- rest, then giving Becky food and an extra shirt. Everything possible went in the garbage cans at Sonora Pass. I was tired of burying my food, and sleeping alone. It was 74 miles to Echo Lake Resort. The best remedy now was to just hike long and hard. The first two days I hiked with Becky, then she disappeared again. On the third day, I reached Echo Lake. That evening I called Rainmaker, and managed to get a ride to Berkeley Camp just a quarter mile down the road. For $10, I had a hot shower, access to a hot tub, full sized pool, and a bed in a shared tent cabin. I was done for now! I still had eleven days until Rainmaker arrived, and I intended to spend the time resting and relaxing.

Intermission

For nine days I stayed at the Berkeley campground, working out a deal with the manager to cook for an hour daily in exchange for room and board. I enjoyed the luxuries of flush toilets, a mattress, a pool, hot tub, excellent food, and human interaction. Frequently other hikers would come down to the camp for a night.

Often, for a couple hours diversion, I hiked back to Echo Lake Resort, to meet friends passing through. I missed them, those hardy thru-hikers. We exchanged stories of bear encounters, food disasters, lost gear, and family contacts. One woman's family learned by reading someone's online journal that she was hiking solo now that her partner left the trail. Another guy, bemoaning the fact he didn't have his wild bear photos, told us how he was conned by two bears into leaving his pack unattended trailside, while he scampered into the woods after spotting one of them feeding. Then, turning back to the trail, saw another bear happily trashing his pack. Thankfully, some friends showed up in the nick of time, and helped drive the thief away. Lesson learned, take the pack with you. I could not restrain my laughter as this hiker expressed his indignation of being conned by bears.

We rummaged through each other's drop boxes, witnessed dog fights, irritated too-clean tourists, traded each other fuel for food, and griped about the resort. Although only a stone's throw from the lake, the store personnel said they could not give anyone clean drinking water because it was a drought year. There were privies, but no water to wash with. Yet the store sold fresh produce, a contradiction in standard health precautions.

The pampered women at the campground surprised and sometimes annoyed me. One lady told me it was such a hardship for her, that this campground was as rugged as she could stand. I thought I had come to heaven! Several campers asked me what made me so different, so strong, and why I wasn't afraid. Amazing. Somehow over these last two months I must have changed, dramatically. Perhaps a long hike is the best therapy for recovering one's identity.

I was anxious to get back on the trail; this soft campground life was boring. Having mailed my tent home from the resort, I had to wait. Finally, the time came. Early one morning I hitch hiked to South Lake Tahoe, caught a bus to Reno, and got a room at the fancy Sands Hotel. Rainmaker would fly in tomorrow evening, and the anticipation was like that of Christmas.

Chapter Four

Reunited And Onward to Canada

I met Rainmaker at the Reno Airport around midnight on the twelfth of July. Last time I saw him in April, he was clean-shaven. The guy who walked towards me now had a full, mostly gray beard. But the confident stride of that long, lean body, those wide shoulders and piercing blue eyes, were unmistakable. We returned to the motel by cab. The next day we rented a car for the one-way drive to Klamath Falls, Oregon, where we dropped it off. Our dear friends Brenda and Ralph met us there and took us to their home for the night. The next day they drove us to Crater Lake.

Suddenly, Rainmaker and I were together again, on the Pacific Crest Trail, with just what we carried in our packs. Our routines were reestablished: sharing a tent, smiles, jokes, and conversation. Sharing, most of all, our love for the trail and for each other.

The rim trail around Crater Lake was spectacular, constantly giving and taking the same 300 ft. of elevation. Crater Lake is one of the Seven Wonders of the World, without a doubt a magnificent place.

It was very cold for July in southern Oregon. The locals told us that it was quite unusual. One cannot count on the usual on a long distance hike. Our clothing was sufficient, but just barely. The multiple layers gave plenty of options, wearing everything at once was effective in the worst conditions.

Nearly every day after my partner joined me, it rained. In spite of all his other accomplishments, his trail name will always be Rainmaker. We had separate tent vestibules and made ourselves hot coffee and breakfast in the mornings before packing and heading out. Our 3-½ pound, double-wall Coleman Cobra tent kept us warm and dry. There had been very few mosquitoes; our theory was they all froze to death previously.

Shelter Cove Resort was one of three resorts where we planned to buy food. The store was very expensive; I needed only three days of food, and in retrospect, should have just bought what I needed, regardless of price. However, ramen noodles were $1 per package, stovetop stuffing over $3 a box and candy bars were 70 cents each. You know something is wrong in life when noodles cost more than candy. So, instead, and in protest, I stubbornly chose some "soak and heat" stuff I'd found in the hiker box. I will politely refer to this concoction as food, and dumped it in with my tad of remaining ramen and mashed potatoes. This medley would have worked had there not been all these little split peas, inedible beans and dangerous seeds mixed in. Just bird feed, I kid you not. I called it Shit Supreme.

Ultralight is definitely the way to go on a long trail. Most of the weight is food, which normally should be a pleasure to deplete on mega sections of 150+ miles. But, if you end up with nasty food, a daily debate to dump this weight, or eat it down, may surface. Dumping food in bear country must be done with care. If cooked and indigestible, carry and bury it at least half a mile away. If dumped raw, do it early morning before hiking away, broadcasting it several hundred feet away from campsites, to feed small creatures and avoid mounds of mold.

Before we resumed the trail, we bought a half-gallon of vanilla ice cream at Shelter Cove. We opened the lid, got our trail spoons, sprinkled hot cocoa mix on top to add some interest, and ate right out of the container, finishing it off amid stares of vacationers nearby.

Elk Lake Resort was a tiny store next to a beautiful lake, full of boating enthusiasts. Thankfully, a friend who lives in Bend, Oregon offered to help us. We resupplied in Bend after she picked us up at the resort parking lot. This resort had hot meals, which smelled delicious. However, the few groceries there could not even resupply one thru hiker, if he or she could afford them.

I bought a beautiful fleece turtleneck in Bend, which replaced my silk button down shirt. That silk layer worked great in the desert, allowing for warmth and ventilation, but it had deteriorated with the sun. The fleece turtleneck was necessary now, vital in cold weather for keeping my neck warm.

In Bend I also bought a handsome Nike daypack, which weighed 21 ounces once I modified it for trail use. I discarded my pack frame, and kept two-silnylon stuff sacks. I had to make a hip belt for it, though. Leaving town, my pack was really loaded with food as a direct result of the poor resupply at Shelter Cove. Now, it seemed quite heavy. All along the trail from Elk Lake Resort to Canada, I made adjustments, sewing with dental floss at night in camp. I cannibalized various stuff sacks, trimmed off some closed cell pad, and customized the hip belt further. This was my first frameless pack.

Bend, Oregon to Cascade Locks

In northern Oregon, the PCT traverses lava flow for many miles. The trail was quite rough in places, with marvelous views of northern mountains and evergreens, white barked trees, and sweet smelling lupine. Rare cloudless skies and moderating temperatures sweetened the adventure. Horses with riders were very common, yet they seemed to have little, if any, regard for hikers. Even though we hiked on narrow ledges, they kept right on coming towards us. Horses have the right of way, yet time is needed to find a safe place to step aside. I quickly learned to scramble down hill, off trail, hoping for enough distance between us to avoid kicks by startled horses.

Thru-hikers were catching up to us now. One group of three young men was so compatible they were still cooking and eating out of the same pot after 2,000 miles. They still shared their 10 x 10 ft. tarp. We exchanged trail news and stories with them. They would bring news of us ahead, and we would have their reports for those who caught up. We talked of the water in northern California, solutions to the cattle problem (a .357 Magnum was mentioned), inquired after the welfare of hikers ahead and behind, traded incredible stories of animals, hardships, sickness, and plummeting down 59 switchbacks. Each hiker is like a small town newspaper. The more trail gossip, editorials, weather predictions, current events and not so current, the better.

It rains quite often in Oregon. Overcast and chilly, I hiked with 3 layers on top, shorts and rain pants. The silnylon jacket did a great job keeping out the wind and rain. The attached silnylon mittens worn over fleece gloves kept my hands warm. Rainmaker was wearing Nike sandals, with Smart Wool socks, both he bought in Bend. Due to a foot injury suffered the first day hiking from Crater Lake, his New Balance Shoes were causing extreme pain. These sandals replaced the shoes and allowed us to go on, over snow and glaciers. I noticed his sandals never got heavier, because the water just drained away, but my high tops with shoe inserts grew heavier and completely water logged. A sharp pain developed in my instep every time I climbed with this additional stress. In the mornings he dried his sandals, and started out with dry feet. My shoes never dried completely for days on end. This is how I got my bright idea of hiking the Appalachian Trail in sandals.

Ollalie Lake Resort, reportedly quite similar to Shelter Cove Resort, was our next resupply stop.

"Maybe they'll have some decent deals. Like ramen, 2 for a dollar. Or, buy one oatmeal, get one free." Rainmaker quietly considered my banter, so I continued, "Maybe like a free motel room with the purchase of every ramen." Rain turned and gave me an incredulous look. We silently regarded each other a few moments. "Ok, maybe not," I conceded.

When we arrived, we found limited food supplies, and expensive. A microwave was available to the public, so I made popcorn. Hot coffee, and hot water were free. Ramen was 75 cents. There were bagels, muffins and pastries for a dollar each. At times like this, one must be creative. We asked to see the hiker box and found a plastic jar of unopened peanut butter, a few packages of oatmeal, and some powdered energy drink. While I sorted through the hiker box, Rainmaker was making friends. One local hiker, leaving the next day because of bad weather, offered his food to Rainmaker, who accepted graciously. Most small convenience stores have candy bars and snack chips. This one also had two loaves of bread behind a glass door. I selected the potato bread. With peanut butter, that would be our lunch. Then I noticed a bit of green mold starting on the crust, so instead of charging the $3.59 cents, the owner gave it to me.

Rainmaker and I took some time on the front porch to split up our finds, examine our food bags, eat, and plan the rest of the resupply. At times like this, it isn't so much variety, as volume. And, money isn't very important when you are cold and hungry, fifty miles from town. A Snickers bar for breakfast, a peanut butter sandwich for lunch, something hot for supper (like oatmeal, soup, instant rice, potatoes or ramen), a few handfuls of corn chips for a second course, then a candy bar for dessert would be this week's menu. It was amazing how much food it took to maintain my energy and stay warm. It takes a lot of calories.

Finally resupplied, we left Ollalie in the rain. Days later, we could see Mt. Hood in the distance. It was appropriate to approach such a place over several days. The mountain itself seemed to own a spirit dangerously aloof. Although it permitted people to come and eat, celebrate and play on its slopes, one could also die there.

We spent twenty-four hours at Government Camp, the town just three miles southwest of Mt. Hood. During that time, I scouted the town, and found that all the gear shops will wax snowboards, sell ski clothing, and stock accessories. This town seems to cater specifically to the snowboarders who practice and play year round on the glaciers of the mountain. Summer school was in session for teenagers wishing to learn and perfect their skills. There was no hiker gear in any shop I visited. All snow gear. I cruised every shop in town looking for a serious hip belt. No luck. Not even close. This town had a great grocery store, with inexpensive fruit pies and candy bars. A trail mix of pretzels, slightly crushed, Fritos, and chocolate chips is pretty decent. I bought a pound of each and mixed them in a gallon bag.

As we headed north, lots of raspberry, thimbleberries and huckleberries lined the trail. At lower elevations the berries were ripe and delicious. The vegetation covered the trail in many areas, making it hard to see the rocks below. Great views then opened up of the Columbia River Gorge, and northerly views of Mt. St. Helens, Rainer and Mt. Adams.

Tuesday, August 7th is a day I will never forget. Southbounders had told us there was free camping for PCT hikers at the RV Marine Campground ¼ mile east of the town called Cascade Locks. That sounded like a great place to camp, with free showers, flush toilets, lights and hot food. So, headed to town after hot coffee and cream cheese bagels for breakfast, we packed and were on the trail by 7:30 a.m. I was strolling along past waterfalls, ahead of Rainmaker, eating ripe thimbleberries at the edge of the trail, daydreaming, and simply enjoying the early morning.

I rounded one curve and heard noises down in a narrow deep canyon, and thought, "People. What on earth are they doing down there?" The winding trail was a narrow ledge, which dropped off into the canyon on the right, with the wall rising straight up on my left. I continued munching trailside berries, rounded another bend, when suddenly there was a "swoosh" by my right shoulder. Thinking a branch had brushed my pack, I turned to look. There was a large black shape next to the tree at the trail's edge. "David, a bear!" I shouted. I looked up, and saw her cub in the tree that was so close I could touch it.

I began backing up, hitting my hiking poles together as a million thoughts raced through my mind. How on earth did I not see her? Oh my god, I just walked right past a mother bear and cub. Not wanting David to walk past her as I did, I called several times, "David, a bear!" I could not see him, but that bear was in full view now. She rose to her full height, looking very angry, and began to huff and woof. I kept backing up, glancing behind at the trail so I wouldn't fall off, and also hoping that I wasn't backing into another bear. I have no idea why I could not scream or yell, but just kept watching her as I anticipated her bluff charge. A bluff charge, I asked myself? Is there any room for a bluff charge? All my senses were getting ready for it, determined no matter what happened, not to run. Determined not to touch her unless, or until, she made contact.

Around the bend David was calling to me, "Carol, don't run! Don't run!" Because of the topography and noise from the waterfall, we could neither hear nor see each other, and had no idea what the other was doing. He had seen the cub scurry up the tree, and then he had seen the mother rise up. Knowing I was just ahead, he kept advancing on the mother bear, yelling to me, hoping I could hear, hoping she would become confused, perhaps be distracted, and even turn her attention to him. It worked. Finally, she dropped on all fours, and ran down into the canyon. Her cub soon followed. Then, Rainmaker came around the bend.

We held each other close for a while, reliving it and retelling our experiences over and over. I had never had anyone risk his or her life for me. I don't think I ever had anyone who was willing to. David took an offensive role to save my life, jeopardizing his own. It is something I will never forget.

Safe and sound, we continued on the Eagle Creek Trail, a marvelous section that brought us past Tunnel Falls, and unpaintable beauty. There is cable embedded in the canyon walls for hand holds along that narrow stretch. We took photos under waterfalls, and strolled into town by 3:30. We hiked down to camp on the designated site, near the six sets of train tracks by 4:30 pm, and later went to supper.

That night I couldn't sleep. Perhaps I had eaten too much taco salad. Maybe it was the Quarterly Hour Special, a freight train roaring past, shaking the ground to pieces. Maybe I'd seen Green Fried Tomatoes too many times. Maybe I was still wound up from the bear encounter. I kept reminding myself that adventure was a trail gift, to see bears so close. Whatever the reason, I made the well-lit public bathroom my office and sat writing my journal and drinking water at 2 a.m. Could be worse. Lots worse.

His Dream

"Would you tell me your dream, David?" We lounged on the side of the trail in a beautiful, intimate spot, snacking under an overhang. He looked at me with those piercing blue eyes. He did not answer, so I assumed he was puzzled

"That dream you had when I was hiking in the desert, the one you mentioned when I called home from Cajon Pass." He frowned and looked towards the ground. Still, he did not speak. I waited a few minutes, then softly said, "Don't tell me if you don't want to, that's ok." I respected this man, this one with spirituality few people could ever attain. Rainmaker has some special connection with the natural world. Forces gravitated towards him, which accounted for all the adventures we shared.

While resting together in a comfortable silence, I watched his face. "Alright, I'll tell you, but it's going to be difficult," he decided. Rainmaker is not one to be rushed. I had frequently thought about this unknown dream since he mentioned it two months ago. It had to be something disturbing, something unspeakable. He had wanted reassurance that all was well, that day we spoke on the phone, so long ago. Yes, I'm fine. Everything is fine, really, I had told him.

"I heard your footsteps, as you came walking down the hall towards our bedroom. I woke up and saw you standing for a moment in the doorway. Your hair was white, you were entirely white," he began sadly. "You came and pulled the covers back, and lay beside me. I could feel you there. I reached over to put my hand on you, and touch your body next to mine. And then, I knew you were just a spirit; that you had died on the trail. You asked the Great Spirit if you could come back to me, just for a little while, because our time had been so short together. I couldn't sleep anymore. At the time, I didn't know if it had been a dream or if it was real, so I got out of bed and sat in my chair, and waited for you. Every day I wondered, and waited, until finally you phoned from Cajon Pass. I couldn't tell you the dream then."

Rainmaker spoke so softly; I could see the dream myself. Sobs began to escape me; my greatest fear had been exposed. Taught for 25 years that if I ever left church God would kill me, every day that passed, I felt was on borrowed time. An angry God was about to strike. The teaching and practice of that fundamentalist church was that someone who left the church for a life of "sin" would be turned over to the devil for the destruction of the flesh, so that the soul could be saved. And, even worse, I feared God would kill David to punish me.

"Yes, that's exactly what would happen. I would beg to come back to you for awhile longer," I sobbed.

The inner spirit whispers: Treasure the time together; love this man who risked his life for you. Maybe that is how life should be lived. Here and now is all we have. But, not to live in fear, for if there exists any dream or hope, now is the time to follow it. The clock holds no illusions of a tomorrow, and the calendar is just wishful thinking.

David knew a God who wasn't angry, who would allow us time together, and permit a shameless love. Tearing down the bars so firmly cemented is very painful. But, like a birth, when the agony is over there is relief.

Onward

Visualize having it
Devise a plan; Write it down in detail
Say no to anything that gets in the way
---author unknown

I had thought over every thought at least five times. I was running out of thoughts. I had redesigned my pack, designed new tents, clothes, and sleeping systems. I asked Rainmaker what thoughts occupied his mind. He replied that he was humming tunes. It had been a long time since I heard any tunes, but decided to hum what I could.

One day while hiking I noticed a lot of frogs on the trail. One even jumped out in front of me, hitting my pole, and bouncing off. Then he hopped away. A hit and run frog. There ought to be a law.

After crossing several water sources, we met three people heading south, towards us. A man in a white dress shirt (how odd), carrying topography maps, stopped and asked, "Do you know of any place these folks could camp with water?" He gestured towards the older couple. "Do you have any water you can spare? Is there any water ahead?" There was supposed to be a spring just off the trail, which they should have just passed. Strange they should be asking us for water. When we questioned them, they said it was dry. Indicating the spring we meant on the topography map, they warned us saying "No, it's dry. There is no water in this whole stretch." I was incredulous, just couldn't imagine. I told them of the water we'd passed, not to worry, that although we had none with us to spare, they would surely have water to drink soon.

David and I hiked about 15 minutes and distinctly heard the flowing spring on our right, exactly where it was supposed to be. Minutes later, we came upon several campsites, with definite trails leading downward, obvious signs to a long distance hiker of water nearby. At the end of a well-worn path was a large spring, flowing happily along, with all the water and flowers one could wish for.

These people brought themselves out here without the ability to find water. Very dangerous. Listening, quietness, and observation, will get you what you need, in almost all instances.

August 16th became a very frustrating day filled with a lot of climbing, beautiful views, and rugged terrain in the Goat Rocks Wilderness. We reached the Packwood Glacier, but the tread seemed to have disappeared. With the actual trail obliterated by rockslides, we tried crossing the scree field that was below it. Our eyes were fixed on the trail, which snaked up the other side. Rainmaker was taking his time, choosing his footing carefully. I had been hurrying ahead, anxious to be done with this off-trail scrambling, each step sending rocks cascading into the void. Being so close to getting back on the actual treadway, I didn't want to give up, yet the slope was becoming quite treacherous. Suddenly, Rainmaker called for me to turn back. All along, it had been iffy. I kept hearing noises from the mountain itself. The glacier above me seemed to be groaning, shifting, and adjusting to the summer sun. I glanced back at my partner, just in time to see a rockslide hurling down, barely missing him. I think that's when he had enough.

An alternate route over Old Snowy Mountain was the only option. My whole body screamed against the injustice of having to climb, when the data sheet said we were done with that for the day. The treadway down from Old Snowy was loose scree, and then began the undulations of the crest walk, as fog rolled in. I wasn't happy, and Rainmaker knew it. Silently, I was punishing him for making me turn back. I rebelled at admitting he was right.

Later, I told him how badly I had been sliding, watching the rocks I had dislodged go tumbling into the abyss. It would have been an absolutely gorgeous ridge walk had it not turned cold and windy, with night pressing us.

Finally, with partial views opening through the fog of high mountains and deep valleys, the trail descended to Elk Pass, and we camped near glacier melt streams in a sweet campsite, above 6600 ft. in elevation. For supper, I had a couple of cookies, a granola bar and glass of instant milk, then I fell asleep.

As we neared Canada, the weather cooled remarkably. I learned that rocks make a poor pot support in cold weather. They soak up all the heat the fuel puts forth. Tent stakes were proving workable, in spite of rainy weather. Again, I had mailed my esbit stove ahead, as I strove to lighten my pack. One who refuses to learn from history is doomed to repeat it. Not sure if an ultralighter said that, but they should have.

One night we set up camp just before another deluge started. I couldn't get my stakes into the rocky ground anywhere, to serve as a pot support. In spite of Rainmaker's offers, I refused to let him boil water for me. Just something about independence, pride, and ego. Finally, in desperation, I lay my hiking poles on the ground, side by side. With the metal ends just 2 inches apart, I placed a hexamine tablet between them on a piece of aluminum foil and lit it. The metal ends of my hiking poles became my pot support, while my partner laughed good-naturedly in disbelief. "Is that rubber I smell burning?" he asked. "Yeah, it's the snow basket gaskets," I replied.

The cry of an eagle or red tailed hawk is a beautiful sound, heard often in northern Washington. While climbing a steep trail, I realized how special it was to be out here. I raised my arms wide to embrace it all, looking skyward, being truly a part of this mountain. How will I ever go back to that job at the hospital? I am addicted to the free life, where my energy is its own reward.

Up in the heights I walk the ridge,
Looked way below, and saw the bridge.
I crossed that log this early morning
In spite of all day hiker warnings.
Wind blowing softly through my hair,
An eagle cries, I'll soon be there.
Never be tame again.

The Waptus River is wide, with many established campsites near the bridge. We had a relaxing supper, and wrote in our journals. Then, I took two extra strength Tylenol, zipped myself snug in my sleeping bag, inside the tent, and slept very soundly. Sometime before midnight, Rainmaker mentioned that "some damn mouse" ran across his arm. Yawn, yeah, ok. I turned over and resumed my deep sleep. Suddenly, it was very real. I sat up quickly around 2 a.m. and yelped, "A Mouse!!" It seemed as though one had just ran past my head.

Like a cougar, Rainmaker all at once and without a word, in three seconds flat flipped the flashlight on, tracked that mouse, located it next to his Therma Rest and beat it to death with his fist. He then unzipped the door and flung that sorry carcass outside by the tail. He zipped up the door, and lay back down. No swearing, no yelling, just pure action. Heavens! So that's how it's done! I could only lay there in total admiration.

That mouse must have been instinctively challenged. He had chewed a hole through the mesh at the foot of the tent, dropped down onto my food bag, and ran up to our heads to see if we were awake. Now he is smashed flatter than an ultralighter's sleeping bag. If I had been him, I'd have munched myself sick, then made a break for it at first light.

One night some critter stole two wads of my toilet paper I kept in my shoe just outside the tent door, for night trips. I was indignant; there's not an endless supply! I decided I would have to start sleeping with it, too.

I love it when the trail goes right through a town, or so close it's within walking distance. Otherwise, one must hitch hike. I've noticed it's never the people with the nice cars, the money or the space that give hikers a ride. It's invariably someone with an old car, having to move book bags, dogs, newspapers, taco chips, fast food wrappers and themselves over to make room. May all their kindness return to them a hundredfold. May gifts come their way, and sunshine be their portion. Those pushing a brand new two-ton vehicle through life, usually traveling alone, may they need a ride someday, and stand helplessly hoping.

Skycomish is a dying town. Only one motel remained in business in the year 2001. Seventy-Three dollars for a tiny room is high priced. However, it did have a microwave and small refrigerator, coffee pot and lots of TV channels. No laundry facilities. No, they couldn't let us use the motel washing machine for our wet and muddy gear. The manager said we should ask a local person to do our laundry for us. Excuse Me? Fine. I washed everything in the tub, hanging it to dry all around our room. The owner thought a load of wash would be hard on his septic tank. How about 2 bathtubs of hot water to wash with, and a couple more for rinsing? We left with cleaner clothes. It's all relative, anyway. We have a saying, Rainmaker and I. It's not actual dirt unless it's real shit. I mean that literally, like horse, cow, bear, fox, or human shit. Now, that's real dirt.

Everything in this town seemed to be closed, or for sale. The deli was for sale. The one restaurant was for sale. They kept whatever hours suited them. When I complained to another hiker that the diner closed unexpectedly at 2:00 one afternoon, he replied, "Well, then, you were lucky!" That hiker had managed to get a meal there the day before. So, we shopped at the Chevron mini-mart, bought food sufficient for a good resupply, and food for our meals, which we cooked in our motel room.

Rainmaker had his fleece bag liner sent to him here. I have needed mine and was relieved knowing he would be warmer. We could see our breath in the tent at night, wind chill must be hovering around 20 degrees.

Fire Creek Pass I believe to be the loveliest place on the entire Pacific Crest Trail. It was certainly my favorite. The evening sunshine brought out the golden hues of the fall colors and the ripe blueberries. The grade was gentle, the mood sublime. Perfect contentment, perfect harmony, and perfect companionship. We stopped and took several photos, all the while knowing it would never suffice. Lingering because we knew this hiking season would soon be finished.

Stehekin would be our last resupply. We were very happy to reach this town, nestled there in the mountains with only eleven miles of connecting road and a daily ferry giving this secluded village access to the outside world.

There were many hikers in this tiny village. Rainmaker and I quickly registered at the visitor center for the last free camping spot across the street. Laundry was done in the same building with the free showers. Up the street, many hikers were hanging out on the front deck of the only restaurant. Anyone who wanted to eat supper there must register early in the day. By the time we had our camp set up and showered, the store and restaurant were both closed. At 8:00 pm, everyone was on their own. Eating the last scraps from our food bags, we planned to do ungodly damage to the breakfast buffet, served in the morning, promptly at 7:30 a.m.

September Eleventh

We woke to a smoky valley. The wild fires were not yet extinguished. During the night, the fires gained the upper hand because darkness called in the fighters. Starving, we dressed and started walking down the main road to the restaurant for breakfast. Many of my friends were leaving for the trail as soon as they finished their meal. I wanted Rainmaker to meet them, especially Dell, a sixty-year-old retired biologist who ran one hundred mile ultra marathons. John and his dog Cyclone were also walking down the road to breakfast. He waited for us to catch up, then asked incredulously, "Did you hear? A ranger just told me the radio said that four planes have crashed. One into the Pentagon. Both World Trade Center towers are gone. The other one, I think, into the White House."

Disbelief, anxiety, and confusion followed us into the restaurant where twelve of us were seated at two long tables. The waiter told us what little he knew about the situation. In this remote town, radio reports were all they had. It was 7:30 Pacific time, 10:30 New York time.

The buffet included scrambled eggs, sausage, bacon, pancakes, fruit, milk, oatmeal, juice and coffee. While we ate, rumors philosophies and theories, from those once united by a common love, now divided us. Some political discussion surfaced, and a hiker angrily left the table. Photos were taken, good-byes and best of luck extended to friends we would probably never see again. There remained just 89 miles to the Canadian border. Only days.

Finally stuffed, and the buffet emptied, we walked next door to the store to supplement our drop box resupply. Ten people stood around listening intently to the radio turned up for customers and employees alike. From the streets of Manhattan directly to backwoods Stehekin, reports came live, transmitting the agony and fear. One woman was crying, telling listeners around the world of the people she saw, even while she spoke, jumping to their deaths. Desperate in their hopelessness, from the upper windows of the World Trade Center people flung themselves towards the pavement. Everyone was fleeing, all of lower Manhattan being evacuated, and the smoke, incredible suffocating smoke was everywhere.

My god, I thought, this is real. This is America. The country was in readiness, our politicians were telling us. We were in an advanced state of emergency. And the question on everyone's tongue "Who are these terrorists?" We are told the Mexican and Canadian borders are closed. No planes are flying; all have been grounded until further notice.

Nothing made sense. A sick feeling came over me. I must get some fresh air. I must do something that makes sense. Rainmaker remains listening while I leave the store to work on my resupply. Not once do we consider not crossing that border. We have come too far, suffered too much, been out here too long. Neither Rainmaker, nor I, will turn back now.

My magic trail spoon disappeared. I carried that same spoon with me since the Lassen Park stream crossing, where I found it last year by the river's edge. I looked high and low, through every stuff sack, and every corner of our tent. I went over the campground five times, checked the bear box, and retraced my steps, over and over. Then, I chided myself. Get real. People have lost their lives today, and you are mourning the loss of a spoon.

Hikers continued coming into town, were met with the news, shared the utter amazement and shock, which turned to anger that someone would commit this horrible act of violence. We thrilled at the story that four men on the last flight, hearing via cell phone of their fate, rushed the terrorists, still crashing, still dying, but as lions, and not sheep. And I think, "Never Again." Never again will a hijacker be allowed to take over, take us anywhere. We are not pawns. Never again will we allow it.

But for now, the trail claims our attention. We rest, resupply, and mail home the final extras, those last few ounces not needed.

I met Zion, a thoughtful, intelligent 23 year old. He expressed concern that he will get drafted. Walking Bob invites Zion to come to Canada and hang out. He was hiking for Parkinson's disease and bought two mousetraps there in Stehekin to eliminate the constant pests beneath his tarp. Jack, who I haven't seen since Echo Lake, made it in. He is looking hungry, much older, and quite tired.

We left Stehekin the next morning after the ferry arrived with the only newspapers that village will see. I tried to buy a newspaper but the tourist ahead of me scooped up the last one. We stood around him on shore, as he slowly opened and paged through for our benefit. A small crowd, reading over his shoulder, standing closer than family, saw photos for the first time of our national disaster. Then, Rainmaker and I took the 11 o'clock bus out of town back to the trail. Eric and Molly, friends I'd met way back at Lake Morena, were catching that bus into town. Introductions were made, hugs and trail news exchanged. We broke the news of the disaster, to the best of our knowledge. The bus was returning to town, so we said our last good-byes and hiked into the wilderness, leaving our nation to deal with its emergency. Until we arrived in Canada, we would receive no updates.

To The Canadian Border and Home

Now there were plenty of thoughts to occupy my mind. The state of our country, body aches and pains mounting up, how we were getting home, and new gear for a thru-hike of the Appalachian Trail. The smoke had abated and it appeared we would not have to reroute around any forest fires.

Border fever was a tangible feeling now. It drew us like a magnet, that last week of anticipation of completion, giving strength to tired bodies. We met Bad Boy Billy Bean and traded stories. He told us about a fellow hiker who awoke to find a bear's face in his tent. He hauled off and slugged the intruder in the nose. The bear retreated, and the hiker went back to sleep. My friend Patch gained lasting admiration when we learned he had driven a cougar off twice in one evening, so that he could camp by water.

Beautiful weather continued. After a couple days, we saw one jet contrail, which meant the planes must be flying once more. What I would have given for a current newspaper!

We were weary, and only time would tell if gear, body or weather would hold up to the end. Early one morning, my trail spoon poured out of my Cheerios bag. Just before dawn, with barely enough light to see, a large object started falling out of my breakfast zip lock bag when I dumped the cold cereal into my pot. At first, I thought it was a mouse, and was both repelled by the notion, yet curious about the creature. Then I realized it was my lost trail spoon. It had returned to me. Rainmaker understood when I kissed it, and reprimanded it for leaving me, for hiding like that and making me worry so.

Early morning hunters with high-powered rifles and scopes were seen everyday now. A buck walks into our camp early one morning, and shares the sunrise with us. He is safe until we leave. My blue sleeping pad was strapped on outside my pack, so we were more visible. I don't mind the hunters. They teach bears respect.

Layers of colors surrounded us; fall had arrived. The weather is perfect. A hawk circled overhead, then a vulture. "Not yet!" we called to him.

Rainmaker taught me so much, and it was always such a joy sharing trail adventures, stories and dreams. We will finish the Pacific Crest Trail together, a continuous unbroken line from the Mexican border to Manning Park, Canada. As we discussed the future, I realized he was contemplating the end of his long distance hiking career, as I was contemplating the beginning of mine. I love this life, and at last have found my peers. At last I feel respected, rewarded and allowed to find out who I am. Our appearance is horrible, untrimmed, ragged, and dirty. Our clothes don't match. We make no fashion statements. Often misunderstood and thought homeless, many of us are economically at the poverty level, and enjoying it.

On Monday, September 17th, David and I neared the Canadian border. Now I stopped, and waited for Rainmaker to lead the way. This adventure had begun as his hike. He had invited me along last year. He has led me to this discovery. It seemed appropriate that he should see Canada first, touch that monument, and rest his pack against the sign that designated our crossing.

The drama was nearly complete, and I would cherish it forever. You never loose things won at such cost, they will always be there for you. The mountains have infused us with their spirits. No matter what happens to us or around us, we will always be strong; we will always have our identity.

I looked up the side of the mountain, and saw a narrow strip of trees torn down at the base. That is one skinny avalanche! Oh, that is the border! We reached the monument, and Rainmaker raised his fist in a victory salute. Section hikers were lounging nearby and they took our photos. We ate some snacks, leaving just enough for supper and a light breakfast. Then we uncapped the monument, dug deep inside the pillar and found the register. We signed it, and read the names of those who came before us.

After many congratulations, we hiked up to a designated camping area near Windy Joe Mountain, in Canada. Twenty teenagers with two chaperones were already camped there. It was full with only one space left for a small tent just a bit off the trail in the main area. Since it was nearly dark, we immediately set up camp, and began cooking.

Kids are full of curiosity. These young people kept coming by asking us about water. They leapt over my aluminum pot, with its one last meal cooking over an esbit stove. I was afraid they would knock it over, contents, flaming hex tablet and all. After I had to change clothes in the tent to avoid the boys' eyes I really started to feel crowded. Finally, a large group came so near, stepping over my stuff, I ceased cooking, and looked them steadily in the eyes. In a soft slow voice I said, "I am drawing a circle around our site. Next one who steps over the line gets shot." They stopped, looked at me seriously, and gave me plenty of elbow space. No one crossed over that line the rest of the evening. Rainmaker was leaning against a tree. Silently, he looked at me with blue smiling eyes, and continued cooking. I sensed approval. The kids went to sleep early and except for the noisy attempts of the chaperones to hang their food bags, by flashlight, our last night on the trail was quiet.

As agreed, we woke at 4:30 a.m. and cooked coffee by red and green photon lights. I hung my red light on the tent door, setting a very mysterious atmosphere. We shared our peanut butter and whole-wheat bread, each getting a sandwich with predawn coffee. Hard to believe. Hard to believe it's finished. I go home now. That was the last night on the Pacific Crest Trail. I had been hiking for nearly five months now. They say it changes you. They say you will never be the same. I think they must be right.

Rainmaker and I packed up quietly and hit the trail as soon as we could see without lights. Only about four miles to go. By 8:30 we came to Gibson Road, a parking lot and "The End". We then hiked on the road until it came to Hwy. 3. We turned left and there was the Manning Park complex; cabins, lodge, restaurant, gift shop, and groceries. We enjoyed a very nice breakfast, and saw other long distance hikers eating there, also. By paying with a credit card, the money change was no problem. If one pays with American dollars, they give Canadian back. Exchange rate was 40% increase in our favor.

We took the Greyhound bus to Vancouver. From there the 5 p.m. Amtrak bus took us to Seattle. The Customs officers were very thorough. The agent had problems seeing the bearded Rainmaker as the clean-shaven David Mauldin, the man on his driver's license photo. After David removed his glasses, and reminded the officer that it had been a long hike, the agent finally let him pass. We flew out of Seattle on our reserved flight, the 22nd of September.

Reflections

So many things lost their influence on the trail. Money only mattered when I was in town, and then, it was spent on real things, like food and clothing. Reduced to drinking out of a plastic peanut butter jar, wearing the same clothes day after day for 5 months, and making all my worldly possessions fit into the pack, proved how little one really needs to be happy. The less I had, the more complete my experience. A materialistic attitude is detrimental to a long distance hiker.

The need for noise was replaced by quietness and focus on life: taking time to look, and see what is before me, observing the bears, snakes, water, wind, weather. Reading the true nature of things. Knowing now, for a certainty, that a person is truly responsible for his or her own happiness.

Society lost its power, and a new definition of the Real World replaced it. It is very real when one faces wilderness elements and life's basic needs daily. Civilization seemed contrived, with all its self-inflicted trappings. Walls are built to keep things in, and out.

What works for me is here and now, and may not work for me forever, or for anyone else, now, or ever. I really learned to live in the moment, and for the moment. Respect is earned by what one does, not what one has.

Chapter Five

Life-Lessons

In the fall of 2001, Rainmaker and I returned from the Pacific Crest trail, and enlarged our website, http://www.trailquest.net. We started selling silnylon tarps, rain pants and rain jackets, in addition to the stuff sacks, pack covers and patterns for our tents, the Lakota and the Cherokee. Our business partnership, Dancing Light Gear, began October 2000. I earned just enough to support my investment in designing, creating and testing backpacking gear for personal use, while maintaining my source of income by cooking at the hospital.

Foolishly, reluctantly, I resumed cooking at the hospital within one week of returning home from the trail. As usual, the kitchen was in turmoil, a true representation of society at its best and most human state. My mind would wander back to the freedom of the trail and the solidarity I felt with all things wild. My co-workers noticed a big change. No longer did I cower at their criticism, but defended my status and myself and made no effort to hide plans to hike again next spring. No one could imagine how one obtains such freedom; I could feel their resentment. There was such a difference between the women I worked with and myself. While they spent a great deal of money on clothing and furniture, I saved it for long distance hiking.

I love my home in the mountains with David, but longed to earn the title of Thru-Hiker. In the traditional, purist sense of the term, a thru-hiker is one who hikes an entire trail in one calendar year. Yellow blazing occurs when one hitch hikes ahead, skipping trail sections. Blue blazing is taking a short cut, or alternate trail. The Appalachian Trail, all 2,168 miles of it, is well marked and maintained with white blazes. My personal goal was to accomplish a purist thru-hike. Rainmaker and I agreed there was no reason to wait, that 2002 was a good year.

Personal issues and nightmares still haunted me. Many times I dreamt that all my freedom had been lost, and would wake up crying, wondering what had happened to Rainmaker. I wrote the poem "Survival Tree" in an effort to confront these fears and attempt an explanation of my moods. And, I hoped, given enough time, unburdened and free, I would no longer resemble a survival tree.

Survival Trees
the ones who could have died,
fallen upon, gnawed on, fire
ravaged,
They are misshaped, ugly, and
deformed.
Perhaps no traces of the torments
remain.
No one can tell why the tree looks
like it does,
this perverse tree reaching for the
sun.
But it lives, and that's what is
important.
It survives, that's what matters.
The big strong straight trees have
fallen,
are rotting.
But the survival tree remains.
That's me. ---*Brawny*

Appalachian Trail Preparations

As I prepared for the Appalachian Trail, every gear item was
scrutinized. My rain jacket and rain pants were still in usable
condition after five months on the Pacific Crest Trail. I realized a
pack made in that same fabric, 1.1 ounce per yard, silicone
impregnated rip stop nylon, would be very light, and strong. Last
year's silnylon stuff sacks were still in reasonable shape in spite of
being used externally (with my packless system) for several months. I
designed the 8-ounce silpack, fashioned as an upright oversized stuff
sack, and sewed it that winter. One tall stuff sack was placed inside a
shorter stuff sack, with almost the same diameters, and stitched at the
bottom. Four exterior pockets were formed by sewing 4 vertical
seams up the sides. A mesh pocket was added later, which brought it
up to 9 ounces, and an estimated capacity of 2,288 cubic inches. A
top flap (the width of the pack) covered the opening and also had a
pocket, providing additional space. All the seams were sealed with
silicone. I added wide shoulder straps, (made from a closed cell pad)
and covered them with silnylon. My water bottles were carried in
their silnylon bags on the shoulder straps. The water provided a
counter balance when the bottles were full. Many people questioned
whether this pack could hold all my winter gear, with enough food to

last between resupplies. I planned to give it a try. I made a hip belt the same way I did the shoulder straps, anticipating heavier loads when leaving town with 6 days of food.

Rainmaker and I began the search for a pair of shower tongs. The only ones I could find weighed three to four ounces. I decided to do without, until Rainmaker made some one-ounce "gram weenie" sandals for me. Made with shoe inserts and cord threaded through ventilation holes, they were light, fit well, and took up very little space. With such a small pack, the volume of an item was every bit as important as the weight. I wore these sandals everywhere in trail towns, shelters, on side trails to the privy and in public showers in hostels. From Fontana Dam to Katahdin, this ultralight footwear received much acclaim.

Rainmaker cut my orange plastic trowel down so that the handle was one inch shorter, and trimmed the blade by an inch and a half. This saved space, and ¾ ounce. To commemorate my special piece of gear, I wrote my name and the date on it with a permanent magic marker.

A silnylon tarp measuring 5 feet x 8 feet weighs 7 ounces and can be successfully pitched for protection from rear and side wind and rain, using only 5 stakes and one guy line. We have used a trapezoidal floor, with the door on the side in several new ways. The resulting shelters and tarps are offered at Dancing Light Gear. We call them Tacoma tarps and shelters.

To pitch any rectangular tarp in a "Tacoma" configuration spread it full length on the ground. Stake down the back two corners, then pull the front forward and inward, forming a trapezoidal floor. This will create slack in the front, which will be taken up when the front pole is inserted. The greater the difference between the back and front lengths, the higher the pitch. Keep a low pitch in inclement weather, a higher pitch to break the wind, in good weather. Stake out the two front corners. Insert your hiking pole; lengthen until the canopy is taut. Tighten the pole and stake it out, using a guy line. The five-point tension will keep the pole in place, if its tip is inserted into a grommet or loop. The pole may be inverted, and the handle uppermost if it is secured with a clip in the wrist strap to the tarp. Silnylon is quite slippery; special care must be taken when using it. A customer requested a "beak" be sewn on for this pitching option. We designed an overhanging panel for various lengths of tarps. While working on this custom order, I saw my Tacoma Tent take shape. Further development led to the Tacoma line of shelters.

The quest for a solo ultralight tent weighing under a pound occupied my mind, on or off the job. By sewing a floor and special drop-down screen door onto my Tacoma tarp, my tent for the Appalachian Trail thru-hike was created. I put a swing-style storm door on my tent. Seam sealed, with six stakes and guy lines, the weight was a very respectable 18 ounces.

Hiking poles form the frame of every shelter I design. Hanging loops are also sewn into the outside peaks for those that do not use poles, for instance, on the massive 41-ounce Cheyenne teepee. This silnylon teepee was designed and put online for all to view in December of 2002.

Sometimes a second pole or lift loop can be used to raise the exterior back wall. All the Tacoma shelters have a loop for that purpose.

We started making the silnylon rain suit available to the public at our online store, Dancing Light Gear. It has a remarkable low weight of 4-5 ounces for a jacket with hood and pockets, and 2 ounces for most rain pants. We did custom sizing and colors on every order. Because they are so durable I knew our customers would have them for a long time, so fit was really important. I was able to quit my job in February 2002, to concentrate on our new business. At the same time, preparations were made for a departure in late March for the Appalachian Trail.

Preparations for the Appalachian Trail Thru-Hike
My Gear List
--- With explanations of later modifications for the Appalachian Trail thru-hike follows:

Tent: The Tacoma, with 6 stakes and seam sealing.... 18 ounces-(no additional modifications).
Pack: My homemade Silpack, after I added mesh pockets weighed 9 ounces. I used it the entire trip.
Both weighed a total of only twenty-seven ounces, and were used the entire trip.

Clothing
Fleece Jacket: I sewed a hood and mittens onto this Columbia pullover. Mittens were sewn onto the sleeves, topside only. This allows them to be folded back and tucked inside my sleeve when not in use. This design originated when I made my silnylon rain jacket for

the PCT hike in 2001. They were very useful, so I put some fleece mittens on my fleece jacket the same way.
The fleece jacket weighed 12 ounces. I kept it the entire trip.
Fleece Tights: These tights were also homemade, so they would fit tightly, and not be too long. They weighed 7 ounces. I sent them home at Damascus.
Silnylon rain jacket: This is the same jacket that won a prize in 2001 on the Pacific Crest Trail. It weighed 4 ounces. As a vital layer all year long, I kept it the entire trip.
Silnylon rain pants: The same rain pants used on the PCT. I used them in my sleeping bag and also when hiking. They weighed only 2 ounces, so I kept them the entire trip.
Gram weenie sandals: Rainmaker made these for me. Weighing only 1 ounce, I carried them from Fontana Dam, NC to the end of the trail at Mt. Katahdin in Maine.
Silk shorts: A friend gave these to me in Harper's Ferry. I kept them for sleeping. The shorts weighed 2 ounces.

    The following items I carried from Springer Mtn., Georgia to Waynesboro, Virginia. There, I packed them into a cardboard drop box and sent them ahead to Glencliff, New Hampshire to be used only in the White Mountains. They were discarded in Gorham, New Hampshire:
Nylon tights: These had the feet sewn in, and weighed only 3 ounces.
Silk long sleeve shirt: This shirt was a pullover and was nearly worn out from previous hikes. I bought a button down silk shirt in Waynesboro, and threw the old one away. Both weighed the same, at 4 ounces.
Smart Wool socks: These socks were my warm layer for sleeping and weighed 4 ounces.
Watch cap: This homemade cap was made of a lightweight fleece and weighed just one and a half ounces.
Fleece gloves: The gloves were not needed in the summer because of the mittens that were attached to my rain jacket as well as my fleece jacket. They weighed 1.5 ounces, and were handy in the cold months and in the White Mountains.

Total weight of clothing when I began at Springer Mtn., Georgia was 43 ounces, or 2 pounds 11 ounces. When I finished the trail at Mt. Katahdin in Maine, the weight of my clothing was 21 ounces.

Cooking System

My **original system** for 1,600 miles contained a 3-cup capacity aluminum cook pot with lid, a plastic margarine container for a cup, and my magic trail spoon. The **soda can stove, pot support, and windscreen** all nested in the pot. I used hexamine solid fuel tablets. With matches, and lighter, this system weighted 10 ounces.

My **new system** for the last 591 miles (Massachusetts Hwy. 2 to Mt. Katahdin) contained the same soda can stove and magic trail spoon, matches and lighter. Rainmaker made a new pot support from a 15-ounce bean can to hold my mini-pot, which was made from a gel canned heat container. A lid for this pot was fashioned from a cat food lid that had been sanded and taped with heat resistant tape. A windscreen was made from aluminum foil. A **cup-bowl system** made from a powdered drink mix was used as my rehydration cook set. It was trimmed so that it was just tall enough for the mini-pot, pot support and soda can stove to nest inside. This new system weighed only 3 ounces. With the magic trail spoon, 8 hex tablets, plastic 8-ounce soda bottle for fuel, matches and lighter the new cook system weight was 7.5 ounces.

Total weight at beginning of hike: 10 ounces
Total weight at end of hike: 7.5 ounces

Sleeping System

Cats Meow Sleeping Bag: This 20 degree synthetic bag was cut down to fit me, yet it weighed 40 ounces. In Damascus I bought a 30-degree **Marmot 800 fill** goose down bag, which I modified to fit my height, forming a soft insulating "nest" of feathers for my feet. It weighed only 24 ounces and stuffed to half the volume of my Cats Meow model.

Closed cell short pad: Trimmed to 19 inches wide and 53 inches long, it weighed 8 ounces. I kept this same pad the entire trip.

Kitchen size garbage bag: Used to line my sleeping bag stuff sack.

Total weight at beginning of hike: 48 ounces
Total weight at end of hike: 32 ounces

Others

Trail guide, and data sheets, credit card, driver's license: The weight varied with the quantity. It usually was about 4 ounces, with a pen. I later reduced it to just 4 sheets of trimmed paper at any given time, which lowered the weight to about an ounce. I used the backside of guide sheets for my journal, mailing them home as often as possible. I burned my data sheets in campfires and bought envelopes at the post office as needed.

Silnylon ditty bag was used as a wallet, and weighed 7 grams.

Silnylon pack cover was 1.5 ounces.

Photon lights, ultralight can opener, razor-knife and watch (minus the band) were all threaded onto an elastic cord, and carried in my pocket. They weighed 1 ounce. I kept all these items the entire trip.

Total weight at beginning of hike: 7 ounces
Total weight at end of hike: 4 ounces

Hygiene/Medical

A **ditty bag** containing the following items (in the smallest, sample sizes available) included:

Tooth brush, toothpaste, floss

cotton balls, 2 oz. bottle rubbing alcohol

Multi-vitamins and Ibuprofen, in snack size zip lock bags

ultralight mirror, tweezers, razor

sunscreen/ Deet/ Vaseline

liquid soap.... 1 ounce

chlorine for water purification in a one ounce bottle

ultralight trowel, t-paper

The only things I eliminated here were the vitamins (which had become bad with the humidity), the soap and sunscreen.

Total weight at beginning of hike: 9 ounces
Total weight at end of hike: 5.5 ounces

Murphy Kit

My **needles** were taped to the tube of Vaseline to keep them safe. I used dental floss for thread.

Free flowing super glue, and a few **safety pins**

Electrical tape was wound around water bottles. I kept all these items to the end.

Total weight: 2 ounces

Wearing

For the purpose of a "skin out", or base weight, I list these items:

Shorts, with pockets made of 100% nylon were 5 ounces. I later found a lighter pair for 4 ounces.

My **sports shirt** had a built in bra, and lasted the entire trail, weighed 3 ounces.

I started in sandals, which hurt my knees, and changed to trail

runners that weighed 24 ounces. The shoes I finished with weighed 22 ounces.
I wear only one pair of **100% nylon socks** at a time. They weigh 1 ounce.
A 100% cotton **bandana** lasted the entire trail and weighed 1 ounce.
My **sunglasses** weigh 1 ounce.

Total weight at beginning of hike: 35 ounces
Total finish at end of hike: 32 ounces

Komperdell Hiking poles, a Christmas present from Rainmaker were not included in pack weight, they weighed 18 ounces.

  At the beginning of my hike, my total pack weight, without food and water, for cold weather (including clothing worn) was 181 ounces, or 11.31 pounds. At the completion of my hike, my total pack weight, including clothing worn, was 130 ounces, or 8 pounds 2 ounces.
  This is a valid weight. The Port Clinton outfitter weighed my pack at 14 pounds. It had four days of food, and 12 ounces of water. After Port Clinton, I lightened my cook system, and stopped carrying the soap and sunscreen. It may be noted that although I am a small person and therefore each item can be lighter, as a soloist I still required all the gear a very tall person would. This final base pack weight is about 7% of my body weight. With food for 4 days, and a quart of water, it is approximately 12% of my body weight. Given the very cold weather situations, including 4 days of food and a quart of water, the percentage would rise to nearly 16%.

Ultralight Passion
  One can survive with very little. I am predisposed to this frame of mind. My mom raised six of us alone; Dad took off when I was only 4 years old. We lived on next to nothing during my entire childhood. I learned to make do with what I had, or make things out of other people's discards.
  When Henry Thoreau was once asked to advise on how one might sell more decorative baskets (as an income), he said that he spent his time figuring out ways not to have to sell them. That's a great ultralight attitude. If I don't need it, I don't have to earn it, and I don't have to carry it.
  A minimalist attitude is not really a change for me. I have never been an accumulator. If I wasn't using it, out it went. While hiking

solo, with a lot of time for deep thinking, I finally realized that part of this mindset is a direct result of the fundamentalist church doctrine that everything a married woman had belonged to her husband. In that case, I reasoned, hidden, honestly earned money was better than anything visible. Part of my minimalist attitude was the sense of impending homelessness; the less I had, the less to leave behind, the less to move. Trinkets of life are beautiful, but they all require energy to maintain.

I still work through those negative feelings, the last remaining bars to come down. I have become self-sufficient; and remind myself that assuredly I have the ability to survive. What still perplexes me is this continuing notion of perceived security in ownership, and its natural corollary: perceived insecurity when without ownership.

In the great quest for the best gear for the lowest weight, I give myself permission to have just what I want. Usually that means making it, or searching through catalogues and store aisles for something that can be modified. This way, it can be cut down to the extreme I am comfortable with.

One of my favorite Thoreau quotes supports this extremism:
"Most men are needlessly poor all their lives because they think they must have a house as their neighbors have. Consider how slight a shelter is absolutely necessary."

Chapter Six

Appalachian Trail 2002

**If I knew then what I know now, I don't know if I would play.
-From My Story, by Michael Jordan**

Your First Game

This is your first game.
I hope you win.
I hope you win for your sake, not mine.
Because winning's nice.
It's a good feeling.
Like the whole world is yours.
But it passes, this feeling.
And what lasts is what you've learned.

And what you learn about is life.
That's what sports is all about.
Life.
The whole thing is played out in an afternoon.
The happiness of life.
The miseries.
The joys. The heartbreaks.

There's no telling what'll turn up.
There's no telling whether they'll toss you out in the first five minutes
or whether you'll stay for the long haul.

There's no telling how you'll do.
You might be a hero or you might be absolutely nothing.
Too much depends on chance.
On how the ball bounces.

I'm not talking about the game;
I'm talking about life.
But it's life that the game is all about.
Just as I said.

But every game is life.
And life is a game.
A serious one. Dead serious.

But that's what you do with serious things. You do your best.
You take what comes.
You take what comes and you run with it.

Winning is fun.
Sure.
But winning is not the point.

Wanting to win is the point.
Not giving up is the point.
Never being satisfied with what you've done is the point.
Never letting up is the point.
Never letting anyone down is the point.

Play to win.
Sure.
But lose like a champion.
Because it's not winning that counts.
What counts is trying. —Author Unknown

Michael then said, "I can't accept not trying."

This favorite poem, found in some obscure newspaper about ten years ago, took me through many rough times, including my divorce and relocating to the southern U.S. When I faced loneliness on the trail and turning points in life, I remembered that this was my first game, all of it. I would not give up, nor be satisfied with the past. I was in this to win, and would die trying.

It started raining last night, but still it was time to begin my AT thru-hike. Rainmaker drove me to the trailhead at Springer Mountain via Forest Service Road 42 on March 12, 2002. This is a 15-mile gravel road, and it allowed me to skip the 7-mile, blue blaze, approach trail from Amicalola Falls State Park. He hiked with me through the mud and mist to the plaque and white blaze that marks the southern terminus of the AT, and took photos. Reality began setting in. We hiked back to the parking lot. Rainmaker took a last photo as I set off into the woods. I couldn't look back. Already I missed him.

Even with the constant rain and considerable condensation, I slept warm that first night out. A price is paid for a single wall, ultralight, silnylon tent. One can't always stay dry, but they can still be warm. A camp towel was used to wipe up the moisture. With last night's deluge, I had proof that my tent did not leak.

I started my journey hiking in Nike sandals. I personally knew other long distance hikers who hiked entire trails in sandals. But, for some reason, my left knee began to hurt. In gear testing hikes with these same sandals, they had ached on the downhill, and I thought it was a fluke, but now even the uphill portions of trail hurt. No matter how slow I went, or how much care I took, nothing except keeping my left knee absolutely straight would stop the excruciating pain. The climb up Blood Mountain was agonizing. Something must change; I could not go on like this.

After consulting with Rainmaker, I finally accepted the fact that these sandals were not working for me. I took 13 days off to allow healing of the ligament and tendon injuries to my knee, and bought some trail runner shoes. The season was early, and there was time, but the compulsion for completion nagged me.

Back on the trail March 27th, I worried how my knees would respond. I hiked slowly; fully utilizing the hiking poles, especially downhill, allowing my arms to bear some of the stress. It seemed I wasn't getting very far. The sun began to set, a full moon rose to the right as I walked a crest. The wind turned cold and I decided to forego night hiking and camped. It was very windy, but I slept well. That first day back, I managed to hike only ten miles.

Rising with the sun is a habit developed last year on the PCT to cope with desert heat. I was right back at it; enjoying the sunrise, greeting and passing other hikers still packing up in camp. Rainmaker supported my hike that first month by meeting me at predetermined towns and bringing me home, where I washed clothes, made minor modifications to gear, and resupplied. Then he would drive me back to the trail the next day.

Badger, from Virginia, earned the dubious honor of having the heaviest pack. At Neels Gap it weighed 87 pounds. In order to continue his thru-hike, he shipped 40 pounds of gear home. Reportedly he was giving stuff away on the approach trail, having begun with an incredible 100-pound pack. In most camps, I was the only ultralighter, and the homemade gear received a lot of attention.

My pack was passed around for a test lift, my tent inspected, and exclamations of various sorts followed.

I felt terrific, my knees adjusted to the terrain, and my pace began to return. The synchronized motion of using my poles and stepping in this fresh mountain air was so invigorating. As the hike progressed, I trained myself to go longer between rest breaks.

Breaks may be classified as:
Type 1= a pee break (may or may not remove pack).
Type 2= pee break, drink water, and eat a snack (may or may not remove pack).
Type 3= remove pack, sit down, remove shoes, eat, drink, and pee (about 15-20 minutes).
Type 4= all of type 3, over the course of an hour, many take this time to air dry tents, sleeping bags, and socks.
Type 5=involves sleep, and all the above.

Note that all breaks involve peeing. If you do not need to pee, you may need to drink more water.

As I hiked alone, and neared Albert's Mountain, the bladder began demanding a Type 1. The knees chimed in "Excuse us, we could use a 3, at the very least!"

"Hello? Who do you think have pounded the dirt for 3 hours straight? We demand a Type 4!" The feet have made themselves heard.

"Ok, ok, everyone shut up, and when we hit that mountaintop, there's a privy and Serious Type 4 coming! Work with me on this!!" I guess that came from the brain, which many times knows nothing at all. I stay out of it, and let them argue. When we get to the top, we'll see what happens.

The last tenth of a mile up to Albert's Mountain is a rough hand-over-hand rock scramble. Hiking poles must be secured by the wrist strap over one hand. On this type of climbing, they are not worth anything. Once on top, a beautiful panorama opens of the Smoky Mountains. A fire tower stands tall, and if one is so inclined, he or she may treat the knees to some more abuse. I took a long break at the base of the fire tower, basking in the sunshine, and ate some granola.

Almost every hiker I met was having some knee problems, wearing a brace, or taking the down hills slowly. Several have bought hiking poles from one of the many outfitters along the way, and are learning how to use them. When the pain started, I wore my two knee braces a few hours each day. Eventually I hoped to discard them. Together they weighed 16 ounces.

On top the switchbacks looking down upon the Nantahala River, the same feelings encountered on the PCT returned: overwhelming stimuli and apprehension. It is like a small town, alive this weekend with kayakers, hikers, and vacationers. On the edge of town I found a pay phone, and called home. David was not there, so I left a message, and crossed the bridge. "Brawny!" A woman sitting behind the Backpacker Magazine information table called my name. Startled, I looked to see who it was. It was Amy, and her husband Brent, who were on a countrywide tour for Backpacker's "Get Out More" campaign. We hugged, thrilled to see each other. Last year, we met while hiking the Pacific Crest Trail. They shared their bunk house with me, and took me to dinner that night; trail magic at its finest.

One morning I complained about my frameless pack's weight. Something just didn't feel right. Charlie from Kansas threatened to trade with me. I gave a good hearty laugh. I probably couldn't lift his pack off the ground.

Charlie and I leap-frogged along. We met again at lunchtime in front of Mollies Ridge Shelter, a stone three-sided structure. A chain link fence reaching the roof made the forth side. Inside were two ancient wooden shelves, one above the other, with slats nailed on to make individual spaces. It was my first glimpse of a Great Smoky Mountain National Park shelter. I was reminded of the Amistad slave ship. No, don't get me wrong. This is "Bad Bear" territory, and I definitely wanted a slot. A dirt floor inside, in front of the fence, and fireplace at one end, completed the arrangement. Outside were fire rings, logs for sitting, and a grassy area big enough for many tents. Signs pointed to the path to water, and the path in the opposite direction to the toilet area. As we hiked on, I had plenty to think about. Two and a half miles to Russell Field Shelter. Do I want a top bunk? Or a bottom? No way will I sleep next to a stone wall, whose crevices contain mouse condos.

We arrived about 5:30, and I claimed a middle slot on the top bunk. Poptart, and Geek were already there. After eating, our food bags were hung on the bear cables 30 feet off the ground. Everything else was brought inside the shelter. Packs were hung on the inside of the fence, the many straps hanging down, obscuring the view outside. Our water bottles were set around inside the fortress. Someone threw a candy wrapper into the fireplace, and already in broad daylight a mouse was chewing on it. A southbounder had a 6-liter Platypus bag, filled with camp water, which he hung outside on the fence, about 5 feet from the ground. Once we settled down, Smurf told us a bedtime story. Off to dream land. About 11 p.m. it started raining; a steady drenching rain. A couple hours later it lulled, and I head a big "Whoosh", banging noises, followed by silence. "Who is tenting out there, dumping the water off his fly?" I wondered.

Early next morning I ate breakfast while sitting on a log as the others slept. Then the southbounder came out to get water from his Platypus. "What the hell?" he exclaimed. His water bag was empty. It still hung on the fence, but a large nearly perfect hole 7 inches in diameter, had appeared. All that remained were teeth marks. "I paid $18 for this thing! A bear bit a hole in my bag!" He showed us, and rehung it. Then he left to get more water in a borrowed soda bottle.

"That must have been his water being dumped you heard last night, Brawny," Charlie said. A bag is a bag, and if it's hanging on a chain link fence, it's liable to be taken for a food bag, fair game to camp-wise bears. A drenching was all he got.

Packing up that morning, I put the bulk of my food in the bottom of my pack, leaving just snack food on top. The food is the heavy stuff. As I put on my backpack, things were right again. I hardly felt the weight. The weight keeps the slippery silnylon hip belt from sliding up. Now it carried properly, with most of the weight resting on my hips.

The mornings were still chilly, but favorable for good hiking. I decided to eat cold breakfasts because it was much more efficient, and I only had to wash the dishes in the evening.

Max Patch, near the town of Hot Springs, North Carolina, is a marvel. You can see it a couple miles ahead, this grassy bald extending for what appears to be thousands of acres. One must follow the fence posts marked with white blazes as you climb, then cross and descend the mountain. Views are 360 degrees, and the Blue Mountains seen from there really are blue. This range of mountains geologists tell us, are older, and rounded because of erosion over millenniums. Western mountains contrast with their rugged peaks, supposedly proving they are much younger, and formed in an earthly upheaval more recently. Astounding earth-presumptions.

One large, dark thundercloud loomed straight overhead as I crossed Max Patch. Not wanting to be struck by lightning, I continued on. A foreign couple was dining on top with their wine bottle, picnic basket, and tablecloth, oblivious to the threatening skies.

As I descended, the thunder began, accompanied by a few raindrops. Roaring Fork Shelter, Where Are You? Hike like mad. Finally, there was a glimpse across the gap, a privy, but no sign of humans. I arrived before 5, happy and pleased with this clean, well-planned shelter with a skylight, and table. I read the trail register, and spread out cooking gear. The April 3rd edition of the New York Times, already two weeks old, laid on the platform. A good read. Hey didja know that Michael Jordan was out for the season with a knee injury?

Corncob, retired and thru-hiking, arrived. Then Wanderer pulled in, sixty-seven years old and backpacking, fulfilling the dream of a lifetime. They set up their little stoves, and each cooked a one-pot meal, exclaiming, "Isn't this the life?" I chuckled, pleased with their company. Watching them set up their own sleeping areas on the shelter floor, get water from the stream, and clean up for bedtime, I thought of how bad a day job must be, that we can love this sparse freedom so much.

The dogwood blossoms were gorgeous against the dark firs, the Blue Mountains and bright spring leaves. The trail rolls up, over and around these hills, yet always descending to the valley at just over 1,300 feet. As the humidity increased, the anticipation of air conditioning quickened steps towards town. I passed a side trail intersection to the Deer Park Mountain Shelter, and noticed a smaller trail to the left. In a tiny clearing was a ring of rocks, and two head stones. I went into the little cove, and read the inscription. A couple, names now forgotten, lay buried there. "Absent not Dead" read one. "Absent not Forgotten" read the other. Inscriptions that speak to the inner being. We reassure each other that we will not be forgotten, and will never forget. Let no one pass through our world and not be mourned upon his or her departure.

Three miles remained to Hot Springs, a slow teasing descent while viewing the town from above. This town was much bigger than I thought. The trail follows the road through town, blazes painted on telephone poles just above the sidewalk. I had a few hours before Rainmaker arrived, enough time to check out the town, stop in the thrift store and barter awhile, have a cold soda, and visit the post office. Life is good. Freedom is fine. But love's what it's all about.

After two days rest at home, I was hiking strong, catching up to friends, and starting to put in longer, high mileage days. It wasn't a matter of hiking fast, but hiking long.

Unfortunately, there was a "war" going on in Erwin, TN, between the two hostels. Some hikers wisely resupplied and headed back out the same day, others stayed at the Holiday Inn. Those staying at one place or another became the pawns in a "turf war". It seemed odd to have so many trail services that we can be fought over, and involved in petty issues of everyday life. I again fought the disappointment with this trail that seemed too easy.

In late April it was still amazingly cold. I had sent home my 20-degree bag, and was using my "summer system", which consisted of a fleece bag with a taffeta outer bag cover. I was very glad I kept my fleece pants. One night I used my tent as a blanket, probably making all the difference in sleeping warm.

By early morning, I could feel the built-up condensation (from the silnylon fabric top layer) seeping through my fleece pants. I woke with the dawn and was on trail at 6:30. The shelter was full of sleeping hikers, so I packed quickly and quietly. After a couple of miles, I began to fear I'd left stuff at the shelter. Nothing was where it was supposed to be in my pack. My data book, tent stakes, and bandana were all "missing". It was a very lousy start and I chided myself a hundred times for being so hasty. I left without breakfast, just throwing stuff in the pack so I wouldn't wake anyone and could warm up while hiking. I found my stakes, and later when I went to my food bag, there was my data book! Then I found my bandana! All was well again. As an ultralighter, these things are dearly missed, and I promised myself that the next time, I would take more care.

In Damascus I stayed at "The Place", a large house with bunks and showers for hikers, sponsored by the local Methodist Church. They accept donations, but it is rumored that few were given. That is how hostels finally go under. I bought an 800-fill goose down bag, rated for 30 degrees from the outfitter in town. It was a full sized, 6-foot long sleeping bag. Not a single sleeping bag sized for women was to be found. It weighed just 24 ounces, and stuffed very neatly. It became a favorite piece of gear, well worth the $260 I spent.

At times, I just need to hike gently and alone. I pondered the meaning of a thru-hike and kept thinking "I must slow down to receive what this trail experience will teach. So far it's escaping me." In retrospect, I had been hiking a reactionary hike. Hiking to catch up to people whose names I recognized in the registers, hiking to escape certain people, hiking to claim a spot in the shelter when it was raining hard or bad weather threatened. This was a busy trail, and I fought disappointment constantly. It was too easy, too many people, too many hostels, too many roads, too many places to bail out and go home. I had to accept this trail for itself. It was my good fortune to hike the PCT, but now my estimation of the AT suffered. Until I quit comparing them, there would be no appreciation for this journey.

The Appalachian Trail is renowned for its constant PUDs, the pointless ups and downs. It is not as though the climb takes you to any views. If there is one, signs will point them out. This trail was completed in 1948 before erosion was a major concern, and subsequent switchbacks were used to deal with it. Some rebuilding and rerouting has been done in the intervening years, but there still remains a need for hill climbing strategies. Here are mine:

Hill Climbing Strategies For Mega Hills
(Over 1,500 ft. elevation gain)

1. Empty bladder before climbing; never haul those extra 8 – 12 ounces up the hill.
2. Take breaks in the shade or on an upgrade, as needed.
3. Do not chew gum. It hinders breathing.
4. Stop and rest if your leg is about to fall off.
5. Think erotic thoughts for distraction.
6. Before passing another hiker, give adequate notice. If they don't acknowledge, be sure that they are still alive.

Charlie and Lost-and-Found met me in Pearisburg around noon, and we shared a tiny room at the Rendezvous Motel. Charlie and I went to the library, then for salad at Pizza Hut. We met a couple, Vagabond and Blueberry, who were thru-hiking with their dog. On their hike into town, they saw the same two goats we had seen. Their dog, Alice, decided they would make a great chase. As Vagabond called repeatedly for her to return, one goat took measures of its own. Over the cliff of Angel's Rest and into the air it sailed. The dog followed, into the fog and over the cliff. The goat knew of a ledge out of sight, just below the leap off. The dog didn't. She fell 30 feet, trashing her pack, and injuring her hip. Her owner found a tree wedged into the rocks, and used it to climb down to Alice and lifted her back to the trail. With that done, they finished hiking into town. She was limping when we met them, but otherwise appeared subdued, and okay.

Virginia is a beautiful state, though some say it is too long. Climbing over many stiles, we crossed pastoral lands. Grazing cattle and horses were shooed off the actual treadway so that we could remain purists. The attitude of extreme purism and righteousness was found early on, while we were still naive enough to think we could actually walk every step of a four-foot wide trail that was under, or on top of, white blazes. These white rectangles were so neatly painted (2 x 6 inches), and regularly placed on trees and rocks, though not necessarily in regard to the life or limbs of the hiker.

Whenever I get close to town type facilities, within 25 miles, the same compulsion to hike into civilization overtakes me. And, why not just do it? I needed to talk to Rainmaker, and I felt strong. Near Troutville, just off Interstate 81, there are motels and plenty of phones. That morning we crossed Tinker Cliffs, as the sky darkened and then the thunder and lightning rolled in. The rocks were exposed and slippery, making the hike across Tinker Ridge exhausting. The rain abated, and then resumed just as I got into town. After reserving a room with another thru-hiker, we ate the Chinese AYCE buffet dinner in Troutville. It was fantastic. "Nothing in the world is accomplished without passion," read my fortune cookie. Seemed appropriate. A small sticker left on shelter register page said, "It is good to journey towards an end, but in the end it is the journey that matters."

The pattern of waking early, getting on trail at daybreak, and consequently deciding to do big days was my hiking style of choice. Perhaps that induced the so-called Virginia blues. On the other hand, seeing the data change, and feeling some sort of accomplishment, kept me going. They say it's not the state being so big; it's the 6-8 weeks away from home taking its toll, with the longing for loved ones. I felt discouraged at this stage, and had serious doubts about continuing. It seemed I didn't have any more hills left in me.

We had heard about the dreaded ascent to The Priest, the knee-jolting descent to the Tye River, and then immediately having to make the 3,000 ascent to Hanging Rock Overlook. It was 30 degrees, and the grass was frosted. Times like this it's just best to dig in, and get started.

The climb wasn't nearly as bad as I had heard; it was graded and beautiful. Once again I reminded myself not to give into the "Fear-Brokers" who sometimes hike the trails. By pelting us with their fears, they justify their own. Maybe they just want to see some dread on our faces.

All the stone "fences" we passed reminded me of the movie "Gettysburg", and the lives that were wasted during the Civil War. There were two head stones marking the burial place of union soldiers, and small confederate flags tacked to a tree. At times, it seemed that the spirits of slain soldiers still lingered in the mountains.

Just twenty miles out of Waynesboro, I read Lightingbolt's entry in the register "Where's Brawny?" This dear friend from the PCT had unknowingly passed me one evening while I sat huddled in a cold shelter. As I crossed the bridge at Rockfish Gap, Lightingbolt called my name. He was returning to the trail from an overnight town stop, and I was heading in to resupply. We ran to greet each other, and exchanged a big hug. He is a fellow ultralighter, and this chance meeting boosted my moral. We took each other's photos and checked out our custom gear. Emotionally, this section had been hard, and I often searched my soul for the reason. Not everything can or deserves to be identified, so simply just celebrating the fact that I had made it this far, I looked forward to the upcoming Shenandoahs and Harper's Ferry. The wet and unexpected cold had taken a toll, and I was ready to get my winter gear back! We hiked north with spring, and occasionally with winter. It looked like we had beaten the summer heat.

After taking a zero day in Waynesboro, I was bored with inactivity and ready to move. Shenandoah National Park is just a mile north of Rockfish Gap. Reputedly, it is very beautiful, with well-maintained trail, plenty of wild animals, many easily accessible camp stores and grills. The enthusiasm for this journey returned; I was nearly half way.

One enters the park, and there is a self-registration box. I filled out the forms, read the rules and tied the white tag to my pack. All food must be hung on the tall metal poles installed near the shelters, by lifting the food sack with the heavy metal rod provided and snagging the hook above with the bag's loop. This was easier said than done.

The trail and weather were indeed lovely during the four and a half days it took to hike through the park. Deer were so tame; they followed hikers, looking for handouts. Everyone was hoping to see a bear. I certainly saw mine.

The first of five bears I saw the next day suddenly crashed across the trail early in the morning. Then she stopped in the brush a few yards to the right. Wondering why she hadn't run further, I called "You're going to have to go farther than that!" while clicking my hiking sticks together. Minutes passed. No sounds. I called again, and then she ran off, her cub scampering behind her.

While hiking that same afternoon I looked to my left, and was startled to see a bear standing on a grassy hill about thirty feet away, regarding me. I called " Hello! Hey, I need to come by here." The bear ran uphill and stopped, sizing me up. To the right, another bear crashed downhill. The stand off resumed until I realized the bear on the left side wanted to cross the trail and join the bear on the right side. I backed up several feet. He turned and trotted north, dropped onto the trail, and halted, watching me again. "Hey, I need to come through here. What do you want me to do?" I demanded, stomping my feet, and hitting my poles together again. Finally after a few minutes, he ran off.

I saw two more bears that were grazing that evening. That day, I hiked 33 miles to Bear Fence Shelter. Seriously, that's the name of it. People expressed amazement at such miles. When someone asked thru-hiker Radio Flyer how one manages to do 28-miles, he replied in his Tennessee accent, "You get up early and haul ass all day."

The food was good at Big Meadows Camp Store & Restaurant. Everyone missed the unmarked intersection, and ended up hiking a one-mile "nature" trail from the Lodge turn off. Contrary to rumor, the store accepted credit cards. At Thornton Gap, the restaurant that is within sight of the trail was closed, but candy bars and chips were available in the gift shop. The Elk Wallow wayside was easy to find, and the best stop in the park. With some creativity, we were able to buy enough food from that store to make it to Harper's Ferry. We left the Shennandoahs to the tourists, and headed north.

The toe box on my 704 New Balance shoes had excess leather on top, preventing them from flexing when I stepped. This caused a raw area on the top of a few toes. Using my razor knife, I cut some leather away from the shoe, and used hydrogen peroxide to keep the injury clean until it could heal. In retrospect, all the top leather should have been cut off at that time; eventually both my feet suffered the same injuries.

The infamous Roller Coaster section of the AT is thirteen miles of undulation built so the trail can avoid private property. It really was not that bad, since I had an ultralight pack and only one day of food.

The next day, one reaches the Appalachian Trail Conference Headquarters in Harpers Ferry West Virginia, where the ATC folks take your picture, put it in a photo album and assign you a color-coded number. I was northbound thru-hiker number 148 in the year 2002. Every year has its own book. I found the 1992 collection, and began looking for Rainmaker's photo. I found the correct date, and his thru-hiking friend's photos. It was impossible to recognize his picture until I finally started reading the names. He looked like a long lanky kid in a yellow t-shirt. Up to that point, he had remained clean-shaven.

I hiked out of town alone the next day; my companions for the last 100 miles wanted a zero day in town. That is the beauty and the loneliness of a soloist. I hike my own hike, and have become accustomed to meeting new people. I camped just one night in Maryland. Several thru-hikers, one section hiker from Australia, and three girls who were hiking only Maryland shared the site. We had a campfire and evening of chatter.

I saw my first AT rattlesnake while climbing over boulders early one morning. A bunch of boys and their leader forewarned me, but the snake apparently had moved from where they had seen it sunning itself. Just as I was descending a large boulder, suddenly to my left the snake slithered out over the rock, its flicking tongue only 10 inches from my eye. Immediately I jumped down and forward, then turned to regard it and started laughing. He was a marvelous creature, and I didn't want to hurt his feelings with such a quick departure.

The concession stand at Caledonia State Park was open, catering to the people enjoying the large outdoor swimming pool. Fellow hikers and I went over to enjoy some ice cream and fries. This was the beginning of Pennsylvania, seemingly the land of concession stands.

The first 150 miles of Pennsylvania are really quite nice, often intersecting with old logging roads and following them for miles. There were also a lot of white splotches on trees, resembling sloppy blazes. I found out they are hunting markers. It can be confusing, especially at dusk or in poor visibility. Many of the shelters have been well kept, several of them just a few years old. The James Fry Shelter, which is absolutely beautiful, has many pegs for hanging gear, 4 large bunks plus a lot of space in the main area. Thru-hikers on a budget take zero days in such places.

Traditionally, a thru-hiker can celebrate the half way point of the Appalachian Trail by eating a half-gallon of ice cream at Pine Grove Furnace State Park. This challenge is an interesting event, and the notebook on the picnic table contained tips and warnings. After reading the register, I decided I was too old for this shit, and just watched my new young friends chose their flavors, and get out their trail spoons. I bought a hot dog with onions, relish and microwave popcorn to enjoy during their attempt. After the participants were all good and sick, I bought an ice cream cone, then a second one when I passed the next concession stand. There is way too much easy food on this trail, but by taking advantage of it, one can keep his or her food weight low.

The trail north of Boiling Springs is mostly level, through pastures, woods and cornfields, then there's a short ascent to Darlington Shelter, and my evening destination. I brought my leftover pizza with me from town, always a treat in a shelter. The water there, however, was some of the worst I had seen so far, needing to be dipped with a small cup and strained though a bandana. Because of my high mile days, it was early in the growing season, and the corn was only a few inches high. I have avoided the southern heat, and have been enjoying mild temperatures, entertained by the many small creatures that are well hidden on one side of the trail. For some reason, they feel compelled to make a mad dash to the opposite side, just as I approach, scurrying as though their tiny lives were in great danger.

The next day, I hiked 11.6 miles into Duncannon, and paid $15.90 for a room at the ancient Doyle Hotel. There were only three bathrooms, and loads of people there to share them. The fourth floor shower drips into the third floor shower while a bat huddles in the corner. Another third floor bathroom has an old fashioned tub. Hikers need a place to rent, even if it's old and dilapidated. This is the reason one brings sandals for the showers in town, and to avoid slivers from the rough wooden floors. The tavern down the street was a great place to relax. The Doyle was in transition and no in-house food or drink was available that year. It could be much worse. Trail experiences are meant to be memorable. I will remember this one for a long time.

Games Soloists Play:

Gorp According To Blazes –Place daily allotment of gorp in sandwich baggie in a pocket. Eat a small bite. Chew slowly. Swallow. Pass 3 blazes before taking another handful. Repeat.
Hiker Factor - Time how long between human sightings. Some days, it's about every 3 hours. Sometimes, it is only once a day. It only counts if the person is actually on the trail, not near a road crossing.
No Thought Game – Time how long between thoughts. No thinking. Each soloist must set his or her own parameters here. "When is the last time I saw a blaze?" counts as a thought for me. The brain is just supposed to register blazes without thinking.
Plan Next Resupply – Plan both for ounces and calories. Obtain these figures, then divide by days and multiply by miles. Subtract from your age. Add to your IQ. If you don't know your IQ, guess. Be generous. Start over. No ultralighter brings a calculator.

While playing my new game **"How Long Does It Take To Pass**

100 Blazes?" I was counting 34, we have 34, 34 and going on 35, we have thirty-fi… when suddenly along the narrow, bramble-bordered trail, came a southbound black bear. We both stopped. We eyed each other. I went into scare-the-bear mode, clanking my hiking poles together. He was not impressed. I called to him, "I need to walk through here." He nonchalantly turned his head, and took a bite of grass and brambles. I tried negotiation, "Hey, bear, I need to use the trail. I know you do, too." The bear, apparently amused, looked at me and shook his head.

Then, I noticed the tagged right ear, and fought back recognition of "Bad-Ass Bear". The attitude of denial did not work; it was time to give this bear some space. I took several steps back, the bear responded by trotting towards me, my heart pounding faster as he closed in.

My god, do I jump quickly into the weeds, and hope he passes by like a day hiker? The gut rebelled at this horrid thought, and I started screaming, "Alright! No more Mr. Nice Guy! Do you want me to rock you? Get out of here!" I stooped and picked up a rock. All I could find was one that weighed about 5 pounds. Where are all the rocks in Pennsylvania when you really need one?

Just then, the bear jumped left, off trail, into the weeds. I decided that was good enough. "Attaboy!" I yelled, "I believe in peaceful co-existence, just like you!" I kept talking loudly, watching the bushes, as I edged past. Then he jumped back on the trail; the passage of two beings was done without bloodshed.

At the 501 Shelter one may order pizza using the phone at the house next door. The bunks, an assortment of good reading material, a big table, and cold shower outside made this old pottery shop a fantastic stay. A guidebook warned us about the dogs there, but they were tied up. Then the rocks of Pennsylvania really began.

With a long day, the next stop was the pavilion in Port Clinton. The outfitter's store is just three-tenths mile off the trail, and sells food, gear, ice cream and cold sodas. Apparently, it has the only phone in town that is available to thru-hikers. There were no pay phones anywhere else. The outfitter asked me to watch his store while he ran another hiker to Hamburg to use an ATM machine. This town only accepts cash. It was near closing time on a Friday evening, no customers. I was too tired to move, so I agreed. When the owner returned, he immediately counted the money in his cash register, and asked to weigh my pack. With 4 days of food and 12 ounces of water, it registered 14 pounds. He was impressed and probably relieved.

Having trusted a total stranger with his life's investment, while he ran another total stranger to town, he gambled and won. I saw 2 rattlesnakes the next day; one was huge. However, it saw me before I saw it, and began rattling furiously. I bushwhacked around both of them and did 32.6 miles to Bake Oven Shelter, which was built in 1937. It is small and dilapidated, but other than the lone deer eating and nosing around, I had it all to myself. This trail section, winding up and through rock cliffs, was not funny. I slid into a tree and scraped my arm, from elbow clear down to the wrist. It bled, but I counted myself lucky to have survived in good shape. The rock scramble out of Palmerton was maddening and very dangerous. Not all hikers are 6' 2". We shorter people could use a rod embedded in the rock to hang onto every once in awhile. If it had been raining, or my pack had been heavy, I might not have made it.

Power Hiking

I hiked the last 20.4 miles of Pennsylvania (into Delaware Water Gap) by leaving the shelter at 5 a.m. and arriving in town at ten minutes past noon. This is what is called Power Hiking. Doing big miles, resupplying and heading out the next day. It's not a matter of trail running, and one does not miss the beauty, trail magic, or animal encounters. It's a hiking style of continual observation, without resting until arriving at one's destination.

From Delaware Water Gap to Massachusetts /Vermont line I carried an ultralight radio with tiny headphones. I loved hearing music, but when it began to rain, the radio had to be put away. Many times, good reception was a rarity, and static was common. One thru-hiker said he carried his radio because otherwise there was too much introspection. That, in itself, is food for thought. The ridiculous chatter and commercials were a distraction, and finally I concluded that for me it was not worth the weight.

The Mohican Outdoor Center, 11 miles from Delaware Water Gap, had better accommodations than the Doyle Hotel in Duncannon. Food, snacks, and insect repellent were available. There was a phone in the main office. With the thru-hiker discount, I paid $12 for a bunk in a large, carpeted cabin. Plenty of clean bathrooms and showers came with the deal, plus the use of a real kitchen with coffee maker.

New Jersey reputedly does not allow bear hunting, resulting in a breed of bears so bold they even venture into town. Personally, I had enough bear encounters, and craved no more. I made enough noise, talking and singing aloud in the perpetual rain and fog, to avert any sightings. In New Jersey I finally caught up to Hammock Hanger at the "secret shelter". The location is discovered by word of mouth. A thru-hiker built it after he completed his successful hike. He wanted to continue the tradition of trail magic, giving back to the hiking community a portion of what he had experienced on his journey. This marvelous cabin had a working dryer, hot shower and electrical heat.

Early next morning, I said good-bye to Hammock Hanger, thanking her for a great night of girl talk, and hiked to resupply in Unionville, New York. Then I headed to a great little pastry and fruit stand within sight of the trail, just down the road on Hwy. 94, that goes into Vernon, New Jersey. Determined not to continue hiking in the rain until I was stuffed, I ate 3 pastries, two bananas, a waffle ice cream cone and drank 24 ounces of hot coffee. Great lunch!

The white blazes took us over Pinnacle and Cat Rocks. After hiking only 12 measly miles, my right knee was already killing me. The blue-blaze trail at the base of these boulders made more sense, but I remained a purist and these choices defined my hike. I slipped badly at one point. The shelter registers recorded the same experience for many others, one guy even swearing over his broken hiking poles.

The trail from Wildcat Shelter to NY 17 (Arden) is 10 miles worth of hills and ravines and graded for mountain goats. They made the dreaded Roller Coaster in Virginia look like a bunny hill on a ski slope. Because of recent rains, water was plentiful.

The second 10 miles were pleasant, grassy and well graded. I arrived at William Brien Memorial Shelter to find some young men on an overnight trip were already there. When other long distance hikers pulled in, they built a campfire.

A Poem, Commemorating this night:

The Night the Hikers Hung
--on that fateful night, June 17, 2002

One by one we stopped there
On a sultry afternoon.
An assortment of AT hikers
That day in early June.

Thru-hiker, sectioners, overnighters
Had a bonfire and evening chatter.

Some cooked, some drank, some horsed around
It really did not matter.

I'm early to bed, early to rise
Asleep before the others,
As smoke from the fire filled the shelter
I prayed we would not smother.

Drifting in and out of consciousness
There on that wooden bunk,
Benumbed from too much Advil
Wasted, like some street drunk.

Then, this scraping, crawling, scratching
Upon the roof was heard,
Too organized to be the wind
Too loud to be a bird.

Exhaustion and darkness claimed me
I could but lay and hope,
Whatever had taken up residence
Was within the human scope.

The sun sought the horizon
I awoke to meet the beast
As I stuffed my gear together
I saw this ungodly feast.

Cookies, chips and salsa
Tuna Surprise left in a pot,
All lay spread on the shelter floor
Overnighters hauled in a lot!

Then down from the roof they clamored
And their heroics must be sung,
Instead of hanging their leftover food
They themselves were hung.

I enjoyed a lunch at the Bear Mountain Inn, which opens at 11:30
a.m. A very tasty steak sandwich, fries, slaw and about 8 cups of
coffee cost $11. Great service and quite posh; one just assumes the
mannerisms of a wealthy tourist. Never mind that the clothes you're

wearing have seen 3 months on the trail. If you have money, you belong there as well. After a phone call home, it was back to hiking. The Mountain Laurel was blooming in such profusion that a scent of perfumed soap filled the air all day. I camped at the Greymor Friary Ball Park Shelter, offered as a place for hikers in 2002 by the Greymor monks. There was a cold shower, sink, soap, and privy. A nice place, but overrun on weekends with local partiers who left their garbage strewn around for the generous monks to clean up.

The first day of summer, June 21st, is the traditional Hike Naked Day, although not a single soul appeared to be participating. I walked into Kent, Connecticut and met thru-hikers who had been ahead of me. Buck 30, a power hiker, got this trail name because he weighed just 130 pounds. The last time we met in Hot Springs, he was doing laundry with a bath towel wrapped around his waist. He was amazed to see anyone catch up to him. After I bought groceries at the IGA, ate a cheese and bagel sandwich (washed down with a quart of chocolate milk), we hiked out of town together.

Kent, Conn. to Massachusetts Hwy. 2

Sometimes rain caused an extra long day. When it started to drizzle about 3:45, I had just begun the descent to Limestone Spring Trail. That blue blaze side trail dove five tenths of a mile steeply into The Pit. Knowing that the dastardly climb would be waiting me in the morning, I figured no shelter was worth such knee damage. As long as I was going to camp, might as well get some miles in. I hiked in drenching rain, madly through Salisbury outskirts while cars passed me. Then, I took refuge from the storm in the privy at the parking area. After adjusting my pack, I headed out for the last 3 of my 27 miles that day. Arriving at 6:30 looking like a drowned rat, four guys happily scooted over, and allowed me to share the shelter. We discussed ultralight gear while I unpacked, dried off and cooked supper. After seeing my minimalist systems, they concluded I knew every trick. What a wonderful compliment and conclusion to a rough day.

Connecticut is the land of lean-tos. You have to laugh at that word "lean-to". They are some of the largest shelters so far, with bunks, upper lofts and full floors. Some could sleep 20 people comfortably, or 35 thru-hikers in storms. I met several southbound youth groups today who were climbing the steep trail as I descended. "Are we almost to the peak?" they asked.

"Which peak?" I replied. Groans followed, and hastily I amended, "Oh yeah, you sure are. Just a bit more!" The leaders smiled their appreciation.

Then the teenage girls asked how long I had been out hiking. "Don't you ever get tired of walking?" one asked. A young man surprised me with the question "Do you even know where you are?"

Making repairs to my shoes in the evenings with needle and thread, I wanted them to give me just 65 more miles for a total of 1,123 on this pair. These 704 New Balance trail runners fit into the Circle-Of–Life category. When you first get them, you love them. Aren't they just the prettiest things? In the next little while, like the teenage years, they cause all kinds of problems and pain. They get another month on them, middle aged, and they are tolerable, yet need more experience. They get trimmed, and cut until they fit right, and do what society expects of them. Then, they start getting old, torn up, and need medical attention. As soon as they're really feeling good and doing their job right, they are ready for the trash can.

There were caretakers at the Upper Goose Pond Cabin in Massachusetts, so the fantasy of pancakes for breakfast became a reality. Rumor had it that for a $3 donation, there would be a bed, and breakfast. Penny gave me fresh homemade bread and butter, and hot coffee when I arrived. Fantastic. Today, the trail was soft and mellow. I counted 38 orange salamanders this morning. From the tiniest to a normal 3-inch fellow, it was simply amazing to see so many of these creatures.

Earlier this morning, I had caught up to an elderly section hiker named Trapper. He warned me of "trouble ahead": boy scouts who would take all the space in the shelter. Laughing, I told him I would catch up and get to Goose Pond cabin before them. He disagreed, saying, "Nope, they are at least an hour and a half ahead." Oh Yeah. That's what I like to hear, tell me I can't do it. I had already done 10 miles that morning, and then caught those boy scouts about a half-mile before the turn off. The weather was fabulous, with light breezes, and 70 degrees. That night, Dale America and Amtrak from Israel showed up, thru-hikers I had been hoping to meet for weeks.

The AT passes right through Dalton, Mass. Resident trail angel, Bob, let hikers stay free at his house. We went to the Shell station, met him, and got directions to his house. For the first time since Delaware Water Gap I washed my hair with Real Shampoo, used hair conditioner and washed all my clothes. Hadn't used a washing machine since Harpers Ferry, but just washed clothes in a bathtub.

Self-Imposed-Deprivation.

From there it was only a 9-mile hike for a wonderful veggie supreme pizza at Christina's in Cheshire. Dale America claimed he ate the best ham sub on the trail there. The next day, Dale and I hiked to Massachusetts Hwy. 2, and hitched into North Adams. Because dangerous storms threatened, Dale and I agreed to share a room at the Holiday Inn. North Adams and nearby Williamstown has an extensive bus system, lots of good eating places, stores, culture and all those things hikers sometimes crave. It is expensive, though.

On June 28 I rode the local bus to Pittsfield to pick up my reserved rental car. Yesterday's terrific storms and lightning were over, and it was cool. I already felt weird, and kept reminding myself I was not leaving the trail, simply taking a short rest at home, and would drive back revived and stronger to finish in August. Since the time Rainmaker and I devised this plan over the phone, my nightmares had stopped. Nearly every night since Damascus, I would struggle with that same horrible dream of losing David, and being trapped in that fundamentalist church again. Once the rental car was reserved, I slept peacefully. I pondered the meaning of these nightmares and wondered if perhaps it was the old doctrine, still nagging me deep inside, that forbids a divorced woman to ever find joy with another man.

This love-hate relationship with trail life is so strange. There are miseries, and there are pleasures. There is the total freedom to walk when and where we will, and there is the total submission. We submit to blinding rain, suffocating heat, record cold, and the whim of white blazes. We feel the physical demands of hunger and thirst, getting up each morning, and facing whatever comes our way. A daily adventure of our own choosing, we learn the balance between freedom and submission.

I chatted with the bus driver while he bragged on the area's heritage, music and art. All I could think of was my home in the Georgia mountains, the peace and beauty of the forests. No way would I trade for this bus driver's complications. Another hiker flagged down the bus, and was treated disrespectfully. He was somewhat dirty, and disoriented. The driver took $2 from him, and misled him into riding five miles in the wrong direction. Neither understood each other. I tried to help, reading directions from the Companion Guide Book that the hiker carried. The bus driver dismissed the experience with his casual observance "What is happening here is that urban life is clashing with you who have just left the woods." Yeah. Right. My lesson here was to keep my off-trail contacts and resupplies as simple as possible, and bring all my own directions.

I got my rental car and drove nearly 500 miles, stopping for the night at a Days Inn, just 80 miles north of Roanoke, Virginia. A valuable lesson was to bring a non-debit/money credit card. A regular credit card was the only type a car rental agency would accept for out of state rentals. Rainmaker mailed my credit card to me. Fond memories returned when I saw the road signs for Pine Grove Furnace State Park, Harper's Ferry, Front Royal, and Waynesboro. Rainmaker told me it would be this way. Driving was such a change, with all its signs, roadwork and traffic congestion. I missed the trail, and knew the last 591 miles that remained would be so fine and enjoyable.

You know you need a "break", especially as a soloist when:
You are willing to listen to static for hours at a time on your ultralight radio.

You have a personal conversation with each of the 38 orange salamanders seen one day.

You experience total refusal to do any "mileage stats" or play any soloist games.

Nothing tastes good anymore.

Your heart is aching for your Life Partner, and there is no other remedy.

Returning to the Trail

Rainmaker and I spent two days driving from our home in Georgia to Vermont, and parking our car at a friend's house. All the next day, July 10th, we used Vermont Transit Line buses to finally arrive in Williamston, Mass. A young woman gave us a ride to the Appalachian Trail intersection, where I tagged the road sign to symbolize the resumption of a purist thru-hike.

We hiked 1.8 miles to Sherman Brook Campsite, both of us officially on trail once more. There I had my first experience rigging a non-freestanding tent on a platform. Using a rope, some found cordage, and stuff sacks filled with rocks to provide tension (instead of stakes), our Coleman Cobra tent stood solidly and was as comfortable as ever.

Our relaxed hiking style permits coffee and breakfast in the morning. We pack up, hike awhile, enjoy a morning break, a lunch break, and an afternoon break, and still average 14 miles a day. We find a little nook to stealth camp at times; anywhere is fine as long as we are together.

Crossing into Vermont marked the actual beginning of Rainmaker's trail, The Long Trail. Everything seemed wilder now, perhaps because of the dense vegetation and many roots snaking across the trail. Old trail friends began catching up. Charlie Foxtrot was leaving the trail and going home to a job of his dreams in Kansas. He will not finish the AT this year. Restless Spirit left to find new adventures, being bored with this one. We met groups of section hikers. I had to admire the teenage girls who managed to carry only daypacks, having talked the guys into being their pack mules. The guys were carrying enormous loads, struggling uphill, but proving their masculinity.

Just before noon, Rainmaker and I hitched into Manchester Center, a sweet little New England town that was alive with tourists. All morning we had heard the highway as it paralleled the trail that was taking us ever further from town. The grocery store was huge; we ate at the pizza place, after deciding not to brave the town's Laundromat, where the atmosphere approximated a very overcrowded sauna. Some things just aren't worth dying for, and clean clothes are definitely in that category. Having finished with Manchester, we hitched a ride and hiked out ¾ mile to the Bromley Tenting Area. The heat and humidity had reached the northern states now, causing frequent afternoon storms. The thunderstorms that had been predicted for that evening blew in, and passed quickly.

Hiking up and over Killington Peak, we passed the rundown, road-accessed Governor Clement Shelter. Few thru-hikers will use the shelter because of harassment by local thugs. We stayed in the Cooper Lodge after a 10-mile day. With such a name, one would presume that shelter is fancy. It isn't. A weekender came to share it with us and had a map showing the newly rerouted AT, along with the old, historic Pico Trail. Being a purist, I grumbled and griped, then took the new route, which added an additional 2 miles of trail. This also necessitated hiking a half-mile south down the Sherburne Spur Trail to reach the Long Trail Inn. Most hikers have elected to do the historic Pico Trail route.

From the Inn, there is a 1.2-mile road walk steeply downhill to the Killington Post Office. Our solo tents were waiting for us there. We mailed home our Cobra tent, my cell phone that I had tried carrying since returning to the trail, my journal and a few other personal things. We secured a room for $59 at the historic Inn, which included breakfast in the morning. Rainmaker and I shared a very romantic evening, enjoying the live music, and living for the moment.

Our trails parted the next morning at the intersection of the AT and Sherburne Trail, his heading to the Canadian border, and mine to Mt. Katahdin in Maine. It was amazingly hard to head off alone once more. I did the 18 miles to the Wintturi Shelter, which had a lot of elevation changes. I felt out of shape and already missed my life partner. Alone at the shelter, eating brownies and drinking sodas left by trail angels, I read register entries left by southbounders that told of the Panarchy Frat house. They allowed six thru-hikers to stay free for one night in the basement, sleeping on old mattresses. It was only 26 miles, so I was determined to head to Hanover the next day.

The trail goes right through the tiny village of West Hartford. A small diner with a convenience store and trail register, made a great lunch stop. That afternoon, I made it into Hanover. Geek, ATR, Chili Pepper, Monkey, Bearded Monkey and Moose were already there at the fraternity house. I found a spot, in spite of being the seventh one.

I took a cold shower with my clothes on, washing the sweat from them and me at the same time. Later, Geek and I went to a restaurant for a snack and a couple beers. That night, Moose, a southbounder, detailed for us the upcoming White Mountains, with their hut and "work for stay" system.

At daybreak, I hiked out of Hanover while the town slept. The trail was well marked, the white blazes being on telephone poles. Drained by the hot, humid weather, I looked into the skies while the haze just seemed to taunt me. Please rain, please just rain and cool off, I silently begged the trail gods. While crossing Lyme Dorchester Road, the thunder began to roll, and the wind roared. The rain made the ascent of Smarts Mountain cooler, but the mountain's open rock face was a bit scary with the lightning. I ducked into the shelter on top, and read that Hoosier and Cheddar had just left, after lunching there. That night, I caught up to Phoenix, Greenbean, Hoosier and Cheddar at the Hexacuba Shelter.

The next day we resupplied in Glencliff, New Hampshire with a post office drop which included an extra layer of clothes for the White Mountains, my remaining data sheets, 4 days of food, and 12 hexamine fuel tablets. Reports by southbounders consistently verified the abundance of food found at the huts in the Whites, so we packed only four days of food.

As we entered the White Mountains, signs warned against wild camping and mentioned fees of $8 per person in designated areas. The trail is very rugged and beautiful, reminding me of the Sierra Nevada Mountains in California.

Early the next morning, we arrived at Lonesome Lake Hut around 8 a.m. and discovered the rumors about food were true. For $1, we filled up on all the breakfast, leftover dessert and coffee we wanted. The cook let us take a wedge of homemade bread for lunch. Three of us stealth camped about 2 miles south of Garfield Campsite after enjoying wonderful views over Little Haystack Mt, Mt Lincoln, and Mt Lafayette.

The next morning we ate at Galehead Hut for $2. The coffee was hot, and the blueberry coffee cake, scrambled eggs and oatmeal was satisfying. We hit Zealand Hut at lunchtime and scored the last 3 bowls of homemade soup, with pie and cake for dessert. Hot food is always a welcome addition to limited food supplies. Phoenix and I were on Food Prowl Patrol, having decided to carry minimal food so we could enjoy light packs through this rugged section.

From Zealand Hut north it was smooth and fast. I enjoyed having friends to hike with these last days. Together, we caught up to Papa Geezer, paid our $8 each to camp at Ethan Pond, traded stories, and shared an old shelter.

Phoenix and I left Ethan Pond Campsite before 6 a.m. and found "trail magic" doughnuts, soda and peanut brittle placed beside the trail for thru-hikers in a cooler. Then, at Mizpah Hut we stuffed ourselves for $1. The crew was mopping and cleaning, so they gave us a pan of blueberry pancakes, gallon of syrup, and pitcher of coffee to enjoy in the fresh air. They donned aprons over their butt naked bodies, turned up the music and had one helluva good time.

Lake of the Clouds Hut, just 1.4 miles from the summit of Mt. Washington, is crowded. Wealthy people in bright colors and perfume, toting fancy gear, crowded the walls. Hikers of every persuasion and destination pulled in. We thru-hikers, who had asked for Work-For-Stay, began our chores. We filled the condiments; helped set the table, and washed dishes. Finally we ate with the crew, getting a taste of the stuffed pasta and free access to the two pots of bean soup. All the vegetables and salad were long gone, but we were okay with soup. There were no crackers or bread to dunk, but for dessert there was some fantastic poppy seed cake with a buttery frosting. At 9:30 the final guests were ushered out of the dining room, our "bedroom". The dining room tables became our bunks. Hikers spread out pads and sleeping bags. Exhausted, it was finally time for lights out.

Early the next morning, determined to eat with our friends, Phoenix and I set tables, packed all our gear, and filed in to eat with the guests at meal call. The weather report was not good: 50 mph winds and gusting, visibility 30 feet, temperatures in the low 50's, and intermittent drizzle, which felt like sleet in the high wind. Papa Geezer has been up here many times. He is somber, and tells us of the bad weather route, the Golf Slide Trail, that goes to Madison Hut. The official white blazes take hikers to the summit of Mt Washington. I am determined to do the white blazes. I have hiked alone, I say, in worse.

Papa Geezer leads with his wooden staff, I follow, Greenbean is next, then Phoenix. At first, I am perplexed by the seriousness on Papa's face. We start hiking; he waits for the rest of us to catch up. The tread is nothing but boulders, and there are very few blazes, some of them yellow. As we head up the mountain, the weather worsens remarkably. I am knocked sideways, and struggle to stay on my feet. Our pack covers threaten to fly away; we stop to tie them on, clipping them to the pack in several places. "Everyone ok?" Papa Geezer asks. Affirmative nods. We continue hiking, the visibility worsens, and Papa stops to analyze each cairn we pass. Phoenix is afflicted with several bouts of diarrhea, and we wait for him each time he has to leave the trail. The more we gain in elevation, the more concerned I become about doing this alone. There are so many intersecting trails in the vicinity, and the AT is poorly marked, if at all. After 45 minutes, we reach the trail junction with the AT and the Golf Slide Trail.

"Its decision time," Papa Geezer tells us; while we huddle close to hear him above the wind. We are all purists, and strong hikers. We look up the mountain. "It will get worse, stronger winds, less visibility. I don't think it's safe," Papa warns. Then, he adds, "But, if you want to go, I will go."

"I can't call it," I tell them, and turn my face aside. I know if I go, they all will go. Greenbean begins swearing ferociously, Phoenix looks really worried. None of us have taken any alternate, bad weather, or high water trails. We have hiked hard and strong. But now, we stood together, all old enough to recognize our own mortality, knowing that over the years, more than 100 people have died on Mt. Washington.

Fighting back tears of frustration and disappointment I say, "If there ever was a need for a bad weather trail it's now, today." We concede we are already at our limits. To attempt another half-mile on the AT with a 500 feet ascent was not reasonable. We swear, vent our frustration, and decide to press on to Madison Hut on the Golf Slide Trail.

The wind picks up, buffeting us as we inch our way those 7 miles. We stop a moment to get our breaths, and start meeting others from the Madison Hut making their way to Lake of the Clouds. We exchange reports with them, and realize it doesn't get any better. A sign reports we have come just 3.2 miles. We approach another sign, which states we have hiked only two tenths more. I look at my watch; it has taken half an hour to do two tenths of a mile? This upsets me, but Papa Geezer smiles and says, "There are too many signs on this trail, Brawny, don't think of the numbers." How he is finding this trail over rocks and boulders, cairn to cairn, is a mystery. I can barely see him ahead of me.

We finally reach Madison Hut around 12:30. We have struggled over 4 hours and arrive to find a happy young cook with a huge pot of bean curry soup, chocolate cake, fresh bread, hot coffee and hot cocoa. May the trail gods bless all such cooks, and their lives be long and merry. We eat our fill and hear reports that it is sunny and warm below tree line. Our goal is Pinkham Notch, where there are bunks, hot showers, AYCE supper and breakfast for $50. Just one mile down, into the trees and things get much better, we are told.

Back in the howling winds, we climb a half-mile to the summit of Mt. Madison. The hiking is reduced to hand over hand, ducking down between boulders, hanging on in the gusts of nearly 70 mph. I shorten my hiking poles, snag the wrist straps over my left hand, and crawl, on hands and knees, dragging my poles. On the top, I feel overwhelmed, and sympathize with the fly on the windshield of a car hurling down the highway at 70 mph. Greenbean, slender and tall, her pack catches the wind, she falls, struggles. Phoenix is repeatedly blown several feet off trail, picked up like some toy soldier. And all the while, Papa Geezer is leading us, waiting patiently, fighting against the wind. He was the sanity of our Moses through the wilderness.

By 4 p.m. we finally reach the trees, with only 5 miles left to Pinkham Notch. We arrive there at 6:30, reserve some rooms, and go for supper. We are late, but the cook sends out excellent food for us, family style. Other thru-hikers come over to our table to exchange reports. They had hiked out earlier this morning, arriving at the Washington summit, and were stranded. There they had waited for hours and finally hitched rides down the mountain with tourists who were happy for the extra weight in their cars. Tomorrow each thru-hiker will make a decision whether to go back up, or wait out yet another day of storm. A woman had broken her leg up there today, was carried by stretcher to the summit, where the train transported her down.

We left Pinkham Notch early next morning in the rain. The other thru-hikers, holed up at the Pinkham Notch bunkhouse, elected to rest, and just take a zero day. Hopefully, tomorrow would be better. Wildcat Mountain offered some great views, once the rain quit. After a day of hiking in the challenging terrain, we camped at Imp Campground, which had bear warnings posted. We pitched our solo shelters, and discussed the situation. I decided to sleep with my food, and when they hung their food bags directly above my tent, I told them I'd rather they wouldn't do that. They rehung their bags out of camp, and no one lost any food during the night.

From New Hampshire Hwy.16, we hitched into Gorham, resupplied at the CVS drug store, and had lunch. I called Rainmaker's cell phone, leaving a voice mail message. I listened to his message to me, missing him incredibly. He was doing well on the Long Trail; and I yearned to be reunited. It seemed he carried my heart with him.

Stepping Into Maine

Phoenix and I stopped a moment to take photos when we crossed into Maine on August 1. Maine is indeed a rugged state, but I am told it evens out after 80 miles.

The next day, we hiked through Mahoosuc Notch. It took us 2 hours to get through that one-mile boulder field, with hidden streams flowing underneath. Climbing over huge boulders, weaving through narrow cracks, and ducking under massive ledges, we scraped skin and gear all along the single worst mile of the Appalachian Trail. The ascent out of the notch, up Mahoosuc Arm, was a scramble over smooth-faced, slippery, near vertical rock.

We then went up and over Baldpate Mountain to reach Frye Notch Lean-to, a 15.5-mile day. Every muscle hurt, but I slept soundly.

We resupplied in Rangeley after an easy hitch into town. Phoenix and I went to the Laundromat after buying trail food and some lunch from the nearby grocery store. We washed clothes, ate our sub sandwiches and repackaged the foodstuff. He picked up some carburetor cleaner fluid to use as fuel, which although it says "flammable", burns sooty and reluctantly. After those chores were done, we got back on trail and camped at Piazza Rock Lean-to. The young caretaker was very friendly, and boys who were eager to climb the Piazza Rocks filled the campsite.

The Saddlebacks, Lone Mountain and Spaulding were marvelous. We decided to hike half-mile up to the Sugarloaf Mt. Ski Shelter. This place has windows all around, with a 360-degree view of the surrounding mountains. We slept on the picnic tables inside, and used the microwave to our heart's content. Earlier that day while crossing the Saddlebacks, I pulled a muscle in my right thigh. Every step caused excruciating pain. It wasn't my knee, but Phoenix insisted I wear his knee brace. I was taking 2 Ibuprofen every 3 hours, and it didn't touch the pain.

My thigh muscle continued to ache incredibly. The 3,000 ft. ascent next morning, in spite of an Ibuprofen tablet every 2 hours, reactivated the agony. But, a thru-hike is about pain. Just before the rains began we called a halt for the day at Horns Pond Lean-to. I gave the knee brace back to Phoenix.

The next morning my thigh felt good until I started rushing to catch up with Phoenix near Little Bigelow. It was time for us to part company. I am a soloist, and slowly but surely we were getting on each other's nerves. I met some section hikers who stopped to chat, and encouraged me with news of smooth trail along the lake, which was just to the north. It became an exceptionally pleasant day of solo hiking, with beautiful lakeside views all the way to Pierce Pond Lean-to. A man and his son welcomed me to the shelter when I arrived. Later, southbounding thru-hikers came and we exchanged information about upcoming trail.

Even though the ferry doesn't run across the Kennebec River until 9 a.m., just 3.7 miles away, force of habit, and some unknown urge drew me to the trail by 6 a.m. I planned to sit, drink instant coffee and watch the river. It is a very dangerous ford; hikers are instructed to take the free canoe ride across.

I enjoyed the lovely morning hike to the river, set my pack down, sat on the stump and looked across. Southbounders would stop there, and together we would wait for the ferryman. About 15 minutes after arriving, someone waved to me from the opposite shore. I smiled and waved back. This southbounder and I would have a long wait, and conversation would be difficult such a distance apart. I started messing around with my pack, and then looked up again.

"Carol?" he called.

I stood up, shading my eyes against the morning glare of the river. Who is this? Who could know my real name?

"It's David," he called across the river.
Rainmaker! I can't believe it. I put on my pack. "Can I cross?" I asked.
"No, wait for the ferry."
We both knew that a woman had drowned in front of her husband a few years back, trying to wade across. David went for coffee at a nearby restaurant, and I made mine with my little stove using river water, wondering if I had seen a mirage. The ferryman arrived on time, put in the canoe, and paddled across. He handed me the release form to fill out and sign. David had returned, and watched from the opposite river bank, while I put on the life jacket, climbed in front and helped paddle across.

Rainmaker and I embraced a long time, looking each other over for signs of wear. Then we went to the Rivers and Trails Cabins, close to Caratunk, Maine, and rented a cabin complete with stove, refrigerator, and shower. He told me about his hike, the storm he had gone through and his bad fall. I was so happy to see him back alive, although visibly worn and thinner.

There is a hiker box in the store, and plenty of good food on their shelves. I asked Lion Heart, a hiker working at the Rivers and Trails. if anyone had ever done the 37 miles between Caratunk and Monson in a day. He said yes, a girl had just done it. It took her 12 hours. I have never slack packed before, but thought this might be a good time to check it out. He brought out the profile maps and showed me first two mountains, then relatively smooth trail all the way to Monson. Totally do-able.

Early the next morning, just as the white blazes became visible, I headed north to Monson. Kissing Rainmaker good-bye, I told him, "See you tonight." I carried one water bottle, snacks and a rain jacket. There were 15 hours of daylight. Still, I didn't take any breaks, climbed the two mountains before lunch, and averaged almost 3 miles per hour. There was plenty of water all along, so I could stay well hydrated without carrying water more than half an hour, just enough time for the chlorine to work its purification process. The trail was well maintained, and the fords were easy. Just after 6:00 p.m. I arrived at Hwy 15. Moments later, Rainmaker drove up. He took me to resupply at the small and very adequate grocery store, then we spent the night together at the Pie Lady's house. I felt tired, elated, strong and healthy. 37 miles!

I have no idea why The Wilderness causes anyone consternation or fear. It is beautiful northern trail, very popular and well traveled.

There are 13 shelters spaced evenly within these 100 miles, and plenty of water. There is vehicle access, and food available at the midway point, White's Landing. Slack packing within the wilderness has been made available by vendors in Monson. Cars drive by every once in awhile on the many logging and gravel roads that dissect this area. Some thru-hikers expressed their deep disappointment. I admit the same feelings.

Packing out 4 days of food, I was so ready to finish this trail. It has been great, but I was ready to go home to the mountains of Georgia. Yesterday's hike did not affect an early start today; David drove me back to the trailhead by 7 a.m. Southbounders were greeting me regularly, and I chuckled at the 3-gallon kettle strapped to a young boy's pack when I passed a group of scouts. Apparently, he was cook's helper for the day. The 26 miles to Chairback Gap Lean-to went over some mountains I hadn't even noticed on the data sheet. Oopsey, what's this? Barren Mountain? Fourth Mountain? Third Mountain? I arrived about 6:30, and to my great pleasure, finally met Ram Bunny, a woman on her third Appalachian Trail thru-hike. The Spaniard, Million Miler and some section hikers were there as well.

On trail at first light, I realized there were just a few more days of hiking left and one thing was still lacking: so far I hadn't seen any moose. Today, while hiking 28.8 miles to Cooper Brook Falls Lean-to, I caught up to the Mass 4, a group of three guys and one girl. They had hiked together, cooked and ate out of one pot, and remained friends this entire trail. The guys were definitely wilder, with long hair and beards. Molly remained as feminine as ever. They did the half-gallon ice cream challenge while I watched at Pine Grove Furnace State Park, carried and shared one guitar, Devin giving lessons as needed. Some section hikers were in the shelter when I arrived. A woman gave me a fantastic foot rub while her grandsons asked many questions. We shared loads of trail talk.

Katahdin was the lone focus now. At last I saw my first moose: a mother and calf just barely off the trail. Truly enormous animals, they lumbered away quietly as Smoky and I passed them. After 21.5 miles, early in the afternoon, my eyes were so sleepy they were missing obvious things on the trail, like the sign for the spring, and a trail intersection. It was definitely time to get a nap. I pulled into the Wadleigh Stream Lean-to and there sat Christopher Robin and Viking. The scary thing was that I was so exhausted that I didn't even recognize them. They decided to hike further, so I took my nap before others arrived.

That night the shelter and the tenting area filled up with hikers. We stayed up past dark, the section hikers worrying aloud about porcupines coming to get them. One couple hung a 10-pound sack of food, which included bacon, on a mouse hanger in the shelter, then went to sleep in their tent. We shelter dwellers felt no obligation to defend this sack. It dawned on me that this would be the last night that I'd sleep on the trail. It seemed very fitting to have it be an adventure. Small creature noises were heard during the night, but no food was lost.

As prearranged, on the fourth day after I'd left Monson, I hiked to Abol Bridge for a rendezvous with Rainmaker. It was very hot and muggy, nearly 90 degrees. Smoky caught up to me at the Rainbow Stream Campground. From the ceiling beam hung 20 power bars, cracker packs, and snacks in gallon size zip lock bags. We praised the trail angels and took several. I caught up to three older women who were day hiking, two miles south of Abol Bridge. With a brief exchange of questions and answers, they learned that I intended to summit tomorrow, and proceeded to warn me it was too far. Couldn't be done. Where have I heard this before? These warnings have followed me all the way up the trail. I told them I had now finished the Wilderness in 4 days, and they expressed amazement. "You have done in 4 days what most take 10 to do," one remarked. Maybe they just haven't met many thru-hikers.

Upon arriving at the road to Abol Bridge it looks like a mistake. Anticipation of some great store with beer, ice cream, supplies, and a campground just conjures up this image of folks, pavement, and Stuff. I saw some trucks hauling logs, a lot of dust, a big bridge east of the trail, and some guy walking away from the bridge. As I neared the store, a few hikers could be seen at a picnic table. Viking! Virgin! Christopher Robin, and most importantly, Rainmaker. "I got a good room with air conditioning, pool, hot tub, and TV in Millinocket, " he smiled. My friends declined a ride to town, so I told them, "see you in the morning" and off we drove to the decadence of a well-appointed motel room.

Rainmaker willingly got up at 3:30 a.m. and drove me to the trail so I could begin my last day in the grayness of early morning. Twenty miles of trail remained between home and me, and I intended to do them with pure focus and energy. The weather forecast called for another hot and humid day. The climb up Katahdin, to 5,268 feet, needed to be done before the heat of the day.

My Journey to Freedom and Ultralight Backpacking

I had no idea how smooth and sweet that first 10 miles would be. By 8:15 I stashed my poles at the Ranger Station and signed in. A ranger working outside came over to warn me about the heat and lack of water. Supposedly, Thoreau Spring was just a trickle, and one could not get water at the summit. I carried capacity of 48 ounces, had been hydrating all morning, and told him so. He still looked concerned, so I told him I had hiked the Pacific Crest Trail last year, through the Mojave Desert, and that I knew how to ration water.

Heading up the mountain, just past the last camper, hung another sign-in sheet. Others were ahead of me. I am late, I thought. Up to Katahdin Falls, the grade is easy. The falls are cold and sweet, a good place to wet the bandana and cool off. There is even a privy just off trail, with toilet paper, too. The trail steepens and I begin to catch up with others. A man with three young daughters. An older couple, taking their time. A group of teenage girls and their leaders. Now we come to little corner rods fastened in the rocks. The blazes just mark the general route, you get over them the best you can. I catch up to a young woman and her boyfriend, then a man who is bagging peaks. He is focused on the task at hand, and I hike with him. He asks many thoughtful questions, making the miles go by. You are not expected to step on the blazes. Some lead past a red rope, some down and around, some on top of an enormous rock. I keep climbing; we top the first level spot. Not quite to Thoreau Spring, we have just 1.6 miles to go.

The spring is running fine; fine enough for any PCT hiker. Now it is hand over hand, and I am glad that I left my poles behind. All the paint had been scraped off the poles when I went over Mt. Madison; they are etched with past endeavors. Only my body will have the scrapes of Katahdin. We reach the sign that marks the end of my journey, but so many day hikers mill around that I just want my photos. The peak-bagger does so graciously, several high-five me, congratulations abound. I have held in my emotions all day, and now it seems non climatic. I head down, meeting Jumpstart, and her husband Balu. She is weeping openly and we embrace. Embraces all around. By god, we did it. Emotions must wait; I just want to go home now. It is 11:30, and pleasant breezes are blowing.

Mainframe is heading up, we shake hands, and he tells me he is tired of this shit. I laugh. A true purist, we have followed the rules. We are ready to go home.

The peak bagger catches up to me again, and I follow him down. It's not nearly as hard following someone, letting them help find a sensible path down insensible rocks. We reach the campground at

2:30. I still have water. Shaking hands, and best of luck, we part. That is the way of the trail. You meet great people, enjoy their company, and never see them again. Rainmaker, freshly shaven, looking young and handsome, is waiting at a picnic shelter; enjoying a new CD he bought. Life is so good. "Congratulations! Let's go home," he smiles.

August 15th and 16th were spent driving back to Georgia. I recognized on the road signs the names of the places I had resupplied: Cheshire, Mass. Pine Grove Furnace State Park, Pennsylvania, Harper's Ferry, West Virginia, Perrisburg, Virginia. Last time I headed south on I-81, there was unfinished business. Now, there is no unfinished business. I am done. I am a thru-hiker. I started to cry as that fact finally sank in. My emotions could no longer be contained. David understood. He, too, is a thru-hiker, and knows what it took, what it cost in soul and spirit.

Reflections

The things we believed would never fade have already been abandoned by your memory-- found in a magazine on top of Sugarloaf Mountain.

The only lasting memories will be of the humor, stubbornness, strength, and friendships. The pain, loneliness, fear, and worry, at one time so overwhelming, have already been abandoned. Did those bad things ever really happen? There will never be a doubt about the wonder, amazement, resolve and growth.

Thoreau said, **"A man generally attains what he aims for, therefore, though at first he fail, he ought to aim high."** I accepted nothing less than a pure thru-hike for myself.

And finally the quote I found in a rare PCT water cache register **"In the end you find that no one wins, and that the race was only with yourself."** It matters not who finished before or after me, but that I finished at all.

My Resupply Points for the Appalachian Trail

I don't like to hitch hike, and town stops take extra time and money. For these reasons, I chose to hike more miles between resupply points. Because of the season, and time of day, sometimes I was able to buy food at concession stands, which supplemented my food supplies. Those places are noted in this list. Whenever possible, I obtained information from southbounders and section hikers of upcoming trail resources.

Neel's Gap, GA-Trail goes right past the store. They hold drop boxes for hikers and charge $2 for this service. Some food is sold at the store, but it's expensive. There was a hostel right next door in 2002, where many hikers stayed overnight. A coin operated washer and dryer were also available.

Dick's Creek Gap, GA-I went home for a day, but it is an easy hitch into Hiawassee, a town with lots of motels, and fast food restaurants.

Rock Gap Shelter, NC-I went home overnight. One could hike 3.8 miles further on AT, and hitch into Franklin, NC, which has full supplies, including an outfitter store.

Nantahala River, Wesser, NC-Trail goes right through this complex. I bought some supplies, and used the hiker box. The restaurant has great food.

Fontana Dam, NC- I went home for two days; most hitch into the resort area.

Newfound Gap, TN-Rainmaker brought me home for a day, but one can hitch into Gatlinburg, TN or Cherokee, NC.

Hot Springs, NC –Last time home, so I stayed two days. Trail goes right through town with full supplies, including an outfitter and hostel.

Erwin, TN-Trail goes within sight of resort (hiker hostel, with supplies). I caught a ride into town with many amenities, good resupply. Town with a hiker-turf war, be prepared to hear negative comments about the competition. There are motels in town, if you would wish to stay out of the fray.

Dennis Cove, TN- A reasonably priced resort half mile east, decent supplies, hot food, and bunks, showers and laundry facilities. Very friendly management, who gave free popcorn with the free videos for the evening entertainment. They also make a great breakfast, but they do want hikers to register for supper, due to limited space in the restaurant.

Damascus, VA –The trail goes right through town, has full supplies including outfitters. One outfitter has Internet access available. The Place, a hostel run by the Methodist Church, has many rooms full of wooden bunks. Donations recommended.

Atkins, VA-Trail goes right past inexpensive motel, convenience store with adequate resupply, and restaurant. It's not really in town, but had all the facilities that I needed.

Pearisburg, VA-Trail goes within one-tenth mile of an inexpensive motel, called the Rendezvous. Very good resupply one mile into town, with a library, Internet access, Pizza Hut and more.

US 220, near Troutville, VA, -Trail goes within sight of shopping center, supermarket, motels, and restaurants.

Jennings Creek, VA-Weekenders took me to a convenience store to resupply; most hikers went into Glasgow, which is 30 trail miles north.

Waynesboro, VA-Easy hitch into town from Rockfish Gap, and there are plenty of stores of all kinds. Free camping and showers at YMCA.

Big Meadows, VA- Had lunch, and bought some supplies, a decent camp store and grill. There is a pay phone outside, and they do accept credit cards. Watch for the one-tenth mile turn-off by the cemetery, this is easy to miss. If you get near the lodge, you have gone too far, and it will be a mile down the nature trail to the grill.

Elkwallow Gap, VA-Great grill and scanty, but sufficient, resupply one-tenth east of trail, last of the Shenandoahs. This one can be seen from the trail.

Ashby Gap, VA, U.S. 50-We walked one-tenth mile east to a taxidermist shop and bought candy bars, raisins, chips and soda. There also were dehydrated suppers for sale, if you need them.

Harpers Ferry, WV –Trail winds right along edge of town. There is a hiker box at ATC headquarters where they take your photo and tell you what number you are southbounding, northbounding, or section hiking. The 7-11 has adequate resupply. This is a good place to send a drop box with data sheets, fuel tablets, etc. This is considered the half way point, emotionally. The post office is about 3 blocks from the ATC. There is a library with Internet access, too.

Pine Grove Furnace State Park, PA-A small camp store with groceries, and hot food, not well marked, just past the huge white house (hostel). There was a concession stand in the park further up as well that the trail went right past.

Boiling Springs, PA-The trails goes right through, takes a right turn, and starts through a farmer's field. There's a hiker box at ATC Mid Atlantic Regional Office, restaurants within a few blocks (turn left off trail) with great Italian food. You don't need much, it's only 26 miles to Duncannon.

Duncannon, PA-Trail passes through town where hikers can stay at the sleazy, 4-storied Doyle. A free shuttle to a fantastic grocery store, convenience stores, restaurants, and bars help this town to be a favorite among hikers.

Port Clinton, PA- Just bought a candy bar, but the outfitter there has sufficient food for a resupply. Bring cash. Not a good town to do anything else in, no phones, no ATM. The motel does not take credit cards, and the rooms don't have air conditioning, private bathrooms, or phones.

Delaware Water Gap, PA –Motels with hiker rates, all the amenities, and a convenience store with adequate resupply, and great restaurants. This is the place to spend money on a motel, if you are so minded, because it has the luxuries you have been waiting for.

Mohican Outdoor Center, NJ- Only 10.5 miles from Delaware Water Gap, it's a great stop. Fresh sandwiches made to order, and some snacks, are found a quarter mile left from the trail. There's also a phone and a bunkhouse.

Unionville, NY-The town is just four-tenth west of the trail, has a small but very adequate grocery store.

NJ Hwy. 94-I could see the store from the road crossing. This place is only 12 miles north of Unionville, and one tenth left of the trail. They sell pastries, ice cream, fruit, and much more. Great place to snack and get some additional treats. No phone available, in 2002.

Bear Mountain, NY- Trail goes right behind this fancy motel, great place to eat lunch. Let the waitress know if you drink a lot of coffee. They don't open until 11:30, though.

Kent, CN-A walk of eight-tenths mile into town. Great resupply at the IGA, by the post office. Little shops are quite expensive, so is the lodging. Not easy to hitch, the locals seem wary.

Dalton, MA-Walk through town, with convenience stores, but with Cheshire only 9 miles away a person doesn't need to carry much food.

Cheshire, MA-Hike along edge of town on the AT. There's great pizza, sub sandwiches, and convenience stores five-tenths west of trail. Pay phone at the gas station.

Mt. Greylock, Bascom Lodge, MA-I went in to use the phone. A friend bought a pack cover, and there was candy, hot food and snacks available. Hikers could rent a bunk if they wanted to. Just 6 miles to Mass. 2 where you decide between North Adams to the east, and Williamstown to the left.

North Adams-It's expensive, but had all one could want in food, restaurants, and amenities. Great interconnecting bus system to nearby Pittsfield.

Manchester, VT-An easy hitch 5.5 miles west, with a fabulously large supermarket, lots of restaurants, and a Laundromat. The whole town was quite crowded with tourists, even on a Monday.

Killington, VT-Stayed at the Long Trail Inn, adequate supplies and post office (shuttle bus available) 2.2 miles east.

West Hartford, VT-Walk right past great restaurant/deli with adequate food supplies. Hanover is just 10 miles away.

Hanover, NH-Trail goes right through this fancy college town. There is a fraternity house, which allows 6 thru-hikers to spend the night free. Town has good resupply, and there's a hiker box at the frat house.

Glencliff, NH-Sent a drop box with food for the White Mountains, extra layer of clothing, data sheets, fuel tablets, hygiene, vitamins.

White Mountains, NH-If you hit it right, like we did, plenty of food at the huts. We left Glencliff with four days of food.

Pinkham Notch, NH-I rented a bunk with complete bedding, and had the room to myself, got two fantastic All You Can Eat (AYCE) meals, showers and phone access for $50. It didn't seem expensive after a long hard day.

Gorham, NH-An easy hitch 3.6 miles west, adequate resupply at drug store next to post office and Laundromat. Great restaurants.

Rangley, ME-An easy hitch 9 miles west. Has a good but very busy grocery store, pay phone outside the store, several grills, and a Laundromat, with no change or soap machines.

Caratunk, ME-Spent the night, day hiked to Monson. Great store to resupply at the ferryman's cabins.

Monson, ME -Stayed at Pie Lady's, adequate resupply at small store. Another town with a turf-war. She rents rooms, and makes breakfasts, for a reasonable fee. There's also a mini-mart with great deli sandwiches (made to order) on the edge of town. Internet access at the small public library near the mini-mart.

Abol Bridge, ME-Small store just past the bridge, which the trail goes right past. I went with Rainmaker to Millinocket for the night, and then carried snacks for the day-hike up and down Mt. Katahdin .

Chapter Seven

My Ultralight Tips and Techniques

Backpacking veterans have seen vast changes in gear, especially over the last five years. I have been backpacking only since 1999, so the wave of new ultralight gear does not amaze me as much as others. What amazes me is the weight hikers carried previously when they went into the backcountry.

I had my first real taste of pack weight variations while hiking the Pacific Crest Trail. The first year I went with Rainmaker, there were times we hauled 5 quarts of water (each) and 7 days of food. As the water was used, the two pounds per liter could definitely be felt. When we neared town, and our next resupply, the food weight was down to a pound or two. It felt like I could really cruise. Then a thought struck me. What if my pack was always this light?

Ultralight backpacking doesn't have to be expensive. Using alternative gear can result in substantial savings for both weight and money. Suggestions for inexpensive, recycled, or free gear are given in the appropriate categories that follow. Of course, all of it is light, and weights in grams or ounces listed when possible.

Most of the time, a change in personal habits can save weight. For instance, if you are willing to eat out of your pot, and drink from a plastic home made cup, forego the extra eating utensils, repackage your food, and cook on an ultralight soda can stove, several pounds can be shaved on the cooking system alone. Part of ultralighting is about self-restriction, self-reliance, and self-discovery, but never self-denial. After all, backpacking is about enjoyment. I find the whole subject totally fascinating, and love to experiment.

There are many brands and types of commercial gear. Also, there are the emerging cottage industries offering homemade gear. What you chose to buy, or make, depends on your own preferences and needs. This chapter is devoted to helping individuals lighten their packs to suit themselves. What works for me may not work for you. My hope is that you can achieve the lightest possible pack weight, and still have everything that you need for a safe and enjoyable trip. Some of the information presented here is just my own opinion, and based on personal experience, observations and research. Please share your ideas with me by e-mail. I look forward to hearing from you, and learning additional ultralight techniques.

Definitions

Base Pack Weight is defined as all your gear without food and water. The systems for carrying food (stuff sacks) and water (water bottles or bags) are included. Some people differentiate with **Skin Out** base weight, which is another way of emphasizing that the stated weight includes clothing worn as well.

Gram Weenie is a term coined to identify people so focused on pack weight that even a few grams (28.5 grams per ounce) would be pared from the lightest of gear. Some gram weenie techniques include cutting down the handle on a Lexan spoon, removing name tags and icons from gear, making sandals from shoe inserts and replacing a cooking pot lid with aluminum foil.

The **Volume** or **Bulk** of an item is very important for an ultralighter, as well as weight. If you only have 2,500 cubic inches of pack space available, the amount of space that the various items occupy is going to be crucial. The final choice between a synthetic or down sleeping bag or quilt might be made for this reason alone.

Silnylon is a 1.1-ounce, siliconized, rip-stop fabric. Once treated with silicone to make it water repellent, it weighs approximately 1.3 ounces per square yard. Sometimes called parachute cloth, it is difficult to find in fabric stores, and often it is necessary to order it from companies offering specialized materials. Ultralight gear made from this fabric is very light and amazingly strong. However, it is not flame retardant.

Vapor Barrier is an item designed to trap body heat and hold in body moisture as well. Vapor barrier bags can be used in emergency and survival situations. Vapor barrier clothing can be worn in or out of a sleeping bag, lowering the bag's rating by as much as 10 degrees. Clothing and fabric is said to **Breathe** if body moisture can escape through the fibers. A waterproof fabric will not allow such transfer, while some fabrics (like silk and cotton) will. By their very nature, vapor barrier bags and clothing do not breathe. In high humidity situations, and pouring rain, anything breathable becomes a study in semantics at best.

Wicking refers to the transfer of body moisture to the clothing, thereby allowing evaporation into the atmosphere. A thin wicking layer, sometimes called a base layer, is usually made of polyester. It is recommended for use under rain clothing in cold weather, or when perspiration is considerable. The clothing itself will not hold much moisture, but dries quickly. Hiking shorts and tops that wick will allow the perspiration to evaporate quickly, unlike cotton.

A System is a set of components that work together to achieve one goal. These components may change with climate or personal needs. Several systems needed for backpacking include a cooking system, a sleeping system, shelter, and pack system.

Footprint refers to the exact shape a tent floor makes. When cutting a custom ground cloth, set up the tent on plastic sheeting and mark its base. Remove the tent, and cut the sheeting one-inch smaller (on all sides) than the outline you just traced.

Pitching a tarp or tent refers to setting it up. **Striking or dropping** tarp or tent means taking it down.

Tarp-A water resistant shelter without a floor. It may have an overhanging panel, sometimes called a beak, or no-see-um netting attached. Variable height and floor area result from different configurations. Partially because of recent concerns over West Nile Virus (transmitted by mosquitoes) and Lyme Disease (transmitted by ticks) a new breed of **Tarp-Tents** has been developed. These tarps have sewn in floors, some still maintaining variable pitching options. The floors can be of no-see-um netting, or waterproof fabric such as silnylon.

The word **Shelter** is now used in place of tarp or tent because of the various designs now overlapping in those structures. Different definitions of tent-tarps cause confusion, so the word **Shelter** may be used frequently instead.

Variable Pitch is a major reason people choose tarps over tents. Nearly every tarp can be configured in a triangular pattern. Height will vary with length. This is geometry simplified. If a storm threatens, the tarp is spread, keeping the windward side low. This gives the shelter a low center height, but provides the occupant a longer area of coverage. In good weather, the tarp is pitched higher, and the area covered will be less. One exception would be a canopy, or nearly horizontal configuration. This style could be used for protection against desert sun, or windless, drizzling rain.

Single wall/double wall tent-A single wall tent is constructed with one layer of water resistant or water proof fabric. It may have screen doors and vents, with storm doors, beaks or windows. A double walled tent has much of the top sewn in mesh (no-see-um netting), with a door opening, stitched to a waterproof or water resistant floor. A fly or tarp is then fitted over the top to protect against wind and rain. A double walled tent is heavier, but will have less condensation problems.

Seam sealing is recommended for all shelters, tents and tarps. Even factory-taped seams have been known to leak on new shelters. Seams sewed into shelters with needles form tiny holes every time a stitch is taken. If a sealant is smeared along (and into) the seam over the holes, leaking will stop. The best seam sealant we have found, which even sticks to 1.3-ounce silicone treated, rip stop nylon, is 100% silicone, manufactured for exterior use. Apply according to directions, and allow it to dry for at least 24 hours.

Condensation occurs in fabric shelters because the shelter usually is warmer than the outside air. As we exhale, moisture from our breath rises to condense on the inner walls. In single wall tents, this moisture can be wiped away with a bandana or pack towel. With double wall tents, the moisture passes through the top mesh, collects on the underside of the fly, and then drains downward. Generally speaking, the moisture will not fall back through the mesh. Exceptions occur when rain hits the canopy. Condensation is directly related to airflow. The more closed and waterproof a shelter is, the greater the moisture buildup will be.

Zero Day in the truest sense of the word means a day when no time is spent hiking trail miles. Having a low pack weight, and a complete system that works can substantially reduce the need for zero days.

A **Resupply** is when a hiker replenishes food, medical and hygiene items, and then resumes the hike. A resupply can be done by buying directly from local stores, using a bounce box, or drop box. A **bounce box** is a box with supplies intended to be mailed ahead after needed items are chosen from it. It is "bounced" ahead to the next post office and the container is generally of a much sturdier construction. A **drop box** is intended to be a one-time shipment, and ideally should only include the items needed for that next section of trail.

Ultralight Philosophy

There are many reasons for backpacking. When assembling gear, those reasons need to be addressed. Perhaps the excursion into the backcountry is to take fantastic photos. One good friend took a 4-pound camera on his Pacific Crest Trail thru-hike. When teased about its weight, he simply stated, "I am taking photos that will last a lifetime." Photography was his passion, and he won awards with some of those photos he took in 2001. I have brought disposable cameras, weighing 4 ounces. At times, I carry a 6-ounce digital camera. Ultralight backpacking is not about deprivation, but about choosing the lightest weight gear for your own needs.

The trip's purpose may be fishing, or perhaps it includes fishing, at a remote spot along the way or at the destination. Some long distance hikers bring just a line, hook and sinker. Others include a light reel as well. They find poles in the vicinity. However, it is not appropriate to cut live vegetation for your fishing rod. Then, there are those who bring their entire rod and reel, along with a tackle box. I have seen these left in hiker boxes, when the hiker tired of fishing. Do not forget to check about the permits necessary for the areas you are traveling to and through.

If the reason for backpacking is just about hiking, and enjoying the trail, then a light pack will enhance the journey. With every mile, and every foot of elevation gain or loss, the work involved in backpacking is increased proportionately to the weight carried.

Perhaps time is limited and long high mileage days are crucial. Paring down every last gram is important. This actually can be quite fun, and looked upon as a personal challenge. I would never criticize anyone who does not want to go this far, but it is an extremism that I enjoy.

The formula that one should not carry more than 25% of their body weight is a good starting point. This figure is used with one's ideal body weight, and includes food and water. That 25 % should be considered maximum weight, including food and water. If one were hiking the desert, where water is an issue, temporarily exceeding that maximum may be unavoidable. Each liter of water weighs two pounds. At times, 6 liters are carried, for a total of 12 pounds. But generally speaking, the 25% is applicable in most backpacking situations. As a 120-pound woman, that translates into 30 pounds for me. If I have to carry two liters of water (4 pounds) and four days of food (about 6 pounds) that gives me 20 pounds of base weight to work with. As an ultralighter, I would look at getting to a 15% maximum weight, or below. That translates into 18 pounds, maximum. I was able to do this on my AT thru-hike in 2002. In Port Clinton, PA, the outfitter weighed my pack at fourteen pounds, which is 11.6% of my body weight. That included food for four days, and 12 ounces of water. My gear list for this hike, complete with adjustments, can be read in Chapter 5 of this book.

The philosophy of ultralight backpacking is to bring innovation and problem solving strategies into the backcountry with us. One way to really lower pack weight is to have carefully planned strategies concerning water.

Some strategies concerning water in well-watered areas include carrying two water bottles, one that is drunk as soon as purification is complete. The other one is kept full until another water source is located. At the water source, the other one is drunk, and both bottles refilled and treated. As you continue hiking, this cycle is repeated, drinking one bottle of water as soon as purification is complete, and reserving the other one until a water source is located. This way a person stays well hydrated, without running out of water.

In the desert, this strategy changes. Compute the miles to the next sure water source, and divide the amount of water carried among the hours necessary to reach that source. The most I carried was 5 liters of water. Try to get started at daybreak, while it is still cool. Then, during the heat of the day, it is a good idea to rest in the shade, preferably at a water source. You may have to create your own shade but hopefully there will be a rock overhang or Joshua tree. Cook and wash the dishes, brush your teeth, and wash your body at a water source if possible. If there is still a lot of daylight when that source is reached, you can hike until dark. Whenever you reach water, tank up, that is, drink as much as you can hold, resting and waiting, then drinking more. This method will get you through a lot of desert miles on a daily basis.

I tried to keep my food at just over one pound per day. I realize this is very minimal for most people. Men might need nearly twice that figure. A 160-pound man, carrying 15% of his body weight, would have twenty-four pounds to work with. That would allow for additional food weight. Some strategies for keeping food weight down include always leaving town very full and covering some miles before camping. Each day's meals are portioned, using chocolate covered peanuts, raisins, nuts and candy for a lot of calories and hiking energy. Supper is ramen noodles, instant rice, instant potatoes or oatmeal. A satisfying appetizer is bouillon cube, dissolved in one cup of hot water with peanut butter cheesy crackers broken into it. This is very filling and weighs only 1.25 ounces. Expect to come into town hungry. Take advantage of any convenience stores, concession stands, or trail magic along the way. With a low pack weight, you can cover more miles. Any additional food that accumulates by eliminating extra days on the trail can be portioned and consumed before getting into town.

Attitude

My philosophy of ultralight backpacking says we can take what we want to enjoy our journey, but it just needs to be as light as possible. If we can redefine or eliminate some of our wants, real progress will be made towards an incredibly low pack weight.

I think this requires a change or adjustment of attitude for most Americans, brought up to believe that two chickens are needed in every pot, two cars belong in every garage, and a home with only one full bathroom is considered substandard.

An ultralight attitude can be developed over a period of time. Henry David Thoreau said, **"How many a poor mortal soul have I met well nigh crushed and smothered under its load, creeping down the road of life, pushing before it a barn seventy-five feet by forty, its Augean stables never cleansed, and one hundred acres of land, tillage, mowing, pasture, and wood-lot! The portionless, who struggle with no such unnecessary inherited encumbrances, find it labor enough to subdue and cultivate a few cubic feet of flesh."**

The idea I get from this is that we don't want anything too big; it just drags us down. We want enough, but just enough. Less material goods does not indicate poverty, but the power of personal restraint. It's actually a very satisfying concept and practice.

This is not to be taken in reference to money in the bank. A wise man once said, "Most emergencies can be solved with the proper application of a Master or Visa Card." Instead of pushing stuff through life, I prefer to live lightly, with back-up funds properly kept safe and accessible.

An ultralighter who is self-sufficient shows personal power. Anyone who constantly needs to borrow gear, food, water, fuel, or guidebook pages from others, is not an ultralighter, but a parasite and drain on the hiking community. I know those are strong words, but I will not advocate that anyone go to a trail ill equipped or unprepared because they have tried to save pack weight, figuring they will come across some good Samaritan or trail angel to bail them out.

Certainly it is fun and necessary to share food and gear occasionally. The goal, though, as an ultralighter, is to have everything one needs or learn how to improvise until they get it. In some areas, a person may not meet another hiker for days or even weeks. Also, it is not fair to put others at risk, obligation or inconvenience because of our lack of planning.

This ultralight attitude transcends the pack and includes our own bodies. Carrying an extra 20 pounds of body fat is unnecessary weight. It is detrimental to our health, and requires additional effort for every mile hiked. We make choices about our gear to eliminate extra weight, and choices are made to lower body weight. It's not a matter of totally cutting out items, it's a matter of reducing portions, improving components (less fats and sugars) and arriving at a weight that best suits our needs. Again, it's about having what we want, but perhaps that also means redefining what we need and how much of it.

There are some who, planning a long distance hike, decide to "bulk up". They intentionally gain weight, knowing that they will be using more calories each day than they will be carrying. This is a bad plan, because unless the weight is muscle, no benefit can be found for carrying extra fat up those long inclines and steep grades. Knees, ankles and feet will suffer with the weight. Extra body weight will cause more stress as the heart and lungs labor to fill the needs of the extra poundage. Once the body is able to shed the fat and build leg muscles, real progress will be felt in trail readiness. The lean hiker is a healthy hiker. Especially on the Appalachian Trail, where food sources are abundant, no extra weight should be gained in preparation.

Reality

Even if we could get our needs and wants pared down to absolute basics, sometimes a bad back, sensitive knees, or previous injuries may necessitate additional pack weight. Special dietary considerations have to be dealt with. Harsh weather and climate conditions also call for additional gear. But once customized, and after reality is paid homage, the result is a functioning, workable, system. There should be no embarrassment with knee braces, back braces, doubled sleeping pads, medicines or vitamins. The mere fact we can do this at all is pretty amazing. Some of the most honored hikers are those the doctors have told to stay home, those hikers who press preconceived limitations, and teach us all about perseverance.

Some things I learned about **proper body mechanics** from Rainmaker have kept me on the trail. More than 35 years of long distance backpacking have given him much understanding about pain, its prevention and relief. Follow these suggestions at home, when applicable, to prevent injuries which will flare up when hiking.

His strategies include:

Never twist your back while lifting, or in preparation for lifting anything heavy. Consider it heavy if it weighs over 5 pounds. Always face the weight, bring it close to your body, and lift with your knees. To lower the weight, reverse these steps. This includes bounce boxes and loaded packs.

Use a knee pad or cushion whenever possible. Do not sit in a position that requires knees to be fully bent, such as those young children use, butt resting on or near your heels.

When hiking uphill or climbing over boulders, take smaller steps so that your knees are not extended at right angles to the ground. Keep the weight centered over the quadriceps as much as possible. Those large leg muscles are designed to bear the weight, not the knee joints.

Avoid running or striding quickly down hill. The knees take the brunt of this type of descent, and although they might show no immediate ill effects, that night and the next day they could ache incredibly. Long-term heavy dosage of Ibuprofen is no remedy for mistreating your body in this manner.

Fully utilize your hiking poles to take advantage of your upper body strength. For people with bad backs or knees, poles have become standard hiking equipment. On an ascent, use your arm strength to assist in transferring weight forward with the hiking poles. On a descent, allow your poles to bear some of the weight downward, again using smaller steps to avoid over-extending the knees.

Warm up in the morning before beginning the day's hike by walking around camp, doing some light, full range of motion exercises with arms, wrists, and legs. Never jerk your pack up, but lift it with a smooth even motion while keeping the back straight.

To aid in a healthy lifestyle, lift weights two or three times per week. Dumb-bells (two identical sets of hand weights) are said to promote better balance and muscle development than one heavy barbell. Walking daily, with or without weights, is always healthy. Never run or hike with ankle weights, which can cause a great deal of damage to the knees.

It is always a good idea to take your ultralight system out for a few consecutive nights to find any flaws before heading out on a long trail. Many problems become apparent only after several days on the trail. Some people hope they can get by on cold food, only to discover that without something hot at the end of a day, they just didn't feel well fed. I twice tried to ditch my pot support, using stakes, rocks and aluminum cans, and finally concluded the pot support was worth the ounce of weight. If the way you have configured your water transport system doesn't work for one reason or another, it is better to find out before you are in the middle of a desert.

Experience

We were nearly done with our journeys, section hikers, thru-hikers and overnighters, all sharing a shelter in the 100 Mile Wilderness section of Maine. A young friend thoughtfully asked me, "So how's your ultralight system working for you?" I told him that it was great, that I was still carrying the same silnylon backpack, Tacoma tent, and soda can stove since Springer Mountain, Georgia. I mentioned that I'd gotten my base weight down to eight pounds. He shook his head and reflected, "I carry more weight by accident than you do on purpose."

I gave him a big grin, for that was a great compliment. It didn't happen overnight. Trial and error played a large part in accruing the experience necessary to become a minimalist. I learned how to utilize everything in my pack and surroundings to stay warm in unexpected, record cold. A couple times I got "burned" trying to go too light, was hungry and cold, fought with troublesome gear, and had to forego the week's journaling. But, that's how you learn. A person won't know their limits until they go beyond them, then you just back up to that point. But by experimenting, enjoying the good and coping with the bad outcomes, I was able to shed the standard approach. I learned to ask for information when necessary, and then make decisions. All this takes time, a willingness to fail, a willingness to learn, and a willingness to recognize success, however marginal.

The gear I used in 2002 will no doubt be replaced by other gear as technology progresses, and I come up with new designs. There is no perfect shelter, no perfect sleep system, and no perfect pack. We are all individuals. What works for me may never work for you; hence by that very theory nothing can be perfect. But, as you read the next sections on various backpacking components, I believe you will be able to shave pounds off your present pack weight. Although some ideas may seem outlandish, give them a go, in the comfort of your own back yard, and I think you will have a lot of fun. You may even choose to adopt some of them.

Remember to always play it safe when bringing children, sick, handicapped, inexperienced or older folks with you. Take those extra precautions, and carry some extra weight. A cell phone raises objections from some outdoor advocates, but without a doubt they have saved many lives by facilitating timely rescues. Let no one tell you what you need, and what you don't. Your needs always remain your own choices. The purpose of this book is to share ultralight techniques, and leave the decisions up to you.

Gear Preference

The biggest changes in backpacking weights can be attributed to the new fabrics and designs now available. There are ultralight alternatives to every piece of gear that was once thought basic. Generally, there is some trade-off when you pare serious weight. As I go through each category, and note the pros and cons, remember I am not saying which one is best. That is as subjective as what kind of pie you prefer.

The use of silnylon for shelters, stuff sacks, pack covers, and raingear can cut respective weights in half. Special care must be used with this waterproof, flammable fabric, but the results are impressive. Favorite existing gear can be remade by a skilled seamstress using silnylon; more about that is in the "Make Your Own" section.

Micro fleece, silk, polyester and nylon have replaced cotton blends and heavy, man-made fibers. Clothing is now more versatile and weight efficient. You may have a favorite fabric blend, or expect a looser fit, which could raise pack weight. Again, that is your preference, but branching out into something unusual may give you unexpected pleasant results.

There are many ways to cook on the trail. There are choices concerning solid or liquid fuels, fast cooking or slow, compatibility with your cookware, and the amount of space in your pack you are willing to devote to this system. How large your system must be will depend on what you expect out of your meals.

Multipurpose gear eliminates duplicate ounces, however, care must be taken not to jeopardize one's health or safety. I personally am not fond of ponchos that serve for both rain gear and primary shelter. As a loose fitting rain cover, they do not offer the protection a light jacket would. With hiking poles, the water tends to drip and run down the arms. They could work as a tarp over a bivy bag, or even a ground cloth inside a tarp. In cold, wet, rainy weather, the idea of stripping off one's raingear to set up as a shelter can be a dangerous concept. Great care must be taken in such weather to stay as warm as possible, even if not totally dry. Rain gear can serve as a very effective wind barrier, and it can hold in body heat. At the end of the day, after hiking has stopped and camp is being made, there is a serious danger of hypothermia. Removing this important layer and setting it up as a very basic shelter should be carefully considered, and tested before making it a part of the daily routine, regardless of how light it is. There are some accomplished hikers who have made the poncho serve them for both a shelter and rain gear over thousands of miles of hiking. There was some true suffering involved, but that was their preference and trade-off for the low weight.

Hikers have considerable differences in their shelter preferences. Before spending a lot of money on expensive gear, especially a shelter, it is wise to decide what you expect from it. One gauge of being a real "gear-head" is when the square footage of your accumulated tents, tarps and bivys equal or exceed the square footage of your house or apartment.

Another remarkable difference in gear choices can be seen by the colors chosen. I like all my colors to blend in with the environment, so that stealth camping and hiking is always an option. This ability to be hidden is a safety issue. The aesthetic issue is to allow other hikers a perception of solitude. Also, bright colors have been proven to attract bears. However, some people feel that earthy colors are dark and depressing, and prefer to use yellow, blue and red. It is definitely recommended to have some bright colors during hunting season. White is a dangerous color to wear during deer season, even in small amounts or as underclothing. A flash of white looks like the tail of a deer to inexperienced hunters. An orange or bright blue bandana is good to have during hunting season.

Partners
Weight can be saved if your adventure includes a partner. Before you try to recruit a partner, perhaps some issues should be addressed.

Not everyone enjoys a long-term hiking partnership. Many concessions must be made to keep both parties happy, including matters relating to budget, town stops, length of hiking day, mileage, and routing. Are you a person who needs solitude, or do you become rejuvenated with human interaction? Is your journey a time to get away from it all, or do you want it filled with company and socializing? Will daily decisions initiate power struggles? It is hard enough to get along with a close friend or lover for long periods on the trail. Be cautious of hooking up with a stranger or someone you know only through correspondence, and know exactly what their actual backpacking experience includes. Honestly talk over your expectations before a commitment is made. You will see the best and the worst in your partner, so be prepared for a variety of moods.

During a long distance hike, a partner might decide to go home, or break off to solo on his or her own. If so, would you continue? How would you adapt your equipment? Could you get by with what you have? Keeping the possibility of a split in mind as the equipment is assembled can alleviate problems later. Especially with shelters and sleep systems, knowing the degree of commitment to the partnership is important. Because there is always the chance of illness or injury, having an alternative plan is wise.

No matter how committed to the partnership, you may become separated for a day or two. When hiking with a partner, divide the shelter so that if you become separated that evening, each person will have something to use. One person could take the ground cloth, the other the tarp. Each should have guy lines to rig a shelter. With a double wall tent, one can take the fly, the other can take the tent. In case of rain, the floor of the tent can be used to shed rain (turn it upside down). Stakes are not a problem, since there are always rocks and roots, or limbs to tie off to.

When sharing a shelter, sometimes partners decide over the course of a long trip that they need more room. As the weeks pass, the small ultralight tarp needs replacing with one just a bit larger. That might be taken into account before you purchase any gear. The one and a half person tent might seem big enough at first, but later it could be too stuffy and confining.

Some couples share one large sleeping bag. Other ultralight couples use one regular bag, unzipping it quilt style. They sew some extra fabric on both sides of the bag (silnylon in one particular case) giving it more width, which helps to keep the other one from "stealing" the whole thing during the night. Another couple I met each had their own bags because in cold weather it actually was warmer to zip up alone, instead of snuggling under a quilt. Rainmaker and I tried sharing a double bag once, but we both slept restlessly and it just didn't work for us.

Some hikers will cook breakfast every morning without fail. For others, cleaning the pot just isn't worth the trouble, preferring to have an extra half hour's sleep, and a Pop-Tart as they pack up for the day. There are hikers who will stop and cook during the day. Then, in camp at day's end, some make coffee upon arriving, others holding off until they cook supper just before bed. If you and your partner have different styles, try to recognize it before the trip and develop a cooking system accordingly. If you are new hikers, and unsure of your preferences, being patient and understanding with each other should allow most differences to be resolved. It is better to talk things out right away than letting them fester.

Food is an amazingly troublesome area for partnerships. Rainmaker and I always cook separately, carrying our own stoves and pots. Since they are small and ultralight, the versatility for us is worth the effort. We both use soda can stoves, which will nest in any pot. It is the weight of the fuel that is the consideration. Less fuel is needed with one stove, so perhaps a larger stove, made from two 25.5-ounce beer cans would be your choice for group cooking.

If you cook together, perhaps it will just be the evening meal. It is wise to carry your own personal food and snacks. Beware of the person who constantly is running short, doesn't carry enough, and asks you for handouts. If they go hungry a couple days, the next time they will resupply decently. This sounds very hard-hearted, but unless they are children, this lesson is well deserved.

Some partners divide weight evenly, down to the last pound. With other couples, the guy may be expected to carry the bulk of the weight. When this happens, the partnership can be put under strain, especially if the woman doesn't pack lightly. As an ultralighter, you should be able to carry your own personal gear. Maps could be shared, but it is good for each person to have a set of data sheets. The shelter weight can be divided. With cook systems, it depends on how elaborate it is. Each person should have a flexible cup for dipping water in dry areas. Other things that couples can share are tubes of toothpaste, containers of dental floss, a comb, a water sack, repair and emergency kits. However, if each one carries his or her own hygiene and medical supplies, the partner's supplies could be thought of as back up. When resupplying, always check with each other before making purchases, to avoid running out.

I would carry my own toilet paper, sanitation kit, purification chemicals, insect repellent and Ibuprofen. If you become separated from your partner for a couple hours, these items need to be handy at a moment's notice.

Packs

A backpack is considered one of the Big Three, the other two being the sleeping bag and the shelter. These three items are all necessary, and the items where the most weight can be shaved.

There are three types of packs, the external frame, the internal frame, and a non-frame rucksack-style pack. Each one will be discussed in more detail later, but right now I just want to mention size and components.

The larger the pack, the more it will weigh. I guess that's pretty obvious, but taken a step farther, it means the more hardware you have on a larger pack, the heavier it gets. A backpack's purpose is simply to corral your gear into one container, and allow you to carry it down the trail. One guy purportedly skipped the pack, and carried his gear in a five-gallon bucket. Then, in camp, this bucket was his campstool.

Silnylon fabric weighs 1.1 to 1.3 ounces per square yard; 400-denier pack cloth weighs 8 ounces per square yard. Ten feet of nylon webbing, just one inch wide, weighs nearly 2 ounces. Each zipper, pocket, or buckle adds weight. A basic pack, with few peripherals, is not only less expensive, but lighter.

How does one determine the correct size? As an ultralighter, you shouldn't need anything over 3,250 cubic inches. If you are a small person, nearly every piece of your gear will be smaller and a pack of only 2,500 cubic inches may work. Volume is going to be critical in keeping weight down, so a smaller pack is beneficial. Carrying a smaller pack will prevent a person from bringing all the extra things that just get thrown in because there is space. The pack I made for my Appalachian Trail thru-hike in 2002 was 2,280 cubic inches. It lasted the entire trail, and was large enough to hold winter gear, and up to 6 days of food. To keep my pack weight and pack volume low, I never carry anything that is too big for me. Every superfluous inch of fabric is trimmed off.

I feel that a pack needs a hip belt. Additional food and water may increase the total, finished pack weight to over 35 pounds, a little too much to be suspended just from the shoulders. Also, hip belts help stabilize the load when you are scrambling over rocks. A hip belt can be bought or made, and added to just about any pack, even daypacks with a 2000 cubic inch capacity. Before you go through the trouble of adding a hip belt to a day back, check the structure. I wouldn't use any daypacks with heavy plastic moldings or lengthy metal zippers that could break and leave gear exposed.

For several hundred miles some of us have tested fanny packs as a substitute hip belt. They were kept fully stuffed, worn backwards, and used to support the weight of a pack heavily laden with food. It was tolerable, as long as the fanny pack was full. The belt did tend to bite into my skin when cinched tight enough to support the weight because the fanny pack belt had no padding.

Pack covers and/or plastic garbage bags used as interior pack liners are highly recommended for essential gear such as sleep systems and food items that must be kept dry. The pack cover should have a way to clip it securely to the pack itself, in case of strong winds. Gale force wind has a way of getting behind the cover, working it loose, and sending it sailing away. Garbage bags used on the outside of the pack are fine for awhile, although they can not be secured well, or fitted as snugly. They eventually tear, and must be replaced, sometimes in a town with poor supplies. If you chose to use a garbage bag for a while, buy the heaviest brand available. Most long distance hikers get a pack cover made of waterproof fabric. Silnylon pack covers weigh as little as 1.5 ounces.

External Frame Packs

Previously, external packs were considered to be standard equipment. The metal frame has a pack suspended from it, with a hip belt and shoulder straps attached by way of adjustable pins. It used to be all you could get, except for an army-type rucksack.

Today, youth groups use external packs for several reasons. The metal frames are very durable; some external frame packs are still in use after over 25 years, and 8,000 trail miles. Various and unusual loads can be attached by using stuff sacks and cinch straps. I have seen kettles strapped to them as well as huge loads of bedding and footwear. The adjustable torso length works well for growing kids because the securing pins can attach the belts and straps in any number of holes drilled in the vertical bars for that purpose.

Some adults prefer the external frame because it carries heavy loads so well, transferring weight to the hips. The frame holds the pack slightly away from the back giving better ventilation. An external frame can be leaned against a tree as a backrest. They are easy to pack even when empty because they retain their shape. If the pack fabric wears out, a new pack can be sewn. If the straps or belt become worn, they can be replaced simply by buying a new set, and attaching at the proper points with the easily removable pins and rings.

Several ways to lighten an external frame pack include cutting off extra loops, and straps. If the pack has sentimental value, I recommend removing it, and letting a skilled seamstress remake it in a lighter fabric, eliminating zippers wherever possible. I remade a pack for Rainmaker out of silnylon, maintaining the exact measurements. The pack weighs only 8 ounces, instead of 24 ounces previously with his original pack. The frame, original hip belt and shoulder straps were kept.

Another way to lighten the external frame pack is to use a "packless" system, described previously in Chapter Three. In preparation for the Pacific Crest Trail in 2001, I removed the pack from my external frame, made some special stuff sacks, and cinched them directly onto the frame. There are instructions for making this type stuff sack in the "Make Your Own Gear" section in Chapter 8.

Internal Frame Packs

I have never owned a bona fide internal frame pack, having gone straight from an external to a non-frame. After trying on some internal frame packs, comparing weights and features, I came to several conclusions.

The hips belts are very well padded. If the torso length is correct, the belt rides comfortably. They are pretty, come with load lift straps, compression straps, and special compartments. However, looking at the weights and the prices was enough to turn me away.

Many packs have a top cover that is removable and can be worn on day hikes. This component alone is about a pound, and overkill for any ultralighting system. If you have an internal pack that you love and it has such a lid system, removing the top portion is an excellent way to lighten the pack.

Backpacker magazine does a yearly gear guide. If you check internal pack stats, you will see that for a pack in the 4500-5000 cubic inch range, weights run nearly 4.5 pounds and more. This is a lot of weight just for the pack. Most internal packs have a much greater capacity, but as already discussed, this weight is wasted because we don't plan to fill this space.

If you decide to go shopping for an internal frame pack, do not let yourself be talked into a heavy, larger pack because the clerk has no experience in ultralight gear. Remember that most of them gain a commission on their sales, and it is their duty to sell you the largest pack possible so that you will buy even more gear to fill it.

Non-Frame Packs

The pack I used for my thru-hike of the Appalachian Trail in 2002 was so light, and so simple, it amazed people. They were surprised that it was durable enough for the entire journey (nearly 5 months) and carried all the weight that was necessary for my hike.

There are several non-frame packs available, and even patterns for sewing your own. Some come with hip belts, and have capacities near 5,000 cubic inches. Most weigh just under a pound. In the "Make Your Own" gear section in Chapter 8, there are directions for sewing my Silnylon pack, which weighed only 9 ounces.

The important thing about non-frame packs is how they are loaded. Mine was so shapeless when empty it resembled a large stuff sack with hip belt and shoulder straps. On really cold nights when I was wearing all my clothes, my pack was rolled up and used as a pillow. Of course, it would make a great vapor barrier foot bag as well, and could be used on the outside or inside of the sleeping bag.

For a sleeping pad, I used a closed cell foam pad trimmed to 19 inches wide by 5 feet long. At this printing, they cost less than $6 and can be trimmed easily. One pad lasted the entire trail for me, about 5 months of hiking. By rolling it up as a cylinder, and leaving room in the center, I could slide it into the pack and form a very stable shape. With the pack's draw cord pulled just enough to hold it up and over the pad, the pack would sit upright when loaded. A shorter pad could be used, but this length was optimal for me, providing insulation in cold weather and also providing a clean area on shelter floors. I always line my pack with a large black garbage bag before loading it

Some people prefer to use a z-rest. They can shape a non-frame pack by folding it over and using a width of two sections. Then, it is placed inside along the back of the pack. A z-rest will lose its loft after much compression, so take care how tightly it is packed. They cost nearly $30. You can make a closed cell pad fold the same way a z-rest does, by measuring it into equal sections and scoring the pad with a utility knife. Then, using postal tape, cover the scored line, to reinforce it.

If you prefer a thermarest, a <u>self-inflating pad</u>, you will <u>not have a rigid pad to use for your pack shape</u>. In that case, just use <u>stuff sacks stacked inside the pack horizontally</u>.

A non-frame pack can have water bottle bags threaded onto the front shoulder straps. Both bottles should have the same capacity, so that they will counter-balance the weight in the pack. Be sure the bags are taller than the bottles, so that they do not slide down and away from the bottles. Otherwise, the bottles may fall out. Mesh pockets sewn to the outside of this type pack work well for carrying a shelter, stakes, a trowel and anything large enough not to fall through. They are easy to add to packs already purchased.

I found that placing the food bag, minus that day's snacks and lunch, in the bottom of my pack kept the weight at my hips, carrying the load better and closer to my body. When the heavy food sack was placed on top, it tended to shift backwards. After the food sack was placed inside the pack, I placed my sleeping bag with sleeping clothes in another stuff sack. That went in next. The cook set in its own ditty bag, my hygiene bag, and Murphy kit were all placed on top of the sleeping bag. On nice days, my tent went inside the pack next. Lastly, that day's lunch and snacks went on the top, and the plastic bag liner twisted and folded over. The pack has a flap-type lid with pocket. The journal and data sheets went in a top flap pocket. If it was raining, or my tent was wet, it went in an outside mesh pocket. My rain clothes and pack cover were put into separate outside pockets of the pack. Each item was packed this way, so in case of sudden thunderstorm, nothing inside the pack had to be disturbed until it was safely under the tent or inside a shelter. My waterproof watch, razor knife, photon lights and GI-style can opener went inside my short's pocket for easy access.

Shelters

While it seems that tarps have replaced tents in the ultralight community, and that a certain status comes with using a tarp, this is not necessarily recommendable for everyone. A close scrutiny of various features and a realization of one's own hiking style should dictate what type of shelter to use, more than the pressure of trend. If you spend a lot of time in your shelter, for instance, in winter or bad weather, space and comfort will be more important than if you are hiking long days during the summer in pleasant weather or dry climates.

Ultralight shelters designed by long distance hikers have features that eliminate problems found in many tents. Any shelter that can be repaired on the trail using only a needle and thread has advantages over those that have complicated hardware, shock-corded poles, or zippers. Shelters that are designed to use hiking poles for the frame or that have exterior loops for suspending with a rope from a branch is also a big plus. Storm doors and vestibules are options not everyone feels are needed. Storm doors provide weather protection and privacy. Vestibules offer a place to put wet gear or extra water bottles. A poncho can serve as a storm door or vestibule with a basic tarp. Sewn-in overhanging panels provide minimal rain protection with or without a door system. No-see-um netting, sometimes called screen or mesh, protect against insects, rodents and larger animals. It can be sewn onto tarps and shelters, and is an advantage tents have. All options will increase the shelter's weight. You must decide if the benefits merit the weight.

Single wall shelters are lighter than double wall shelters. They do cause more concern over condensation. A wide door and center height of at least three feet reduces problems associated with condensation. With all shelters, pitching in tall grass, camping in damp areas, and closing it completely will increase condensation. When a shelter is closed completely, you can use a camp towel or bandana to wipe off condensation.

An important consideration is the ease of setting up, or pitching the shelter. Always practice pitching a new shelter on a nice day. This is a good time to look for hidden weight. If you need more stakes than anticipated, more guy lines, or to read the instructions, it will be much easier than on the trail in driving rain. Some shelters require more stakes, many guy lines, additional seam sealing, or a ground cloth. Check to be sure your shelter can be pitched so that there is no sagging. Rain will pool in such conditions, and eventually can wick through. Most fabrics will stretch even after being pitched tight. Readjusting the guy lines before bed is a good idea. If a storm comes through, your shelter will be taut and it will shed rain. A shelter with many seams has potential for more places to leak. Pitch the shelter aerodynamically, with the low side into the wind.

When taking down a shelter, remove the stakes by pulling up on the stake itself, never on the staking loops. Sometimes, one stake must be used to pull another out. This can be done by placing one stake vertically through the hook of the impacted stake and pulling upwards. Place the stakes in a bag separate from the shelter, to prevent the stakes from puncturing the shelter. Shake out debris, match all Velcro closures and close the zippers. Lift one corner of the fabric and begin stuffing into its stuff sack, ending with the window, or screen. That way, all the air can escape. If you have stuffed a wet or damp shelter, air-dry it as soon as possible. Even silnylon will grow mold and deteriorate if left in a dark, moist environment. Shelters should not be folded because the creases, especially if done the same way time after time, will wear the fabric on the folded line. Just stuff it into its sack when packing up. That's why it's called a "stuff sack".

Tarps

A tarp generally doesn't have an attached floor. Some hybrid systems, called tarp-tents, have sewn-in floors which may be made of mesh or waterproof fabric. Some benefits of a tarp are: variation in pitch, larger covered space per ounce of weight, more pet friendly (without the floor), cooking fuel cannot burn the floor, and cleaning and airing is easier with no floor to trap debris. Poles, guy lines and stakes may weigh more or less than a tent, depending on configuration.

An efficient way to pitch a simple, flat, rectangular tarp is to stake out the back corners of one long side. Place this back side into the wind. Pull the parallel front length of the tarp forward and inward, forming a trapezoidal floor shape. Stake the two front corners. Then, lift the slack created in the front with a pole, or suspend from a limb. This forms the door. Many flat tarps are pitched in simple pup-tent configurations. Another way to pitch a flat tarp is to stretch a rope between two trees and stake down the back side into the wind. Bring the front over the rope and have it hanging over the line, then guy-out the front two corners.

Structured tarps with overhanging panels, beaks, doors and floors are usually easier to set up, and they provide a sure pitch every time. However, if you prefer different configurations, a flat tarp will be the better choice, and less expensive. Directions for sewing silnylon flat tarps of various sizes can be seen in the "Making Your Own" section.

Weights of silnylon tarps: For a solo hiker: 5 x 8 ft. is seven ounces; 5 x 9 is nine ounces. For one to two persons, an 8 x 8 is 11 ounces; an 8 x 10 is fourteen ounces; a 10 x 10 is nineteen ounces. For two or three people, a 10 x 12 weighing twenty-one ounces should be very adequate.

Tents

A solo, single wall two-pound tent was a breakthrough just a few years ago. Now, two person tents are in that weight range. The first Tacoma shelter, with all its guy lines and stakes, weighed just 18 ounces and was used for 5 months on my 2002 Appalachian thru-hike. My tent was smaller than the new model, which is 20 ounces and will fit most adults. It is not free standing, but that never was a problem.

Handcrafted, ultralight tents are expensive but if you decide to spend hundreds of dollars on a heavier tent found at outfitters, you may not be satisfied. If you are planning a long distance hike, I suggest putting that money towards an ultralight tent or tarp system. Having a low pack weight will make your hike more enjoyable. You may need fewer zero days for recovery, have fewer injuries and therefore spend less time in trail towns. These benefits will more than repay the expenditure for a good ultralight shelter.

The advantages of tents include a sewn-in floor, screen and storm doors. Everything is predetermined, and once you know how to set it up, it goes quite easily, even in the dark. A freestanding tent is one that does not require tension from guy lines. It relies on shock-corded poles crossing one another, providing a frame, which enables the tent to stand alone anywhere. While this can be nice when pitching on a tent platform, they are much heavier due to the necessary length of the poles. Dome tents are the most common of freestanding tents.

Double walled tents are heavier, especially if the fly is made with heavy 70 (1.9 ounce) denier. If the fly is remade in silnylon, usually the tent weight will decrease by half the weight of the fly, which could be a pound or more.

Before purchasing a tent, make sure the center height is adequate. If it is for two people, try to get a tent with two separate doors so that each person has equal access. Having only one door can become a great inconvenience if one must climb over the other to exit. Having two doors also allows each person to control ventilation.

Hammocks

I have not used a hammock other than for day lounging, so I can only relate some observances.

There must be trees stout enough to hang the hammock from. In the desert this would be a problem. However, the tarp that forms the canopy could be used separately. The hammock could be used as a bivy sack, or sent ahead to be used later in forested areas. Some hikers have merely tied-off one end (the head), to a low branch or guyed-out hiking pole, allowing the hammock to rest lightly on the ground. This may also help in cold weather when good insulation is needed below your bag in the hammock. Reflective blankets can be used under your sleeping bag, on top the sleeping pad.

Before taking a hammock on a long hike, try sleeping in one for several nights in a row. Those I saw using one seemed to be balled up in the middle of it. If you have back problems, a hammock may aggravate it further. Some hammock users told me that animals came up and nosed around under the hammock at night, while others say they love not having to sleep on rocky ground.

Backpacking hammocks range in weight from 2.5 pounds down to 1.5 pounds. The tarps commonly used as canopies measured 6 x 10 ft. down to 9 x 6. Be sure you are comfortable with the canopy overhang, knowing you may need to change clothes and cook under it in driving rain.

One of the most widely used systems is the Hennessy Hammock. By typing this name into online search engines, you can check on specs and gear reviews.

Bivy

My limited observations of bivys come from my Pacific Crest Trail hike in 2001. A couple good friends had them. In the High Sierra when the bugs were bad, they had a lot less room to use for lounging after setting up camp. Their bivys weighed as much as my solo tent. They were simple to use, however. Upon reaching camp they pulled out their bivy sack, which resembled a large bag liner, and placed it on the ground. Their sleeping pad and sleeping bag were already inside it. In anticipation of heavy rains in Oregon, they planned to buy tarps to sleep under, in addition to their bivy sacks. I did not meet anyone with a bivy on the Appalachian Trail.

Ground cloths

Ground cloths are seldom necessary for tents. If used, be sure to cut it smaller than the footprint, so that rain can not run down the side of the tent, catch on the plastic, and pool under the floor. This will cause your gear inside to get wet when the weight from the interior presses the water into the fibers, and eventually through the floor.

With a tarp, some sort of waterproof protection is needed on the ground. Hammock users may wish to have something to place gear on, under their hammock. It could be a small plastic bag, no larger than 3 square feet. Common materials used for ground cloths are Tyvek, which weighs about 1.8 ounces per square yard, plastic sheeting available in rolls varying from 1-3 mil, large black plastic bags ranging .9 mil to .65 mil, and light shower liners with the magnets and reinforced hanging loops removed.

If you have a mesh drape or mesh skirting sewn onto your tarp, carry a large enough ground cloth so that it can overlap the mesh. This will keep mice and bugs from crawling in.

Stakes for Your Shelter

Taking the right kind of stake is important. In rocky or sandy ground, the corkscrew type (18 grams each) is great. For typical ground, gutter nails found at hardware stores, (12 grams each) can be brought. They are lighter, but more difficult to remove when pounded in completely. Use them at an angle away from your shelter, to keep the loop from coming off the head. Those big yellow plastic ones are 30 grams each, and 1 ½ inch longer than the corkscrew type. It is a great stake for car camping, but has no application for an ultralighter's pack.

To facilitate removing a stake from hard ground, insert one straight end into the hook of another and pull upward. For the gutter nails, removal is facilitated by placing the hook end of a skewer type stake over the nail head of a gutter nail stake, can opener style, and prying a bit sideways. Using this method, they usually can be extracted without too much difficulty. Never pull up on your shelter's staking loop or grommet. It could weaken the loop or rip the fabric.

Carry the exact amount needed to set up your shelter, preferably in a separate ditty bag, to prevent them from putting holes in your shelter. A lightweight stake weighs from 8-18 grams. However, having too many can add unnecessary weight. When packing up in the morning, count your stakes before leaving. Rocks and limbs can be used as tie-off points for some stakes should they become lost or misplaced. I usually carry the minimum required, and use natural items for the non-essential stake-out points. This way, if I camp late, I can set up without scouting around. Yet, with enough time, I can stake-out lift loops and back walls by finding suitable limbs or rocks for tie-off points. In high winds, or when camping in sandy loose soil, place rocks or logs on your stakes to keep them from working loose in the night.

Some people use their stakes as a pot support. This can work but some notes from my experiences follow:

Stakes become somewhat bent and crooked over time, making it difficult to get them level enough to be used as a cooking pot support. They can become sooty, and this soot can be transferred to the shelter. More stakes may be needed if you like to set up your shelter before cooking, or if you cook in the mornings before taking down your shelter. At the end of a long day, you may not feel like leveling stakes in order to cook. A pot support is much easier. Some ground is so rocky; it is very hard to get three stakes leveled and close enough to provide an adequate pot support.

Sleep System

The sleep system includes a pad to cushion and insulate the body against the cold ground, a sleeping bag or quilt, and any pillows or bag liners you may use.

There are three types of sleeping pads generally used. A closed cell pad sells for about $6 at Wal-Mart. They are easy to trim to size, and weigh approximately 1.6 ounces per square foot for 3/8-inch thickness. I used one for my entire AT thru-hike.

A Z-rest is folded in sections, hinged like an accordion. It has egg carton type padding, and costs about $35 for the full-length model (72 inches long). The full length weighs 16 ounces. Sections may be cut off to lighten it; a 51-inch length weighs 11.6 ounces. An advantage of this style is they always lay flat, are easy to carry and easy to trim. They will flatten over time and much use, losing some insulating effect.

Self-inflating mattresses are by far the most comfortable, but care must be taken not to puncture them. Patch kits can be carried, but the main thing is never let them touch the ground unprotected. Watch for nails in shelter floors. An ultralight 72-inch long model weighs 24 ounces, and cost $70. A 47-inch long model weighs 16 ounces and costs about $55. These cannot be trimmed. The prices and weights were quoted from a mail order catalogue in December 2002.

In order to save weight, the sleeping pad can be shorter in warm weather hiking. The shortest pad I carry is one that begins at my neck and ends just below my hips, at mid thigh, and measures 36 inches long. It is trimmed to 19 inches wide, and the corners are rounded. If I have enough gear to make a pillow, my head rests on that. If not, I scoot down so my pad is below my head, but still is long enough for my hips.

However, in cold weather, the pad should extend beneath your feet. If you use a hammock, a sleeping pad will insulate the back side of your body. This is a common concern for cold weather hammock users. In very cold weather, or if you have a back or hip injury, consider using a full-length pad on the ground, with a three-quarter length pad on top. This is not considered ultralight, but it might be weight efficient and cost effective overall. Much of our body heat is lost in transfer to the ground beneath us. By using a double pad for winter backpacking, your current sleeping bag may still be usable.

If you plan to sleep under a tarp or on a shelter floor, a full-length pad will protect your sleeping bag from moisture, dirt, rips and abrasion.

A **sleeping bag** is considered one of the most important gear items a backpacker will buy. It may very well be the most expensive. Unless you plan to make a quilt, expect to pay a couple hundred dollars to get a high quality, lightweight bag. Bags made of goose down are lighter, can be stuffed smaller to reduce volume, and cost a good deal more than other bags. A higher number fill, for instance 800 compared to 600, indicates a better down because smaller feathers were included in the process. This results in a denser insulation for increased warmth and better resiliency, which enables the sleeping bag to regain its loft when fluffed and aired. My 30 degree 800 fill goose down bag was as warm as my new 20 degree synthetic model. It weighed a pound less, and took up only half the space. These important facts should be considered before spending money on a sleeping bag.

You can look through catalogues to get an idea of what's available. First, find a sleeping bag with a temperature rating that meets the lows you expect. A 20-degree bag will satisfy almost everyone's needs for 3-season backpacking. One British friend summed up the rating system by saying those numbers are for survival only, not comfort. If you get out in weather below the rating, you are on your own. Try not to buy a bag too large, or too long, because it is harder for your body to heat larger areas, and the weight and bulk is wasted. I have used a bag designed to fit someone an inch shorter. It was as tight a bag as I could tolerate.

Some companies still do not make women's models, and yet they have great gear. If you have a good sleeping bag, but it's too big, there are two ways to shorten it. First, a bag can be shortened by pinching together the excess length near the top, just below the hood. You may need to cut back the zipper also. With that fabric pinched together, stitch near the insulation. Do not sew all the way through to the inside or you will lose the loft at that seam. The loft gives the insulation value. Trim off excess fabric, and finish the seam by rolling it under.

It is a little complicated, but allows one to modify an otherwise fine sleeping bag.

Another easy way to shorten a bag is to tuck-up the foot end into the interior. My Hydrogen Marmot (800 fill goose down), 30-degree bag, was designed for a 6-foot tall person. My feet could never get warm with those extra twelve inches. But, that same excess fill, tucked up inside the bag, and hand stitched across the bottom to hold it there, provided the proper length and extra insulation where it was most needed.

To shorten or modify your bag this way, first lay it flat, right side out. Get in, zip it up, and extend your toes. Have someone mark with a safety pin where your toes touched. That is the desirable length.

Now, with your sleeping bag flat, right side out, take your hand and push the extra inches at the bottom into the inside of the bag.

Smooth the bottom out, so that the sides of the concave "hole" created are flattened against each other. Do not cut anything, you are just repositioning the fill.

Pinch the bottom fabric together, still working on the outside of the sleeping bag. Scrunch up all the insulation above that fabric. You aren't sewing-through any insulation, just fabric. This way, you do not compromise the insulation.

Stitch the fabric together with a small needle, using locking stitches every few inches. This will keep it from coming out when you are sleeping, and turning over.

This will make more sense if you get your sleeping bag out, and do it step by step. It works really great.

When you turn your bag inside out to air it, you can't tell that it has been shortened, because those extra inches folded to the inside will appear to be part of the normal length. When turned right side out, the stitching prevents the bottom inches from returning to its normal position, and holds it up inside the bag.

There is a great debate concerning which material (down or synthetic) makes a better sleeping bag. Whichever bag you buy, it will last many years with proper care. Sleeping bags should only be stuffed, not rolled, into their stuff sacks. When stored at home they should be hung by a bottom loop from a hook, or stored in a large pillowcase-type sack. When you arrive in camp, unpack your sleeping bag as soon as possible. Air it, fluff it, and allow it to regain its loft. Airing both inside and outside is a good practice, and some hikers air their sleeping bags even while on lunch breaks.

Quilts are an ultralight option to replace a heavy sleeping bag. They are much easier to make and do not require any zippers or closures. The quilt is designed under the premise that the bottom side of a sleeping bag is compressed, and therefore loses its insulating benefits. If you sleep only on your back (and could lay perfectly flat), this is basically true. If you toss and turn, the air spaces change and any outside air admitted must be warmed. Before spending money on an ultralight quilt, test a small sleeping bag that has been unzipped and laid over you on a cold night. This test won't work if the bag is large. Some quilts are designed to have a pad velcroed to the sides of the quilt to maintain body heat. Compare weights and ratings of a quality down bag and pad to this quilt system before making a purchase. If you have or buy a quilt, a bottom layer of fabric can be sewn-in to keep your sleeping pad inside, and under you, all night.

Your sleeping bag is your most fundamental guard against hypothermia. When all else fails, you can set up camp, climb in your bag and get warm, but only if you have kept that bag dry. Rainmaker taught me that four layers of protection for your sleeping bag and lounging clothes will keep them dry in the worst of deluges. A silnylon stuff sack, lined with a plastic garbage bag, comprises the first two layers. The sleeping bag is stuffed into that. Then, the stuff sack is placed in your pack, which is the third layer. A pack cover provides the fourth. Some hikers even line their packs with a large garbage bag. Remember to have your shelter available for pitching without disturbing your sleeping bag. You should never expose your sleeping bag (even though it's in a stuff sack) to even a small amount of rain or drizzle. Keep it protected until you are under a good shelter.

It is a bad practice to sleep with a water bottle to prevent it from freezing. The bottle could burst, or leak from its seal. Even Nalgene bottles have broken seals and leaked. If it is so cold you fear your water may freeze, it is no time to be taking a chance getting your bag wet. Instead, fill your cooking pot with the morning's water, and thaw it on your stove.

A tent or bivy will add about 10 degrees of warmth over sleeping in the open air. If a tarp is lowered and pitched out of the wind, it will add extra warmth, depending on the enclosed area.

Bag liners made of silk or fleece will add warmth to the sleep system. You can sew a silnylon stuff sack into the foot-seam inside your sleeping bag, to serve as a vapor barrier for those really cold nights. Then, the stuff sack is used for packing up your sleeping bag. Vapor barrier bags, or dry rain gear can be worn inside your bag on cold nights. For more cold weather tips, you can check out Chapter 8, Winter Ultralighting.

Clothing

Hiking clothes are generally shorts, a light top, socks and shoes, and in sunny areas, a brimmed cap. In 2002 on the AT, several guys and a few women I met were hiking in skirts, sundresses, or kilts. If you chose to hike with a skirt or kilt, underwear or a "privacy button" (that closes one side to another) is necessary when lounging in mixed company. The skirts and kilts were said to be cool, comfortable and to prevent chafing. Some people prefer to hike in long pants to decrease sun exposure or to have additional bug protection.

Whatever you chose to hike in, look for something loose and comfortable in a nylon or polyester blend. Silk is very comfortable but breaks down after prolonged sun exposure. However, silk dries quickly and is about as light as you can get, about 2 ounces for a pair of shorts. Lycra shorts are lightweight and quick drying, weigh between 4-5 ounces, but have no pockets. Pockets are a definite plus. With the right shorts, a fanny pack can be eliminated from the gear list. I don't bother with the zip off style pants. They are heavy, expensive, and the zippers could get jammed, or break.

The next clothing layers are to provide warmth, promote wicking, and give wind and rain protection, without any duplication. Brian Robinson began his successful Triple Crown hike on Springer Mountain, Georgia, January 1, 2001. The ultralight system he used to keep warm worked very well. I have used the same system in temperatures down to 5 degrees while testing gear, with winds gusting to 30 mph. Basically, all your clothing should fit you so that they can be layered and worn at the same time. They should permit enough movement so you can be comfortable while walking in the coldest conditions that you expect to encounter. All this clothing should fit inside your sleeping bag to keep you warm enough in the coldest nighttime conditions you expect. By doing this, you can get by with a lighter sleeping bag. Your sleeping bag will be used in camp while you cook and lounge, so you do not need a warm jacket for camp use only. A down bag allows some moisture to evaporate without soaking the bag, so that when damp clothes are worn to bed, for instance, a fleece pullover, they will dry from your own body heat.

For fall, spring, and summer time mountain backpacking, I recommend 4 layers for the entire body. The outer layer is the rain/wind jacket with a hood and rain pants. Mine are made of silnylon and both weigh 6 ounces. They can be used as a vapor barrier inside a sleeping bag. If you plan to wear your rain gear while washing clothes in a trail town, be sure it isn't transparent. Only black or an opaque silver silnylon have been found to be acceptable when worn alone.

(2) A micro-fleece jacket, and fleece tights are my preferences for the insulating layers. Chose a jacket with a hood, and sleeves that are plenty long. Your jacket should not be too loose, though. Extra width and length will add up in volume and weight. The tights should be snug and fit next to the skin. Fleece is lightweight, dries quickly, and feels warm even when wet.

Fleece gloves or mittens are good in all but the hottest weather. Do not take down your shelter in the morning with the gloves on, however, since they may become wet with condensation that has accumulated overnight. This will make your hands cold until your gloves dry. Instead, take down your shelter with bare hands. Dry your hands, and then put on the dry gloves or mittens. In cold weather, I usually take one small set of each. When cooking, the gloves can be very useful as potholders. Mittens are great for sleeping, and can be worn over that small pair of gloves. Fleece or wool socks for sleeping are the insulating layer for the feet.

The mid weight top layer is a silk or a polyester blend, long sleeve shirt. I really like the feel of silk, and it weighs only 3-4 ounces. It dries quickly, wicks away body moisture, insulates and takes up very (3) little pack space. Previously, silk button-down shirts were very fashionable. You can find them inexpensively priced at thrift stores. Get two, one to carry and one to bounce ahead in your drop box, because they will break down with sun's rays over time.

The mid-weight bottom layer is heavy dance tights, or silk bottoms. Either weigh about 3 ounces. They have just the right amount of warmth for those cold hiking days, and can be worn under rain pants. wicking away moisture. I keep a fleece watch cap and back-up nylon socks for the midweight head and foot layer.

(4) My basic layer is nylon shorts with at least two pockets, sports top with built in bra, nylon socks with a cuff so they will stay up when hiking, and hat when hiking in the desert.

When the four layers were worn all at once, I was comfortable hiking in temperatures of 5 degrees, with wind chills of 10 below zero.

Hats vary with personality. For unshaded, desert, snow or mountain hiking, a broad brimmed hat is important. It will protect your eyes from glare, your head from sunburn, and hold in heat or provide shade. Be sure to have a safety cord attached so that in high winds you can secure it either under your chin, or to your pack.

Some hikers bring an extra set of shorts and top to be worn in town when their clothes are being washed. You can wear raingear, pushing up the pant legs and sleeves to keep cool.

You may want to consider bringing a light set of sleeping clothes to keep your sleeping bag clean. A pair of silk shorts weighs 2 ounces, and a sleeveless silk top is 3 ounces. A polyester sleeveless sleep shirt, measuring 32 inches long by 22 inches wide weighs only 3.5 ounces, 100 grams, and can be worn in town with shorts or rain pants. Many times hikers will sleep in their mid weight layer. At times, this layer can be wet or dirty. Sleeping naked can be a problem in full shelters, and if camping with others. Also, it will cause your sleeping bag to pick up unpleasant odors.

Footwear ~~2 pair~~

Running shoes and athletic footwear have taken the place of heavy hiking boots for many ultralight backpackers. The saying is that one pound on your feet is equivalent to 5 pounds on your back. I don't know if any tests exist to support that claim, but my body seems to agree.

A well-built trail shoe will last from 500 to over 1,000 trail miles. They dry quickly, do not require breaking in, and are much easier on knees and ligaments. Some do not have sufficient inserts, or arch supports, but otherwise are fine shoes. Inserts can be bought separately, if necessary but remember you may need a shoe about a half size larger to maintain enough toe room. Examine the tread for a good pattern, especially under the ball and heel. A close, deep tread is necessary. Tread that is spaced too far apart will allow rocks or roots to injure your foot.

When trying them on in the store, bring along the same weight and size socks you plan to use on the trail. Your foot is larger in the evening than morning. Adequate toe room with a good fitting heel is important. My rule is that if any part of the shoe hurts my foot in the store, it is unacceptable. Trail Runner shoes will relax somewhat with wear, but time will not change leather reinforcements that are rubbing in the wrong places.

My checklist when shoe shopping follows:
1-Check price. If it is less than $80, continue. That's very subjective, you may be willing to spend much more.

2-Before trying them on, lift one shoe. Does it seem heavy? If so, reject!

3-If not, then check the tread pattern. If it is low, and has a lot of spaces, especially beneath the ball of the foot, reject!

4-If the pattern is deep, and closely set, especially under the ball of the foot, check inside. If it has a junky padding, reject. Inserts can be added later. If you generally wear inserts, bring them with you to the store.

5-If the interior looks reasonable, check for flex by the laces, just at the instep area. If it refuses to bend, your foot may become injured while fighting this rigidity when climbing and descending trail. If it is too soft, the foot bed is not strong enough and will wear out quickly. If the flex is firm, requiring some muscle to bend, yet yielding, then continue.

6-Try the shoe on. You may need to try on a few different sizes, depending on style, time of day, and for women, the time of month. If any part hurts, reject. If it feels reasonable, some trail wear may work it out.

7-If it feels terrific, buy. I don't care how inexpensive, how "On-Sale" it is. If it doesn't feel good in the store, it won't feel good on the trail. The fitting is such a crucial thing, what works for one, may injure another. I take it on a shoe-by-shoe basis.

Don't limit yourself to just brand names. My favorite trail shoes remain a pair of relatively inexpensive Faded Glory high tops, which gave me over 1,400 miles on the Pacific Crest Trail in 2001.

Extra length in the shoelaces should be trimmed and heat-sealed, not so much for the weight as the tendency for longer laces to become untied when hiking.

Over the course of a long hike, examine the inserts and tread for wear. Sometimes it's easy to forget about the tread, while only noting the upper wear. Amazingly, I have worn the tread off shoes while the upper remained totally fine. Also, if the inserts are nearly worn out, they can cause blisters to form. Replace inserts if necessary. Some long distance hikers buy an extra pair of shoes or inserts and mail them in their bounce boxes. If they don't need them then, they simply bounce them ahead.

Socks

The socks you choose will depend on several issues. If you find some that you love, buy several pair. Be sure they stay up when hiking. Ship some to yourself in a drop box or bounce box on long hikes, because you can never be sure what you will find in towns along the way. When mending any portion, keep the stitches small and the fabric flat. Sometimes, I just leave small holes alone rather than risk the chance of blisters forming under seams. Some hikers swear by sock liners, a thin nylon sock worn under a heavier wool or synthetic blend. I double sock only in very cold weather, and then the inner liner may be the foot in my tights. If the foot of the tights wears out beyond repair, increase the size of the hole until your whole foot will fit through, and wear them as leggings. That is a Thoreauian approach to ultralight gear.

Weight is important. Weather is a factor, as well as the amount of space you have in your shoe. If you sleep cold, be sure to bring a pair exclusively for camp use. Keep them dry at all costs, along with your sleeping bag and sleepwear. Fleece socks are ideal for sleeping, and Smart Wool is pure luxury anytime.

Weight and bulk of socks vary according to size and fabric content. A pair of my Smart Wool socks weighed 120 grams; a pair of fleece was 58 grams; 100% nylon socks weighed 20 grams. As you can see, if one takes three pairs of socks, weights could vary from 360 grams down to 60 grams, a difference of 300 grams, or 10.5 ounces. The volume difference is noticeable as well. I use 100% nylon in all but the coldest temperatures.

Three is a good number because it gives you one pair to sleep in, one to wear, and one for back-up or washing. I have seen hikers bring as many as six pairs, one for every day of the week. Besides the bulk, I just wouldn't be able to keep up with that many items. It is recommended to air-dry socks every night, even if you don't get a chance to wash them. I have tried hiking without socks but the seams in the shoes caused abrasion, which would have turned to blisters later.

To keep feet happy and reduce blisters, regardless of which socks you bring, or how many you wear at once, remember to allow feet to air-dry as often as possible. If you take a break near a stream, soak your feet, and allow them to dry completely before putting your socks back on. When dry camping, we clean our feet at night with a cotton ball soaked in 70% rubbing alcohol. At night, once your feet are cleaned and dried, rub lotion or Vaseline on them to keep the skin supple and to prevent painful cracking, especially on the heels. In preparation for long hikes, and just for the sensory pleasure, I go barefoot around home and in the yard. This will strengthen the ankles, toughen the soles of the feet, and accustom them to mild abuse.

Cook Systems

I learned a lot of things about cooking while trailside, things I'd like to share before describing my ultralight cooking methods.

With ultralight stoves, the fuel's cost, availability and weight are the greatest concerns because the stove itself is just a quarter of an ounce. To save fuel and keep food hot, be prepared to insulate it if mealtime is delayed. Imagine you have cooked your supper, and something unexpected comes up, like a nature call, or furry visitor. Maybe you thought of something to write in your journal, or want to put on more clothes. To keep your food warm for five to ten minutes without having to reheat it, insulate your pot. If you still have some heat at the bottom, but no flame, do not remove the pot, but insulate it from the sides and especially on top by wrapping your windscreen and then your camp towel around the sides. On top, place some small article of clothing, like mittens, a bandana or hat. You can use your hiking boot as a cup holder to keep coffee hot longer. Some people bring a pot cozy made of closed cell foam sized just big enough for the pot to fit inside. A foam lid can be made to go with it.

Hot salsa is risky on trail, even those little individual packages of free salsa found in hiker boxes. At the time, they look great for spicing up rather bland corn tortillas. Beware. If it is too hot for your taste, you may not have enough water with you to alleviate the ensuing pain.

Most things cool off considerably at night. If you have cheese and soft breads, they will keep much better if allowed to cool at night, then wrapped in clothing and stored deep in your pack during the day. After using, return the food to its place in the pack. At night, place it closer to the outside of the food bag where it is less insulated and able to chill with the nighttime air. Chocolate candy bars are easier to eat when they are cool, and solid. Licking wrappers from melted candy bars is a mess.

Don't mix food that must be cooked with food that can be eaten raw. Ramen noodles are great eaten straight out of the package, uncooked. However, if you mix them in zip lock bags with cooking-required-for-digestion foods, they become less available. Angel hair spaghetti cooks fine in about 5 minutes. It's very hard to eat raw, though. Once, running short on lunches, but having plenty of mixed pastas, I started picking the edible ramen noodles out of my supper pasta blend. Quick cooking raw oatmeal can be eaten raw, as well as cheeses, jerky, and nuts, which make them great emergency foods. If these are mixed with macaroni, or dehydrated vegetables in a bag, they aren't so accessible.

Breads and cookies make great crumbs. Be prepared to eat cookies, pastries, and corn tortillas with a spoon. The first days after a resupply, when they are whole, you can spread them with peanut butter. Once they turn into crumbs, they can be sprinkled on cold breakfast cereals, or stirred together with peanut butter and eaten out of your pot. Pretzels will leave a lot of salt in the bottom of a bag. Be careful of adding that to your breakfast cereal and milk.

Powders, such as coffee, lemonade mix, sugar and dry milk escape the best of zip lock bags. For that reason, I double bag them into a "powders bag", a gallon sized zip lock bag containing small zip lock bags of various powders. Remember to label each bag. Sugar and salt look similar. A hiker once tasted some white powder to find out if it was laundry soap, or dry milk. It was laundry soap.

Life is too short, so buy the best zip lock bags you can find. A zip lock bag that won't hold a seal, or tears at the top when you use it, is not worth much. Buy the good ones, and they will last you for several hundred miles. Poor quality bags will cause you hours of discontent, and even cursing, when food escapes into stuff sacks or when cold fingers cannot negotiate a successful seal.

Making hot food by boiling water and pouring it directly into plastic bags is a mess. It is harder to eat out of, and you may not have a pot to wash, but you end up with a ton of wet, smelly plastic garbage. Some hikers try to burn this garbage, which is not environmentally safe or practical.

Always test your gear and food recipes before leaving on a long journey. Hiker boxes are filled with the same trail mixtures. Made at home in vast quantities, and packaged into various drop boxes, the long distance hiker soon tires of eating the same healthy concoction, week after week. The same meals of corn pasta, tomato leather and 8-bean-soup-mix get left behind, town after town.

Before adding all those healthy legumes to corn meal and rice mixes, try cooking them at home under trail conditions. Regular brown rice takes an eternity to cook. It doesn't rehydrate well, either. Some hikers plan to rehydrate beans and brown rice while they walk. That means carrying an extra pound of water in a wide mouth quart-size container, and letting the food soak somewhere in your pack. Hopefully, it will not spill or ferment. If you choose to rehydrate while hiking, use treated water. Otherwise, all that time spent rehydrating will also be time spent feeding harmful bacteria. Some hikers grow alfalfa, radish and bean sprouts daily, which requires a rotation system. All unusual recipes should be tried at home, under realistic trail conditions.

Cooking separately works for many hiking partners. It may seem unusual for committed partners to cook separately but Rainmaker and I have always done it this way because we have separate methods and evening routines. When resupplying, we each buy and carry the foods we like, estimating our weights and food cravings separately. Sometimes his experience causes him to choose things I would never have thought of, like whole-wheat tortillas. Thinking to outdo him, I bought corn tortillas. Mistake. The corn tortillas dried out quickly, broke into pieces and tasted very bland. But, at least I was the only one to suffer the consequences. There never was an argument over food choices, or who ate what, or when. I like coffee first thing in evening camp. Rainmaker would wait and have his with dessert. I never presoak food, but instead bring my water to a boil, then dump in my food. Rainmaker puts his food and water into his pot. He allows it to rehydrate there, then heats it. We each carry soda-can stoves with hexamine tablets or liquid fuel. This solo method of cooking allows one member of the team to continue hiking if the other needs or chooses to leave the trail.

Every hiker needs one good spoon. You can eat anything with a spoon. Anything that needs cutting can be broken apart, but every hiker should have one decent spoon. After a bad experience of stepping on and breaking my only plastic spoon, I began carrying a metal unbreakable spoon, which weighed 18 grams. After finding out that a Lexan teaspoon, the handle trimmed by one inch, weighed 8 grams I switched. They are very durable, but not unbreakable. I do not carry a pocketknife, using a round, 5-gram retractable razor knife instead.

The Cook Set

A successful ultralight cookset nests together, and then fits in a small ditty bag. My 8-ounce system nested within the pot itself, and was used on the Pacific Crest Trail in 2001, and the Appalachian Trail in 2002, although not exclusively. As told in the previous journals, I was always testing new ideas to lighten my load. Making gear from the lightest available materials is a hobby of mine. For the last 591 miles of the AT, I switched to a 3-ounce cook set which nested within a plastic bowl and lid, and required a new technique for ultralight cooking. I had considered going to cold food to save the weight of my pot/stove/cup system when I realized this new idea was so light it would actually save the weight of carrying heavier cold food.

David made the soda can stove for me. This was the only stove I used while hiking the entire AT, approximately 2,168 miles. It was fired 1 - 3 times per day every day when on the trail from March 12 to August 14, 2002. The stove and the rest of the set are still in usable condition. This stove, made from two aluminum cans, and weighing only 12 grams, is used with both cook sets.

The pot support for the 8-ounce system is made from half of a 13 ounce coffee can and weighs 28 grams. The pot support for the 3-ounce system was made from a standard 15-ounce can that originally contained black beans and weighs 10 grams. Both have 1/8- inch holes drilled along the bottom perimeter, 8 on the small, and 14 on the large. This allows sufficient air to feed the flame. There are two identical sections of metal cut out at the top of the pot support, to increase oxygen flow.

A windscreen is made of a length of aluminum foil, folded over 3 times for strength, to surround the pot support. Its purpose is to direct heat upwards to the pot, and save fuel. It can be folded up, and placed within the set when not in use. On long hikes, extra aluminum foil can be sent in your bounce or drop boxes to make new windscreens when the first one wears out.

The capacity of the aluminum pot for the 8-ounce system is 30 fluid ounces, has a lid and weighs 106 grams. The pot for the 3-ounce system is actually an empty Handy-Fuel Canned Heat container, which has a lid made of aluminum foil. This mini-pot is 3 1/4 inches in diameter, 2 1/4 inches tall, has a capacity of 10 fluid ounces and weighs 14 grams.

I cooked and ate directly out of the larger pot, using a plastic cup for my coffee. This cup was made from a one-liter soda bottle, which had been cut off about one inch taller than the desired height. Then, duct tape was wound around the lip of this container. Boiling water was poured into this cup, allowing it to shrink. Tests have shown that the plastic will shrink only once, and the tape was necessary to maintain the shape of the cup. Once cool, the water was dumped, and the cup was cut short enough to nest within the cooking pot with its lid in place. The cup's final weight was 12 grams.

The bowl and lid for the new 3-ounce cook set were made from a container that originally contained powdered drink mix. The containers can be found at grocery stores and cut down to the desired size. Together they weigh 46 grams. Although the capacity of the pot is only 10 ounces, by continually heating water I could enjoy a variety of items each night. When the first pot of water was hot, I poured it into the plastic lid, and made coffee or soup. This sturdy lid had a capacity of 8 ounces and made a great cup, which did not shrink at all even when boiling water was poured into it.

While the stove was still burning, I added more water to the little pot, set it back on the pot support and brought it to a boil. My meal of instant potatoes, rice, Ramen, or oatmeal would be prepared in the bowl. The dry food was placed in the plastic bowl and the boiling water poured directly over it. I stirred a few times with the spoon, then covered it with the aluminum pot lid, and allowed it to set for 2 minutes. The pot never needed washing, because nothing was ever cooked in it.

If you wish to use this ultralight cooking method, try hot instant cereals. If you eat a cold breakfast, two packages of hot cereal taste great at night. Bring a baggie of raisins, chopped dried fruits, instant milk, and nuts to enhance this meal. If you wish to cook instant cream of wheat, cornmeal, or grits, pour boiling hot water into your bowl, then sprinkle in the grain while stirring constantly. That way, it won't get lumpy. Cover it and let set about a minute. If you cook oatmeal, put it in the bowl first, then add the hot water. Stir just enough to mix, then stop stirring or it will taste pasty. Let sit a minute or two.

Instant soup with flavored crackers is an excellent appetizer for the boil and rehydrate method. Instant 4-Cheese mashed potatoes are fantastic, as well as the chives and sour cream flavor. You can add some bacon bits, or even broken up pieces of beef stick. Beef jerky, is too chewy for this dinner, whereas the beef stick is vacuum packed meat, resembling summer sausage.

Lipton dinners are somewhat expensive, not very filling, and take too long to cook. They do not work with this rehydating method. Regular pasta or regular rice will not work, either. It requires instant foods.

A variety of liquid fuels can be used for the soda can stove, including denatured alcohol, rubbing alcohol and fuel-line antifreeze. Estimate about one ounce of liquid fuel per meal. Soda can stoves will not burn any gasoline-based products. It will not burn Coleman fuel. Hexamine or Esbit, both solid fuel tablets, can be used by inverting the stove and placing the tablet on the bottom, which for this purpose, becomes the top. Alcohol soaked cotton balls, previously used for personal hygiene, and small twigs can also be burned next to the fuel tablet to supplement the fuel.

There are other models of the lightweight stoves, including a cat food can stove, photon stove, tea candle burner and esbit stove. None of them have the versatility of the soda can stove. Stoves that are sold commercially and burn Coleman fuel and gasoline remain a mystery to me. They flame up, weigh nearly a pound, have moving parts, become clogged, and require technical maintenance.

Since you may be cooking in camp while sitting in your sleeping bag to stay warm, be sure to practice with your stove. Maintain safe cooking habits, especially when lighting your stove so you don't burn yourself, your sleeping bag or your gear. Shelter protocol varies. Some people feel one should never cook in a shelter. The other extreme is a hiker who will cook right next to your gear. Because the value of your gear exceeds his expectations, move your gear to a safe place, and don't trust anyone to cook closely to your sleeping bag. I have seen stoves blow up, and have seen others set the shelter on fire. Apologies don't keep you warm at night.

Water Capacity/Treatment

Water capacity is important in desert situations, places where little data is available, areas where you are uncertain of upcoming water sources, and those times when camp is made early in the day. Although it is not always necessary to carry maximum capacity, the ability to pick up additional water can really be useful at times.

Some important considerations when planning water capacity are the weights and sturdiness of each container. Below are some types of bottles commonly carried with their corresponding weights:

Nalgene-1 quart bottle.... 5.2 ounces
Plastic soda bottle-24 ounces...1.2 ounces
Plastic soda bottle-1 quart.... 1.2 ounces
Plastic soda bottle-1.5 liters...1.5 ounces
Plastic soda bottle-2 liters.... 1.8 ounces
Platypus plastic bag-2 liters.... 1.25 ounces
Silnylon Water sack-5 quarts.... 1.5 ounces

As the list shows, if you need 4 quarts for total capacity, there is quite a range of weights possible. If you elect to take only Nalgene bottles, the total weight would be 20.8 ounces. If you take four 1-quart soda bottles, the weight would be 4.8 ounces. If you take two

1.5 liter bottles, with one quart bottle you have 4.2 ounces. If you choose two 1-quart bottles for hiking, with a water sack for evenings, you would have 3.9 ounces.

Each water bottle needs a pocket or bottle carrier, and the bottles are bulky even when empty. A silnylon bottle carrier, attached to the pack for carrying a water bottle, will last up to 6 months on the trail and weighs half an ounce each. Water sacks and Platypus water containers will roll up and occupy very little pack space. The type and number of containers you take will depend on water availability. On the PCT I carried two 1-liter soda bottles, and two 1.5-liter bottles because of the desert conditions. On the AT I carried only two 24-ounce bottles, and a Platypus just for camp use.

Plastic soda bottles are remarkably strong. Rainmaker still has his from the 3 year hike on the Pacific Crest Trail. Both 1.5 liter bottles survived the airlines, and over 7 months on the trail. I use soda bottles on my hikes, and carried a 2-liter Platypus for a while. The Nalgene bottles, while strong and attractive, just weigh too much. People trust them to the point that they fill them full of water, and sleep with them inside their sleeping bag to keep their water from freezing. It doesn't always work; one couple had the seal pop and their bags got wet. A better plan (learned the hard way) is to pour water in the pot at night, and then thaw it on the stove in the morning.

The Platypus can be rolled up small and stored until evenings at camp. I have seen a lot of them develop leaks in the desert, so as a preventative measure, never trust all your water to one or two large containers. Be careful never to place a full one on top of your clothes or sleeping bag while hiking. Bears will tear a hole in them if they are left hanging outside the shelters in the Great Smoky Mountains National Park.

The water sacks are very useful when you are stationary at a campsite, or lunch break. You wouldn't be able to haul water in them in the desert for many hiking miles. If they develop a small leak, repair them with 100% silicone, and allow to air dry at least 12 hours.

There may be times when you must pick up water from shallow or murky places. If you are carrying soda bottles, you may need to get out a small plastic cup to dip with. You can strain out the debris with your bandana by placing it over the mouth of the bottle, and pouring it through slowly. Having at least one wide-mouth soda bottle would be very handy at these times. After straining the water, add your chemicals. If you have a filter, you may be able to find a spot deep enough to pump. Sometimes, there is only enough to dip. Plan to have a small receptacle flexible enough to catch water from a trickling stream. An 18-ounce empty plastic peanut butter jar, an 8-ounce margarine container, or a cut off 16-ounce soda bottle bottom all work well. All these containers will hold boiling water, but will shrink the first time. They can double as soup mugs and coffee cups in camp. Preshrink them at home by pouring boiling water into them when they are in the kitchen sink to avoid any accidents.

Water treatment is such a controversial subject that I suggest each hiker research the issue and decide for him or herself which method he or she is most comfortable with. One important caution, however; never hike into the backcountry with only a water filter. They can fail, and often do. Handles break, seals fail, inline filters clog and become useless. Always carry some chemical to use as back-up water treatment. While boiling water is effective, sometimes a person doesn't have enough fuel to rely on this for their back-up method. Boiling times differ for higher elevations and water concerns. A Wilderness First Aid text stated that:

"The common diarrhea-causing microorganisms are sensitive to heat. The protozoa Giardia and Amoeba, which cause amebiasis, die after two to three minutes at 140*F (60*C). Viruses and diarrhea-producing bacteria die within minutes at 150*F (65*C). Diarrhea-causing microorganisms are killed immediately by boiling water (212*F). By the time water boils, it is safe to drink. A five to ten minute boil sterilizes water. Remember, boiling point decreases with increasing elevation but does not affect disinfection. The boiling point at 19,000 feet is 178*F (81*C), sufficient for disinfecting water."
NOLS Wilderness First Aid, pp. 288-9.

If you have Internet access, a search using "backcountry water treatment" will yield good links. The best one I have found so far is http://www.yosemite.org/naturenotes/Giardia.htm. It is written in lay terms, and just in case it becomes unavailable to future readers, I will list some of the highlights. Most of this deals with giardia, but there are also charts at that site concerning other bacteria.

Highly respected wilderness physicians wrote that although hundreds of gallons of water have been tested in the backcountry of America, only one or two giardia organisms might be found in any one spot. This is generally not enough for infection. The danger is likened to a shark attack at a beach.

Giardia is a protozoan when active, and attaches itself with an adhesive substance to the upper intestinal lining of the host animal. It feeds and reproduces by dividing about every 12 hours. A single parasite can theoretically create more than a million in 10 days and a billion in 15 days. Once the host starts shedding these parasites into the environment, other animals can become infected. A human may shed as many as 900 million per day. A really important note is that even though cysts can survive for as long as 2 to 3 months in cold water, they cannot survive freezing. This means that the high country in winter and early spring is not likely to have viable cysts.

The gut wrenching symptoms take an average of nine days to appear, sometimes not even showing up for four weeks. They can disappear suddenly and reappear later. They may lay dormant for months or not appear at all. Contaminated food or water, and direct fecal contact can cause infestation. Twenty percent of the world's population, and an estimated seven percent of Americans, are infected. Reportedly up to sixty percent of the children in some day-care centers are infected with giardia. Institutions for the mentally retarded, public swimming pools, promiscuous male homosexuals, international travelers, patients with cystic fibrosis, and family members of these individuals all have high infestation rates.

Several people became ill when a cook prepared a salad with her hands. She didn't test positive for giardia, but her child did. The lesson to be learned here is to wash hands thoroughly before preparing food, and to be careful whose food bag you eat from.

Another good link is I found in my search is http://gorp.com/gorp/activity/hiking/medical/water.htm It deals with water treatment, and is from GORP, The Great Outdoors Recreation Page. Studies have shown that filters do not decrease the reported illnesses of backcountry hikers. One study wrote that in their survey, 59% of filter users became ill within just a few days of beginning their hikes. One habit filter users may develop is judging water to be safe because they don't feel like pumping it through their partially clogged filters. If you carry a back up one-ounce bottle of chlorine, you can treat the water instead of taking a chance.

Many hikers use iodine. It is lightweight, inexpensive, and comes in tablets or drops. However, note the small print on the bottle. Some brands state that the water must be at least 50 degrees for the chemical to disinfect it properly. Also, the Iodine taste may affect your food. Adding half of a vitamin C tablet will clear the color of the water, and improve its taste. However, some people develop stomach distress if they use too much vitamin C because of the acidity. Just a little bit goes a long way, and it also inactivates the purifying compound. Therefore, allow sufficient time for the purification process before adding anything containing vitamin C, including powdered drink mixes.

Chlorine is used all over the world, in cities and in the backcountry, to treat unsafe water. It is also used in municipal water treatment plants. The Environmental Protection Agency has a great report about the safe treatment of overflow water using chlorine. You can find this report at this web page: http://www.epa.gov/safewater/dwhealth.html. You can get an in-depth report at that site by typing "chlorine" into the search format. Over time, chlorine does breakdown in warm water and sunlight. Chlorine is ineffectual in very cold water. However, chlorine is easy to obtain, requires only a few drops per liter, and will dissipate with time in treated water. The amount of debris in water will affect how many drops are needed for saturation and disinfection, a good reason for straining murky water before treating it. Rainmaker has used only chlorine to treat water for 10 years of hiking, and reports no ill effects. I have used chlorine exclusively for all my hikes, and I have never been sick from tainted water. Chlorine can be carried in small, leak-proof bottles, which allows the liquid to be used in droplets. I carry mine in a small pocket on my hip belt.

Boundary Water Magazine, found at http://boundarywatersmagazine.com/features/0801_water.htm, has a great article with other resources for further study, which deals with the combination of filters and chemical treatments. Also, further down their web page, a look at how the absence of sanitary practices leads to illness.

Proper hygiene can eliminate most of the gastrointestinal problems that hikers encounter. Always be sure that hiking partners practice proper hand cleaning if they share any eating equipment or food with you. If you take food from hiker boxes, precautions include not eating from any opened or partially used containers of food. When using a privy, or after any bathroom procedure including digging cat holes, it is recommended to use sterilizing hand gel or rubbing alcohol on your hands after you finish. Rinse out your multi purpose bandana in cold running water and dry in sunlight whenever possible. Clean your cooking utensils at night. Periodically bring water to a rolling boil in your pot. In town, clean cooking utensils with soap and hot water, especially any rims on pots and cups. Do not use a single Styrofoam cup over an extended period, which cannot be sterilized.

Hygiene

The purpose of good hygiene is to smell and look decent, prevent infections, and stay healthy. To accomplish this I bring just a few all purpose items.

My list follows:
Toothbrush (half size) with its cover, and the traveler's size **toothpaste.**

Waxed, mint flavor **dental floss**. It makes great thread for repairs, and may save you costly dental bills later on.

About thirty **100% cotton balls,** which will burn, though the synthetic fiber blends will not. I use them dipped in **Isopropyl alcohol** (common 70 % solution rubbing alcohol), every evening under arms, feet and private parts of the body. This eliminates most odors and reduces inflammation and chaffing. After using a privy, I clean my hands with just a dab of alcohol to prevent serious stomach illnesses. Fifty percent rubbing alcohol will work for hygienic purposes, but cannot be used as a stove fuel. If I intend to use it for stove fuel as well as hygiene, I bring about 8 ounces. If it's just for hygiene, I bring 4 ounces.

An **ultralight trowel** was designed for its savings in both weight and volume. With a smaller pack, every item is reworked, if possible. My trowel is the standard orange hiker's plastic trowel, with 1-inch cut from the handle, and 1 ½ inch cut off at the bottom of the blade. This saves ¾ ounce. Some say they use their boot heel, a rock or stick for digging a cat hole. It is difficult to dig a 6-inch deep hole, the depth recommended by Leave No Trace, in rocky or root embedded ground. You will be especially frustrated at this task if nature has given you a "red alert".

Toilet paper is estimated on a town-to-town basis. I never bring an entire roll. Make sure you have enough when you leave town, placing it in a zip lock bag for protection against weather and critters. Shelter and privy mice love this stuff for nesting material. If it gets wet in the rain, it's worthless and very heavy. You are duty bound to pack out unused toilet paper.

A **small comb**, which is useful when going into town, and avoiding impossibly tangled hair. A paradox is that while some women suddenly decide to shave their heads when starting a long hike, the guys decide to let theirs grow. In both decisions, I suppose it represents freedom. If you want long hair, braiding or ponytails will prevent it from becoming too damaged. A plastic comb makes a great back scratcher as well.

A **disposable razor**, because I shave under my arms. I wear sleeveless shirts and like the way it looks. A case could be made for ticks sticking to hairy legs, or for shaving before applying medication to wounds. But the honest truth is, I bring it for vanity. One disposable razor weighs 6 grams. I put extras in my bounce box.

Vaseline, lotion or sunscreen are good items for keeping skin soft and healthy. Do not bring perfumed and fruity smelling brands into bear country. Healthy, moisturized skin is less likely to crack in the desert, which is really important for the feet. Sunscreen should never be underestimated because a serious sunburn can be life threatening. Studies show prolonged exposure to ultraviolet rays can cause skin cancer. Buy the best you can find, and apply every few hours between 8 a.m and 5 p.m for desert, unshaded, snow-covered and high elevation hiking.

Bandanas and camp towels have so many uses, it's hard to imagine leaving home without one or the other. To keep from losing it, sew one corner back to form a large loop. Thread your pack strap or hip belt through. Bandanas can be used for dipping in streams to cool off during the day and for wiping condensation off your shelter. Of course, they can also be used when getting a sponge bath in the evenings. It can be used as a potholder, but only if dry. Otherwise, you may end up with a serious steam burn. Mittens are better potholders. I bring a bandana, but no camp towel. It's the only thing in my pack that is 100% cotton.

Medical/Emergency/Repair

First, my credentials and a disclaimer. I am not a doctor or a nurse. My medical training is limited to current certification in CPR Adult, Child and Infant, and First Aid, through the Red Cross. I raised six children with all their various health needs and adventures. I worked at a hospital for three winters, and am certified in Food Sanitation in the state of Illinois. In the last 3 years I have hiked over 5,000 miles.

So, with that in mind, please take all ideas, personal stories, references and gear lists as suggestions only. Consult your doctor or a medical professional for all your health concerns.

One of my favorite quotes is, "Most emergencies can be handled quite nicely with the proper application of a Master or Visa Card." Even though it may take a few days, or require a runner to hike out to a place that accepts plastic, this statement is true. The application of money to any given situation will usually generate action.

There is the opinion that a person is strong enough to carry in his or her pack only enough things to solve the simplest of emergencies. I tend to agree with that. But, I also think we usually have things in our packs or our surroundings that can be utilized for more serious medical needs. Some of these items may have originally been intended for pack repair, hiking poles, or clothing.

This is what I bring on long hikes:

Super-Glue, the kind that is free flowing, and can be reclosed. Although I wouldn't recommend it to others, Super Glue has been used instead of stitches to close wounds on animals and humans. It also secures a piece of electrical tape to silnylon packs and shelters, for emergency repairs.

Cotton balls and Isopropyl alcohol. The 100% cotton is preferable to any synthetic blend because it will burn, and can be used as fuel. The alcohol is for cleaning and sterilizing hands and wounds. I usually list this in my hygiene category, and carry just one 6 or 8 ounce capacity bottle, which is sufficient for these purposes. Some well-respected hikers bring hydrogen peroxide for this instead, because it is not damaging to tissue.

Tweezers, the standard kind with the angled edge weighs 6 grams. I found one in a Red Cross toothache medication kit that did not even register on the electronic gram scale. Tweezers are useful for removing ticks, splinters, and small tablets from vials (if you use Iodine tablets, for instance).

Sewing Needle with a medium size eye, to use with the dental floss for sewing gear, removing splinters, and popping blisters if you do that. There are other applications for advanced emergencies.

A **Nail Clipper**, weighing 16 grams, is much better than a knife for trimming nails that could become ingrown, have blackened and died, or become ragged and snagged. By maintaining short nails, you will cut down on dirt, possible infections, and pain associated with torn finger and toenails.

An **ultralight mirror**, especially for a soloist, can be used for examining your body for ticks and removing things from the eye. It could also be a signal mirror, if necessary.

Electrical tape wound tightly around water bottles can be used for repairing gear, and taping cotton over wounds when necessary. Some hikers use duct tape, but I find duct tape to be heavier, less dependable in wet or humid conditions, and leaves a sticky residue. I use electrical tape with a cotton ball for anything that would require a large band-aid. I don't bring band-aids.

A **9-foot length of 1/8-inch diameter cordage** can be used in a multitude of ways. It doesn't take up much space in the pack, and weighs only 6 grams. A 9-foot length of 1/4-inch diameter cordage weighs 10 grams, and takes up twice the space. Use nylon or polyester, and heat seal the ends to keep it from unraveling. Do not bring a three-ply braid; it will fray when you need it most, fulfilling Murphy's Law of Backpacking.

Ibuprofen should not be underestimated. It relieves pain, reduces swelling, and can help you hike out should the need arise. Always take these with a few bites of food, to avoid stomach problems. Some hikers bring Aleve, because it is a more concentrated pain reliever. Sometimes I vary the dosage, using as little as 200 mg to a maximum of 800 mg at once. With tablets of 200 mg, I can self-medicate as needed.

A **cutting implement**, such as a knife or scissors is important. A dull knife is more dangerous than a sharp one. I use a tiny retractable razor, designed for cutting envelopes, and found at office supply stores. It weighs 5 grams, but is sharp enough to cut fabric, paper, and dental floss. I do not bring a pocketknife, for various reasons. Some say a knife is a defense weapon. I feel that it would probably be used against me if the attacker ever saw it. The razor knife is small enough to be hidden in one's hand, yet do some real damage should the need arise. Some use a knife to cut their bread and cheese. Food items taste just as good broken into pieces. Knives are definitely not needed for snakebites. Snakebite kits are not recommended, because studies show that most methods of self-treatment cause more harm than good, leaving a dangerous wound without solving anything.

A **bandana or synthetic camp towel**, measuring 12 x 8 inches is already listed in the hygiene category. I bring only one, and it has multi-purpose use. It can be used to stop bleeding, clean larger areas, and provide a compress when cold stream water is available. A bandana can also be used for straining water at murky sources. Rinse it well as often as possible, and subject it to bright sunlight whenever you can.

Two photon lights, one red, the other white, and each one weighs 6 grams. I use them sparingly and both have lasted for over 10 months of trails, the PCT and AT, besides numerous short trips. So far, I've not changed the battery on either one. The minimalist way of utilizing light is to rise with daylight, hike, write journal entries, read maps and books, set up the shelter, cook and wash before dark. When it gets dark, you talk, sleep, or otherwise entertain each other. When there is a full moon, one seldom needs additional lighting. Applying these methods will prolong the life of batteries and photon lights, saving money and weight. When there is a lot of darkness, one gets plenty of rest.

Luxury Items

Cell phones, radios, and Pocket Mails are becoming quite common on the trails now. A case can be made for each one. Remember, they all take batteries, which can add up in weight and expense. When the batteries go dead, they are worthless weight.

Cell phones have many calling plans. If yours is geared towards local use, you will probably use it only for emergencies when out of your calling range. I decided after a week that its 6 ounces of weight didn't merit any perceived advantage. If you get the nationwide plan while hiking, you may find that the folks at home expect you stay in touch. That has its own set of obligations, which again may not merit the advantages.

There are ultralight radios, weighing a few ounces, but reception and headphones aren't always good. Some hikers use theirs only in camp for weather and news updates. I finally sent mine home after falling asleep with it on, battling commercials in the quest for music, and general disgust with reception. Remember, it is poor trail etiquette to play or use any electrical device that makes noise without checking with the other human inhabitants of your campsite.

A Pocket Mail, an electronic e-mail and document-keeping device, is handy for those who keep online journals, have e-mail correspondents, or have bad penmanship. They are very useful when you are in areas with only satellite phone access. By writing e-mails, then downloading on the satellite phone for one minute, you can contact everyone with one call, saving vast amounts of money.

Almost everyone brings a camera, though it is not strictly necessary, so I have placed it in this luxury category. A 5-ounce digital camera has the advantage of instant confirmation that the photos taken are acceptable. These photos can be kept on memory cards, downloaded to your computer's hard drive, and e-mailed later. These cameras will not work without batteries, however, and you will not have a hard copy unless you chose to print.

A disposable camera is a neat item, weighing about 4 ounces, and is self-contained. They can be mailed home when finished, and if lost or destroyed it is only a matter of $5 and your lost photos. They are susceptible to light and heat, so do not set them in the sun, or leave them in a hot car for any length of time. Camera buffs will bring their own special model, regardless of weight. Of course, there is always the risk of losing it. Mark all your gear with real name, trail name, address and phone number. One thru-hiker I know left his $400 camera in a car when he hitched into town.

The portable CD players, with various music disks and headphones, are carried by hikers who cannot or will not do without their music. Again, trail etiquette mandates that permission be requested and granted unless you are using headphones. Not everyone enjoys heavy metal or rhapsody in blue.

Each electronic device can be kept dry by placing it in a quality zip lock bag and then a silnylon ditty bag. Place your trail name, real name, and address on each item, in case you lose it.

Some people will pack knee braces, just in case of an injury. My set weighed 16 ounces. If you feel you need to bring them, try bringing only one, and alternate which knee receives the benefit.

Reading material and books can be very relaxing on easy hiking days. Some hikers bring magazines or newspapers to share, leaving them behind in shelters or hiker boxes when they finish. But, books and magazines are heavy. Paperback books can be cut apart, and the sections mailed ahead to post office drops. When a section is finished, it is left at a shelter, and hikers following behind read the same novel. Opinions vary whether this is good. The shelter maintainers may decide to carry reading material out as trash if the publication is offensive to a segment of the population.

I never could remember the Mace in my fanny pack when it was most needed, so I quit carrying it. Some people think it would come in handy against mean dogs, wild animals or human intruders. If one chooses to bring it, a test fire and safe carrying place would be wise.

Pets are a luxury and a headache on any long trail. They will have health issues just as you will, perhaps even requiring medical attention. They need a lot of food, and water. Sometimes they become weary and cannot carry their own supplies, which means you will have to do it. Dogs chase small animals, as well as bears, and they can get lost. Dogs have chased goats right off a cliff. Cats have been known to wander off completely, or needed to be carried on top of the pack.

Pets are illegal in National Parks, and you will be required to board your pet, skip that section, or try to hike through and risk fines and expulsion. Not everyone likes animals, however well behaved. Before bringing your pet, research the terrain, services available, and back-up plans in case they are injured. Pets make great companions, but they require energy, money and wisdom to keep them safe, happy and inoffensive to others.

Perhaps I shouldn't list rope as a luxury. It can be used to guy-out non-freestanding shelters on wooden platforms. It is useful for hanging items, like food bags, packs, and dirty or wet laundry. Not much is needed, but if you decide to carry some, a test weight of about 40 pounds would be adequate. I never carried more than a couple feet of cordage, as listed above, and then got rid of that on my AT thru-hike. I just never used it.

Chapter Eight

Applying the Techniques

In this final chapter, we will apply all ultralight tips discussed in Chapter 7 by beginning with 12 patterns for gear you can make your self.

Make Your Own Gear

An important benefit to making your own gear is that you can have it the exact dimensions you need, and use the lightest fabric available. Clothing and raingear that fits well is not too large, packs easily and keeps you warmer. Tarps can be pared down and shaped for your preferred configurations. You can choose how many cubic inches your pack will be, adding custom shoulder straps and a hip belt, if you want. A pack cover can be made to fit that pack specifically. Stoves, windscreens, pot supports and cups can be made to nest within your pot, which is much more efficient concerning both space and weight.

Special features can be added in the process. Ditty bags sewn on to rain jackets and ponchos serve as gear pockets when hiking, and as self-stuffing bags when the item is not being used. A stuff sack sewn to the inside of a sleeping bag serves as a vapor barrier on cold nights. Tarps can have ditty bags sewn in for gear pockets, which then serve as self-stuff sacks. No-see-um netting can be added to tarps, making them nearly bug proof. Loops and ultralight hooks can be sewn onto just about any gear item and are useful for hanging it when drying, clipping on various items, or securing it to your pack. The list of potential features is limited only by your imagination.

If you simplify designs and eliminate extra zippers, closures, seams and other breaches in the fabric, it will make the piece lighter, cleaner, and less likely to tear or leak. By using tucks and folds, and cutting the fabric correctly, the weight of seam sealing material can be reduced.

Among the many shelters I designed and used extensively are the Cherokee and the Tacoma Solo. Reading my comparison of these two ultralight solo tents should be helpful before you design your own. Both had seamless canopies, reinforced silnylon-staking loops, and were designed to use hiking poles as the frame.

The Cherokee weighed only 19 ounces, and needed a minimum of 4 stakes for pitching. It was shaped like a long tapering pup tent, was aerodynamic, and had reinforced stitching and side pulls. While testing it on the first 1,089 miles of the PCT, I noticed that the Cherokee held up very well in high winds. None of my staking loops ever tore lose, even when rocks were required to keep the stakes from pulling out. However, the back pole, a café curtain rod, bent from the wind. This tent required both hiking poles for the front, so a third pole had to be brought along to support the back. The Tacoma design solved this problem. Only one hiking pole is required to set up this spacious tent, which is pitched like a 5x9 tarp with a floor and beak. Some backpackers use only one hiking pole, some don't use any hiking poles. A tent that required 3 poles seemed excessive.

The Cherokee could be set up with only 4 stakes. However, being long and narrow to save weight, the sides tended to slope inward. So, I found myself using the side pull-out loops often. Then, with the high winds encountered in the desert, and in the Sierra, I would also stake each loop by the front poles. This brought the total stakes needed to 8. The Tacoma is exceptionally stable, being a steep angled design. My Tacoma held up to storm and wind with only 6 stakes. I didn't bring any stakes for the side lifts, and they were less important than those for the Cherokee. When I was hiking the AT, I usually found something to tie those lifts to.

The tapering foot end of the Cherokee was only 20 inches tall which resulted in the bottom half of the tent being used basically just for sleeping. The Tacoma design made the entire floor space accessible; with one entire side being used for the door, which in this trapezoidal configuration, measured 5 feet. When packing up in rain, or confined in the evenings due to high mosquito activity, that spacious feeling was very welcome.

The Cherokee had the mesh door opening to one side and attached on the other. A long Velcro strip held the screen bottom, side of the screen and vestibule door closed, and this represented a total of about 10 feet of Velcro. When taking down the shelter, all Velcro had to be matched carefully, to prevent damage to the mesh. With my Tacoma, the drop-down, draping mesh door had no Velcro, and simply tucked under the bathtubbed floor. The storm door was sewn in on one side, and clipped tightly to the other side, nestling under the beak. This simple design saved weight, prevented damage to the screen, and facilitated a quick take-down and stuffing in the mornings.

They both were gray, single walled, silnylon tents, and worked well as stealth shelters, being nearly undetectable when pitched off trail.

It is difficult to compare condensation, because the climates are so different. In the PCT desert and High Sierra where the Cherokee was tested, it was either dry, or the elevations were over 9,000 feet. When we were in high elevations, the condensation was due to the coolness of the night. On the AT thru-hike, where the Tacoma was tested, it is very damp and rainy. Condensation was wiped down with a bandana on several occasions. On nights that I could leave the door open, very little condensation occurred.

The weights of each tent are similar. The Cherokee weighed 19 ounces. It had an inferior seam sealant. The Tacoma, with its high quality seam sealant, weighed 17 ounces. It is reported as 16 ounces, but after we applied the sealant, it increased to17. With the two additional stakes and back pole needed for the Cherokee, the difference between the weights went up to 4 ounces.

Hopefully this dissertation will aid you in your shelter designs.

You will need to decide which fabric will work for you. One great resource for purchasing all types and weights of fabric and hardware is Quest Outfitters at 4919 Hubner Rd., Sarasota, Florida. Their toll free number is 800-359-6931. They are very helpful and send out a free catalogue upon request, with a lot of useful information. Another supplier is Outdoor Wilderness, at 16415 Midland Blvd., in Nampa, Idaho. Their toll free number is 800-693-7467. Ask for their free, informative catalogue as well. Comparison shop, and ask questions in order to avoid purchasing the wrong materials.

Once you get your fabric, do only minimal cutting to eliminate seams. Practice with a paper or plastic model to get the right angles. Think about doubling fabric over the top of a pocket in order to add a flap, instead of sewing on a flap. The whole piece of gear is stronger when uncut, and will require less reinforcement and seam sealing. This is especially important in shelters, canopy seams, packs and raingear. Eliminate something whose only purpose is decoration. If it's not functional, then it is wasted weight.

Estimating the Weight

To estimate the weight of any new project, determine the following factors: weight per square foot, or per square yard of any fabrics you intend to use, weight per linear inch of any web straps, Velcro or cordage, and the weights of any hardware or clips which will be needed.

For instance, I had a large piece of egg-carton type foam padding to use for car camping. It weighed 2 pounds, 14 ounces and measured 48 inches wide by 69 inches long. First, I found out how many square inches of foam I had by multiplying 48 by 69, which equaled 3,312 square inches. There are 144 square inches in a square foot (12 x12), so I divided 3312 by 144 and found that this piece of foam is 23 square feet exactly. Two pounds and 14 ounces are 46 ounces. 46 ounces divided by 23 square feet shows me that each square foot will weigh 2 ounces. A sleeping pad, which measures 20 inches wide by 40 inches long, would weigh 11.1 ounces. Twenty inches times forty inches equals 800 square inches. 800 divided by 144 (inches per square foot) is 5.5 square feet. Multiply square feet by its weight and you get the total, which, in this instance, is 11.1 ounces.

Perhaps the weight is given per square yard. This is different than linear yard. A square yard is 36 inches by 36 inches. Some fabrics are 64-66 inches wide. A linear yard of 64-inch fabric actually is 1.7 square yards. Silicone impregnated rip-stop nylon is 1.3 ounces per square yard, no-see-um netting is 1.1 ounces per square yard, and tyvek is 1.85 ounces per square yard. Pack cloth varies in weight, and the weight will usually be listed in the catalogue. 420 denier is quite heavy, weighing 8 ounces per square yard. An oxford 200 denier is only 4 ounces per square yard.

If you are making a project that requires a 120 inch piece of silnylon by its full width, generally 65 inches, we will need to find out how many square yards that is in order to get a weight, because that is the value we know. We are starting with inches and dividing down until we get to square yards. A quick estimate would be 120 inches equals 10 feet, 65 inches are 5.41 feet. Ten feet times 5.41 feet is 54.1 square feet. There are 9 square feet in a yard. So, divide 54.1 square feet by 9 square feet and you get 6.018 square yards of fabric. If the fabric weighs 1.3 ounces per square yard, you have a total of 7.82 ounces. If the fabric is pack cloth, and weighs 8 ounces you have 48.14 ounces. If it's no-see- um netting, the weight is 6.61 ounces.

A 30-inch lightweight nylon zipper will add about an ounce (28.5 grams), 6 feet of 1 inch wide web strapping will add about 34 grams. Light, plastic buckles weigh 3 grams each, cord locks are 1 gram each, 5/8-inch Velcro is about 10 grams per yard, which includes both hook and loop sides.

Seam sealing of 25 feet of shelter fabric will add between one and two ounces, if used directly on the seam, for a width of no more than ½ inch.

These weights only represent estimates. Fabric weights may vary by 10 % from those listed in the catalogues.

Equipment

A **good sewing machine** is the first thing you will want for making your own gear. You don't need decorative stitching, so an older machine is fine. It just needs straight stitching, with reverse. If you plan to sew any knit fabrics, using a zigzag stitch will help keep stitches from breaking when the fabric is stretched. Some of the older models have variable needle positions, which is useful when applying zippers. Get to know your machine before embarking on a large or difficult project. Improper threading is the biggest culprit in broken threads and poor tension. If stitches are uneven, or tension is wrong, the seams will be weak. A good cleaning and oiling, and installing sharp, new needles can solve problems, too. I have two older Singer models, made with metal parts, and I love them both.

Sharp shears should be used for the initial cutting of any fabrics. If your scissors are dull, they will not cut precisely, and may even tear the edges. Using your shears on paper will dull them, so keep them separate from other household tools.

Small craft scissors should be used for fine trimming, snipping around corners and cutting lose threads. You don't want to use the big scissors then, because one small clip can ruin gear. These need to be sharp, and pointed.

Thread should be the best you can find in either a 100% nylon or polyester. Do not use a cotton-coated brand. Serger thread, sometimes labeled "for overlock machines", is high quality, comes on a large cone, can be set alongside the machine on the work surface and threaded directly onto your sewing machine.

Sewing Needles of the proper size and make are crucial to good stitches. If you insert the needle backwards, or bend the needle, you will have no stitches.

A ballpoint needle is used for any knit fabrics, including fleece.

Standard points are used for any woven fabric, including rip-stop. If the fabric stretches, or gets runs, it needs a ballpoint needle. If it frays, or the treads come off in rows, it is woven and needs a standard needle. The size of the needle is also important. Use a smaller size (11 for Singer machines) for silnylon and no-see-um netting. A 14 or 16 can be used when sewing Velcro strips to this fabric. Pack cloth will also require a heavier, size 16-needle. Be sure you buy the brand that fits your machine. Periodically change needles to maintain a sharp point.

A Cord threader that can be made from a plastic margarine lid is useful for threading cords through the casings of hoods, ditty bags and stuff sacks. At one time, I used a safety pin, but that caused some scoring of the silnylon casing, which would rip later. To make a threader, cut a piece of durable plastic the size of a whole almond. In the center of this shape, cut a small hole. To use your threader, pull the first 6 inches of cord through the hole and fold the cord over, as you would thread a needle. This will keep the cord from coming out of the threader and getting lost inside the casing. When drawing elastic cord through pack covers, tie a double knot to prevent trouble. The perimeter of a pack cover can be nearly 15 feet long, and if you lose your elastic half way through, it's quite aggravating.

Safety pins are useful for holding silnylon together. Some people use straight pins when sewing, but they will slide out of this slippery fabric. Straight pins will work fine in fleece and taffeta. Place pins in the seam allowances to prevent small holes, which could cause leaking, if not seam sealed. Lay heavy objects like books on top of silnylon when cutting on a flat surface. This will help hold the fabric in place without marring it.

Chalk and black marking pens are used to mark the positions for staking loops, cutting lines, placement of Velcro tabs, zippers, and pockets. Chalk works well on silnylon. Marking pens can also be used, but may rub off before drying. They may also permanently discolor the main area. Try to mark in seam allowances, or where a loop will cover this mark. You may not be able to remove any marks later.

Measuring devices such as a metal carpenter's square, plastic tape measurer 120 inches long, and a heavy-duty yardstick are all great tools. A 25-foot retractable metal tape measure is wonderful, too. When cutting large projects you will want a long straight edge, such as an 8-foot long 2x2 or "quarter-round" for marking long, straight lines.

A **seam ripper** is actually a small tool with a plastic handle and sharp pointed end, tiny enough to "pick" out the smallest stitches. If you ask anyone working at a sewing department, they will show you. Maybe they call it a ripper because that's what you feel like doing. But, your patience will pay off when you pick out the seam and resew it neatly.

A **Candle** or other method is needed for heat-sealing the cut edges of silnylon and rip-stop. Some people use a hot knife or a soldering tool with flat blade. Allow the soldering tool to get good and hot, and keep the blade at a 45-degree angle, to prevent tearing. Place some protective board under the fabric to prevent marring of the cutting surface. Silnylon will catch on fire, so be very careful when heat sealing the raw edges of any fabric. While the tools are cooling, they are still capable of burning the fabric, so take precautions to keep your project well away from heat sources.

Other Useful Items or things you might really like to have are paper or plastic **real size patterns**. These can be transferred from scale drawings to 2-mil plastic sheeting before tracing the figures directly to your silnylon. A **simple calculator** for figuring angles and weights is very handy, enabling you to double check figures if you have a basic understanding of geometry. An **electronic gram/ounce scale** for keeping track of weights on your projects in progress is good to have. I always keep **a pencil and notebook** handy to record notes as I go, for future reference. A **large work area, with table and space** to spread out the fabric, some good music and a pot of hot coffee, is a sewer's heaven.

Getting Started

This book about ultralight backpacking and all the patterns have been copyrighted. They are the result of countless hours of sewing, designing, testing, and writing. A lot of energy, time and money have been spent on this project. Please respect my rights to this material, and do not copy it for another's use.

Hopefully there will be many projects you plan to try once you have the tools listed above to sew your own gear. I encourage you to start with something simple, especially if your experience with a sewing machine is limited. A ditty bag, or fleece watch cap would be a great beginning project. They require few seams, and not a lot of fabric. You can make either out of a remnant of fabric not suggested, just to get the feel for the instructions.

There are several ways of doing anything. The directions here are my ways, in general, with compromise and consideration given for the benefit of a new sewer. Over the years, a person develops shortcuts, but I avoid describing the more difficult ones, and instead give the ones that are easiest to follow. Unfortunately, no video has yet been made for demonstration purposes. Hands-on is always the best teacher, but the written word has served to relay the world's cumulative knowledge for centuries.

Keeping a Positive Outlook

If you passed kindergarten, you learned to follow directions. Sometimes, a whole page of directions seems to make no sense. At that point, simply stop, get a cup of coffee, and read the first line.

Even though I encourage you to read everything before proceeding, to sort of see where you are heading, still it's always one step at a time. Then, having read the first line, do it. Repeat all through the pattern. Soon, you will find yourself reading several steps, and seeing the trend, and proceeding with confidence.

My method is to do everything possible to each single piece before adding it to the main project. That way, you are working with small parts, and combining them last. If a mistake is made on one detail before adding it to the main project, it will be much easier to fix, and you won't have to rip it all off if it needs redoing. I think you will be successful with this method.

If you learned to ride a bike, you can learn to operate a sewing machine. I met one man who sewed extremely well, but he did everything by hand. His internal frame pack was an excellent product, but it took him weeks to complete. Learning to operate a sewing machine is a worthwhile endeavor, and each encounter will make the next one easier.

I doubt there is a sewer alive who hasn't ripped out a seam, or discarded a mistake. If you see a large project you would like to try, but are uncertain, get some inexpensive material to practice with. Fabric can be manipulated easily with a scissors, needle and thread. It can be marked, pinned and tested. You can add fabric back to your project by using another seam, or you can take in another seam and trim it down. Field repairs are always possible, because you made it.

Common Sewing Terms

Seam Allowance
The seam allowance is the fabric at the edge of the pieces where they are joined together by stitching. In some patterns, the seam allowance is 1 inch, in others it is only ¾ or ½ inch. Stay within the seam allowance to mark or baste so these aids won't show on the finished product.

Heat sealing the fabric edges.
Unfinished cut edges of rip-stop nylon, siliconized nylon, web strapping or pack cloth will fray if subjected to pulling and friction. These fabrics are flammable, so be careful if you choose to heal seal the edges. Light a candle, and run the length of the cut edge about 1/4 to 1/2 inch away from the flame, but do not let it touch the flame. It will shrink back just a bit, and form a tight, crisp edge. Practice on a scrap first, being careful not to scorch or burn your fabric. It will be

easier to do it piece by piece, rather than at the end, when the project is larger and more complex. By heat-sealing the fabric, you prevent raveling later on, and avoid problems of failing seams.

Seam Sealing

One hundred percent silicone works best on all waterproof fabrics. You can buy this in caulk tubes in the hardware department, which are designed to be used with a caulk-gun. Smaller, squeezable tubes are available, but they are more expensive.

Place a small amount of silicone in a plastic jar lid. With one finger, or a soft application tool, spread the silicone smoothly into flattened seam. Be careful not to let the fabric get bunched up, or it will dry this way permanently. Within half an hour of application, recheck the seam to be sure it is properly set and not attaching to itself.

Allow all seam sealing to dry completely before packing it away, for a minimum of 24 hours. If it is the least damp, it could become sealed together permanently.

Seam Finishing

A good method of finishing seams on silnylon projects is to heat seal them, then double roll edges together and topstitch. This prevents raveling and strengthens the seam. If you are using a fabric blend that doesn't respond to heat-sealing, you can either double roll the edge and stitch, or use a zigzag stitch to finish the edge, or use a pinking shears to finish the edge. If it is fleece or a knit, the seam does not require any finish. A second row of stitching, 1/8 inch from the first seam, is always a wise move on high-use items.

Double Rolling

This term I use to refer to an edge that is folded over once, then once again, so that the raw edge is tucked inside, and underneath the seam. Usually this is used to form a drawcord casing. When double rolling to form a casing, stitch close to the edge folded under. This procedure will use up about one to one and a half inches of fabric.

Basting

This means sewing a preliminary seam with large stitches, a very useful procedure that allows you to see if the project is sized correctly. If something is incorrect, large stitches are easier to remove with a seam ripper.

Basting can also be used to hold many pieces together. If you have several layers like a beak, door and screen that must all be sewn on to a canopy, first baste the beak, door and screen together, all facing upwards. Then, add it as one piece to the canopy. When basting, stay within ½ inch of the edge, which is within the normal ¾-1 inch **seam**

allowance. This way, your basting stitches will not show when the project is complete. When the project is turned right side out, all seam allowances will be on the inside. When the basting is done, and checked for mistakes, you can sew the pieces on together with smaller stitches.

The Right Side, sometimes referred to as the outside, is the side that will be visible when done. The **Wrong Side**, or the inside of the project, is the side which will not be seen. Mark on the wrong side. When right sides are placed together, touching each other, the seams will be sewn on the wrong side. Then the project is turned right side out, and no seam allowances will be seen.

Backstitching

Reverse stitching to secure the ends of seams is like tying a knot. Backstitch periodically on large projects and seams that are under stress for reinforcement. If a portion of the thread gets broken, the whole seam will not come undone, and the stitches will stop coming lose where it has been backstitched.

The Fabric Content

This refers to the type of thread used in fabric. For backpacking gear, man-made threads like rayon, polyester, nylon, and spandex are preferred, being less likely to rot or shrink. Fabrics with little or no cotton content will dry quicker and hold less water. Sometimes percentages are listed, as in a 50% cotton/polyester blend.

Some General Sewing Tips

Always cut out the large pieces first. Allow an extra inch for seam allowances on all silnylon projects. Fleece and no-see-um netting will need only one-half inch seam allowances. From your scraps, you will be able to cut out the smaller pieces, stuff sacks, stake bags and fabric loops.

Always be sure you are working on the correct side. Usually, right sides should be touching when sewing seams, so that the seam allowances are on the wrong, or inside of a project. Before cutting or trimming anything, remember the old adage "you can always trim away more, but it's hard to add it back on."

Siliconzied rip-stop nylon can be quite slippery to handle, but following a few simple suggestions should make it a little easier. When handling bigger sections, place all the material in your lap. Match seams and feed through the sewing machine. Do not let the sewn sections fall onto the floor in the process. The weight will cause the fabric to slide away from you. In order to keep it in your control, have a table or desk to rest the finishing sections while you are in the process of sewing these long lengths. A mesh-silnylon interface is extremely slippery. Remember to concentrate on matching the edges, and feeding the narrowest section through the machine. The bulk of any project should be on your left, and not under the sewing machine itself.

When using safety pins, try to stay in the seam allowance. This will eliminate any holes in the actual project. Always read through every section before beginning that step in the gear-making process. Try to visualize, even set up the components. If applicable, check to make sure you have the left side and the right side of the item. Especially with tents, make sure the inside and outside are correct. It is much easier to double-check than rip out stitches, and it saves on the amount of seam/hole sealing you will need to do later.

No-see-um netting has a stretching factor both in width and length. If it is cut across the grain, at an angle, otherwise referred to as the **bias,** stretching or warping of shape will occur. Be careful when adding this fabric to a tarp or shelter. If it is stretched tight, it will cause binding of non-stretching seams. For this reason, always set up your shelter before adding final touches.

And the last tip; a very important lesson learned the hard way, if you are tired, stop. Give yourself a break.

Ditty Bags

A ditty bag makes a great first project. Make these ditty bags using scraps of silnylon, rip-stop nylon, or even no-see-em netting. All the sewing directions are the same.

Supplies:
Silnylon, rip-stop nylon, no-see-um netting
1/8-1/4-diameter cordage (100% nylon, acrylic, or polyester)
Cord lock

Determine the size bag you will need and add 1 1/2 inches to these measurements for the top, bottom and sides for seam allowances. Lay out the fabric. Cut out the rectangular shape, at least 5 inches wide by 10 inches long. Heat-seal edges, if necessary, by lighting a candle and passing the edge of the fabric within 1/2 inch of the flame. Hold the fabric firmly, and take care not to scorch.

Hem the top edge, at the same time creating the cord-casing by folding 1 inch of fabric over, then turning 1/4 inch under and stitching close to the edge of the fold. This will be referred to as double rolling the fabric.

Fold in half, with right sides together and the casing at the top. Stitch the side and bottom beginning just below the casing, turning the corner and going along the bottom, also. Always backstitch at beginning and end of seams. I also backstitch when I turn the bottom edge corner to add strength to the seams. Do a second row of stitching, if desired, 1/8 inch from the first row.

Turn right side out. Using the cord threader described above, draw the cord through the casing. Put on the cord lock. Tie a double knot at end of cord, heat seal.

Fabric Strips

Make these strong and useful strips out of the scraps of silnylon, rip-stop nylon, or pack cloth fabric you are working with. They can be used for loops in almost any piece of gear. Cut fabric strips 3.5 inch wide. Fold each edge towards the center, lengthwise, and then fold that in half, so that the strip is 4 thicknesses. Stitch close to both long edges. Cut into lengths as needed.

Stuff Sacks

You will need:
rip-stop nylon, pack cloth or silnylon
6 inches of web strapping or fabric strip, for pull loop
1/8-1/4 inch diameter cordage
cord lock

Decide how large you want your stuff bag, then add 3 inches to the length and 2 inches to the width for seam allowances and draw cord casing. For instance, if you want a 9 x 12 stuff sack, cut a rectangle that is 20 inches wide by 15 inches long. If you would like a collar on this sack, cut a semi circle with a 6-inch radius. If you will be using these stuff sacks for the packless system, described in Chapter 3, make each stuff sack 5 inches longer than the width of your pack.

Lay out fabric, cut and heat-seal the rectangle and collar by passing
edge of fabric 1/2 inch from a candle flame. Take care not to burn or
scorch. Heat-seal your hold-loop while you're at it.

Form draw cord casing by hemming the top of the rectangle, folding
over the top edge, or double rolling it, and stitching close to the
folded edge. If you would like a collar, tuck it under this casing as
you sew.

Fold in half the long way, with right sides of rectangle facing each
other and casing and collar facing outwards, at the top. Pin the hold
loop at the bottom of the sack, so that the loop is going up into the
right side of the sack, and the ends of it are sticking out into the seam
allowance. You should not be able to see this loop, if it is in the right
place. If this stuff sack is to be used for the packless system, while
sewing the side seam, add two fabric loops in the same manner as the
bottom loop, so that this bag can be cinched on to the frame
horizontally.

Start stitching just below the casing, using a ¾ inch seam. Sew side
and bottom, backstitching at the beginning, and end of your seams.
To reinforce seam, either do a second seam 1/8 inch away from the
first, or better still, roll the seam allowance and stitch it down.

With your stuff sack still inside out, form the squared off bottom by
matching the bottom seam with side seam, and stitching across the
imaginary line to form a triangle. You are actually spreading the
bottom of the bag out, and sewing little triangles into each end of the
bottom seam. Do both sides the same way.

Turn right side out. Using the cord threader described above, draw
the cord through the casing. Put on the cord lock. Tie a double knot at
end of cord, heat seal.

Sleep Net

When the bug situation gets really challenging, use a sleep net
during the day on your upper body when you stop for breaks. It can
also be worn sitting in camp while you are cooking, eating, and
writing in your journal. When you wear it while sitting, this size sleep
net will provide almost total body protection from flying insects.

When used in shelters and high traffic camping areas, a sleep net can
keep mice out of your sleeping bag and hair. The hanging loop on the
front can be used to suspend the net above you, keeping it away from
your face.

Applying the Techniques

Supplies:
2 1/2 yards no-see-um-netting
Cord lock, 3 yards cordage
Fabric strip 6 inches long

Cut a piece of no see-um-netting 82 inches long by 47 inches wide. Fold netting in half, so that the side seams will be 41 inches long, and the width will be 47 inches. Sew both side seams. There is no seam across the top. The top is on the fold.

Form squared off corners by matching the top fold line with a side seam, and stitching across the imaginary line to form a triangle. You are actually spreading out the top of the sleep net, and sewing triangles into each end of the top. Do both sides the same way.

Stitch the corners down towards the side seam to form a box-type construction. Then, turn right side out.

Measure 25 inches up from bottom to place a hanging loop on the front of the sleepnet. Sew a loop onto the front side of your sleep net, reinforcing with an x stitch.

Hem the bottom of the sleep net by folding over and sewing a casing, double rolling the fabric just as you would for a stuff sack or ditty bag. Leave a few stitches open to thread cord through. Thread cordage. Add cord lock. This net will weigh about 2-3 ounces.

Pack cover

For a pack with about 4,000 cubic inch capacity, you will need:

50 x 60 inch piece of rip stop nylon, or silnylon
7 feet round elastic cord
Cord lock
Clip
8 inches ¼ inch flat elastic
6-inch fabric strip

This method produces a seamless pack cover. Take the silnylon rectangle; carefully fold into fourths. Trim the corners so they are rounded. Unfold and heat seal all the cut edges of fabric, taking special care not to scorch or burn your fabric. Mark half way down both long sides for the safety elastic clip and fabric loop placements.

Make a casing for the elastic draw cord by double rolling the perimeter edge toward the inside, and stitching close to the edge. This is the same method used for a ditty bag or a stuff sack draw-cord casing, but going around the corners will be more difficult and result in some small tucks.

To facilitate threading cord later, when you sew the casing near the rounded corners, keep a generous, evenly tucked method. Fold the flat elastic in half, inserting the clip, and sew into the casing as you stitch. Backstitch for reinforcement. Add the fabric loop on the opposite side of the pack cover while sewing down the casing. These two loops can be clipped together when high winds threaten to blow the pack cover away. Leave a small opening at top of pack cover where the cord will be inserted.

Insert draw cord using the plastic threader described at the beginning of this section. If you use a safety pin, it may score the fabric, making it prone to tearing. Securely attach the elastic cord to the threader by tying a knot. Draw the cord through the entire casing. This takes patience. You don't want to lose cord while threading it or you will have to start over on this part.

Once the cord is threaded through, add your cord lock to the ends of the cord, and heat seal the ends. Make a good-sized knot to prevent the cord lock from falling off, or even use a small bead at the end before tying the cord.

Single Bag or Liner

Directions are based on fabric that is 60-65 inches wide. You can make sleeping bag liners, outer shells, simple bivy sacks, summer bags or vapor barrier bags, depending on fabric choice.

Supplies:

2-2 1/4 yards of fleece, silk, taffeta, tyvek or silnylon for a vapor barrier bag.
 Zipper or Velcro, at least 42 inches long, if wanted
1/4-inch diameter cordage, 6-foot length
Cord lock

Fold fabric lengthwise so that it measures 30 inches wide. Cut to the desired overall length, which includes the top of the hood, and 3 inches extra for hood casing and bottom seam allowance. A regular bag is about 86 inches long.

Cut out the face area from the topside of the bag, a 25-inch wide by 14-inch long rectangle. Trim all corners so they are round. Round the corners at the bottom of the bag.

With right sides together, stitch the bottom and up the side to the beginning of your closure, using a 3/4-inch seam allowance. If you do not want a side opening, stitch all the way up to the top, where the face opening has been cut out. Always backstitch at beginning and ending of seams to lock stitches. Sew another row of stitching if desired. Turn bag right side out.

Form draw cord casing for the hood by folding fabric to the inside all along the top of the bag. Stitch close to the edge, about ¾-inch from the fold. If you are using fleece, do not attempt to roll under the cut edge, simply sew it down flat. All thin fabrics should be rolled and folded under, a double roll, just as you would for the stuff sacks and ditty bags.

Leave an opening in your casing on the opposite side of the bag, away from the closure. Thread the cord through the casing and add the cord lock. If you do not have a side closure, you have hemmed the entire top and are finished. If you want a side seam/closure, tack the cords down at the closure seam, and bring a loop of cordage through the opening at the side of the bag. Add the cord lock there and tie a knot so the cord lock cannot come off. By placing the draw cord this way, you prevent any interference from it when you get in and out of your bag.

If you chose a Velcro closure:
Cut Velcro 42 inches long.
Fold over 3/4-inch fabric to outside of topside of bag. Lay loop side of Velcro over this. Stitch close to all sides of Velcro.
Fold to inside, 3/4 inch of fabric on bottom side of bag, and apply the hook side of Velcro. Matching the first inch of Velcro at bottom of closure, reinforce by sewing an X over the end.

If you chose a zipper:
Beginning just at the bottom of the draw cord casing, fold over 3/4 inch of fabric to inside of bag. Lay zipper teeth facing up; stitch down one side, and up the other, as you would for any zipper application. Have the fabric overlap the zipper teeth. Reinforce zipper by backstitching over beginning, bottom, and ends of zipper.

Double Summer Sleeping Bag / Bag Liner

Directions are based on fabric that is 60-65 inches wide. You can make sleeping bag liners, outer shells, summer bags or vapor barrier bags depending on fabric choice. This bag will fit a 6-foot tall person.

Supplies:

13.5 feet of fleece, taffeta, silk, or silnylon for vapor bags
2 zippers or Velcro, at least 42 inches long for each side
13 feet, 1/8-1/4 inch diameter cordage, cut into a 6 foot length, and a 7 foot length
4 cord locks

   Fold fabric end to end, 72 inches from one end, salvages touching, so that it measures 60 wide. The back of the bag will measure 90 inches long. This will form the hood.
   Round corners at foot area if desired, and at top of hood. Right sides together, stitch up the sides to the bottom of your closure, using a 3/4-inch seam allowance. Always backstitch at beginning and ending of seams to lock stitches. Turn bag right side out.
   Form front draw cord casing by folding an inch of fabric to the inside and stitching close to the edge, about 3/4 inch from the fold.
   Thread cord through, end to end, and anchor midway by stitching crosswise over the middle of the cord. This prevents the cord from being inadvertently pulled all the way through by your partner. Add cord locks to each end of cord, tie knot and heat seal cord ends.
   Make the hood casing by folding the top and side edges of the hood area to the inside. Thread cord, secure in middle with stitching. Add cord locks to each end.

If you chose Velcro:
   Cut two loop and two hook sides of Velcro, each 42 inches long. Fold over 3/4-inch fabric to outside of bottom side of bag. Lay loop-side of Velcro over this. Stitch close to all sides of Velcro. Fold 3/4 inch of fabric to the inside on top side of bag, and apply the hook side of Velcro. Matching the first inch of Velcro at bottom of closure, reinforce by sewing an X over the end.

If you chose a zipper:
Beginning just at the bottom of the draw cord casing, fold over 3/4

inch of fabric to inside of bag. Lay zipper teeth facing up; stitch down one side, and up the other, as you would for any zipper application. Have the fabric overlap the zipper teeth. Reinforce zipper by backstitching over beginning, bottom, and ends of zipper

Headgear and Mittens

You will need:
Fleece:
...1/3 yard for Ski Band
...1/2 yard for Neck Gaiter
...1/2 yard for Watch Cap
...1/2 yard for Mittens

These measurements for yardage are linear. Fleece is sold 60 inches wide, so if you are making two or more things, you may still only need 1/2 yard, because there will be remnants left from one project for another. For instance, the watch cap and mittens would fit side by side on 1/2 yard of 60" wide fleece. It is necessary to have the stretch in the right direction, that's why the linear measurements are important. Be sure, when you lay out your fabric, to check the direction of the stretch. This is important to insure the garment "gives" in the correct direction. Cut with a sharp scissors. Sometimes the fuzz will build up in the bobbin case of your sewing machine. Clean this with a small, dry paintbrush after sewing to prevent tension problems later. Use 100% polyester thread and a size 14-ball point sewing machine needle. Stitches are 10 per inch, seam allowances 1/2 inch. Always backstitch beginning and ending of seams to secure.

Ski Band

Cut a rectangle 9 inches wide by 14 inches long. The length should be stretchable. With right sides together, sew long side. Turn right side out. You should have a long tube. Tuck under 3/4 inch of fleece (to the inside) on one end of tube. Slide other, unfinished end into this and pin. Hand or machine stitch these ends together.

Neck Gaiter

Cut a rectangle 18 inches long by 28 inches wide. The stretch should be along the width. Fold rectangle in half, so that it measures 18 inches long by 14 inches wide. With right sides together, sew along side edge, forming tube. Turn right side out. Hem bottom and top by folding to inside 1/2 inch of fabric and stitching.

Watch Cap

Using a favorite cap as a pattern, trace around it on a piece of plastic or newsprint. Cut out this pattern, leaving one extra inch all along for seam allowance. If you want a cuff, add an additional 7 inches on the length. This will increase the weight by about two ounces. The cap must have the stretch on the width.

Lay out fabric, place pattern piece on top. Cut two. With right sides together, stitch all curved sides together leaving the end open. Leaving it inside out, fold fleece up 1/2 inch for a basic hem, or 5 inches for a cuff. Stitch close to raw edge. Turn right side out. The cap may be folded up to form a cuff, or pulled all the way down.

Mittens

To make pattern, lay your hand on a piece of plastic sheeting or newsprint. Trace around it, or copy the pattern as you did for the watch cap. If you want a longer cuff, add the additional length to your pattern. Add an additional inch for seam allowances. Lay the pattern on fleece, with the stretch going the width of your hand. Cut two mittens out, two for each hand, providing a total of 4 pieces. To be sure you have a left and right, lay them side-by-side, thumbs facing each other. Unless the fabric is different on one side, this won't matter.

Stitch all curved edges, leaving wrist edge open. Hem wrist-edge by folding under 1/2 inch and stitching close to raw edge. Snip curves between thumb and index finger, and at top of thumb. Turn right side out.

If you plan to sew them onto a fleece pullover or jacket, do not hem first. Put on the jacket, then the mittens. Pull the sleeves down and bend your elbow. This will insure that you have enough movement. Mark the top of the mitten where it overlaps the jacket. That will be the stitching line. Leave the underside of the mitten unattached, with a longer cuff, which can be tucked in. Sew in the top of the mitten; trim away unnecessary fabric, leaving the unattached part longer. Hem the raw edges.

Flat Tarps

Directions are written for using **1.3-ounce silicone impregnated rip-stop nylon**, which generally is sold in 65-inch widths. You will need 2 inches extra for hem allowances on each side, meaning the raw piece will be 4 inches longer, and 4 inches wider than the finished product. Center seams are based on a one-inch seam allowance, sufficient for double rolling and stitching to finish seams.

You can use **web strapping or gross grain ribbon** for the staking loops, or make fabric strips from silnylon, as described previously. Cut into lengths as needed. I use 7-inch lengths for my center seam double loops, 6-inch lengths for the corners, and 5-inch lengths for perimeter hems.

If you want a **5 foot wide tarp**, cut the length desired with an additional 4 inches for hem allowances.

If you want a **10 foot wide tarp**, cut two of the lengths desired with an additional 4 inches on each piece for seam allowances.

If you want a tarp width between those two measurements, you will need to trim the fabric, and heat seal the entire edge. For an **8 foot wide tarp**, cut two lengths, each 51 inches wide. This gives you one inch for the center seam, and 2 inches for hemming the perimeter. If you want a **9-foot wide tarp**, cut the widths 57 inches for the same reasons.

If you have a center seam:
Start by preparing the center loops that you plan to add as you sew the center seam. Mark the placements for the loops with chalk. Sew both lengths together, inserting double folded loops at placement markings. Back stitch while adding the loops. One loop should be on the underside, and one loop formed on the top side, sticking out of the seam allowance. Double stitch this center seam by folding over within the seam allowance, and stitching close to the first row.

Next, cut 4 lengths of staking loop fabric, 6-inches each for the corners. Cut the other 5-inch staking loops. Place them in different piles. Mark within the seam allowance where you will insert the loops as you hem your tarp. Heat-seal any cut edges before you begin hemming.

Fold over the perimeter edge twice, a double roll, and stitch close to the inner edge. Fold prepared fabric strips in half to form staking loops, and insert them into the hem at markings. Backstitch the loop, then fold the loop towards the outside and stitch over again. Continue around perimeter in this manner. When you get to the corner, you will want to place the loop at an angle, so that when it is finished, the loop can be used from either direction. Sew a second roll of stitching close to the edge, including loops in this process. Reinforce corner loops with an x pattern. If you have a center seam, seam seal it, and allow to dry 24 hours before stuffing into stuff sack.

My Journey to Freedom and Ultralight Backpacking

My Nine Ounce Appalachian Trail Silpack

This is by far the most difficult pattern. Read all the steps through before proceeding. If you have a daypack, book bag backpack, or internal frame pack, set it out for referencing.

This pack was made totally out of silnylon, closed cell padding, plastic buckles and web strapping for the shoulder straps, reinforcements and hip belt. Later, I sewed a mesh ditty bag onto the front. My design is based on the idea of one large stuff sack set within another. The bottoms of those sacks are sewn together.

Outside gear pockets were then formed by stitching 4 vertical side seams, one on each side, and one in the center of the front and the back. A cover flap with Velcro closures can be added for each pocket if wanted. All reinforcement stitching was done in triangular and x-patterns, which does not rip out like a straight pattern will. A one-inch seam allowance was used for extra strength. Every seam was seam sealed with 100% silicone, as described above for tarps and shelters.

Silnylon fabric loops were sewn into the bottom seam, in order to cinch a stuff sack or closed cell sleeping pad underneath. All my AT gear for cold weather fit inside the pack and in the pockets. The extension collar/cover flap had a pocket for those really important things like toilet paper and data sheets. A hip belt was sewn-in with webbing reinforcement. The belt measured 3 inches wide and ½ inch thick. A tiny pocket was added to the hip belt to carry my 1-ounce bottle of chlorine for water treatment.

Shoulder straps were made from closed cell padding covered by silnylon. Mine were 3 inches wide, and ½ inch thick. Initially appearing too wide, these straps proved to be quite comfortable because they distributed the weight so well.

My two 24-ounce water bottles were carried in silnylon pouches threaded onto the front straps. A shock-cord band held the neck of each bottle snug against the strap. Water carried in this way serves as a counterbalance for pack weight, and provides quick, easy access. Also, I was always aware of how much water I had, and could refill and treat water trailside without taking my pack off.

Please keep in mind that I am five foot 2 inches. If you are much taller than that, adjusting the length on pack and shoulder straps may be necessary.

Applying the Techniques

Supplies to make this Silpack:

2 1/2 yards silnylon
3 yards of 1" wide web strapping
2 yards of ½ inch wide Velcro, if wanted for pocket closures
Mesh ditty bags for outer pocket, if wanted
Closed cell pad
Draw cord for pack
3 Cord locks
2 ultralight plastic clips
Hip belt buckle
Shoulder strap buckles
Seam sealer

To make this pack, begin by sewing two large stuff sacks, one shorter than the other. The shorter one will serve as the outer layer, and form outside pockets. When one is placed within the other, the bottom will have a double thickness. Use one-inch seam allowances, heat seal, double roll and stitch every seam

My 2,288 cubic inch capacity backpack is made with a rectangle of silnylon, measuring 30 inches long by 40 inches wide. Cut a generous collar for the large stuff sack. The second, shorter stuff sack was made from a rectangle 22 inches tall by 45 inches wide. As you can see, the outer one will be wider, and will give the pockets some slack, providing additional space. Sew both stuff sacks as described in the directions above, omitting the collar on the shorter one, but still hemming the top of it. On the shorter one, add bottom loops for gear if desired. When both the stuff sacks are made, turn right-side out. Insert the longer one into the shorter one. Match the bottom seams and sew the bottoms together.

You can thread some ¼-inch wide elastic though the casing of the outer sack, and draw it tight to keep gear from falling out. As you sew this pack, any seam can have a loop and an ultralight plastic clip inserted. It is easier to do it now, and reinforce the loop, than to add a loop later. At this time, you can sew in the two clips for securing the top pack lid in place. Place them near the top of each of the front gear pockets. Each loop of silnylon will add about one gram additional weight.

Now, pin the side seams, the center and back seams, marking a straight line with chalk where you will sew. Then stitch these lines vertically to form gear pockets. Add Velcro closures to the pockets, if wanted.

The shoulder straps are made of two rectangular silnylon pieces, each measuring 8 inches wide by 18 inches long. Fold the pieces in half, and sew the long seam. Double stitch to reinforce. Insert an 8-inch length of web strap up into the inside of one end of this tube, so you cannot see the strap. Stitch through the web strap as you sew the bottom of the silnylon tube closed. That will be the bottom of your padded shoulder strap. Turn this tube right side out. Your web strap will be hanging down from the end of the tube. Reinforce from the outside with an x stitch pattern. Sew the plastic buckle on the end of this web strap for the bottom section of the shoulder straps to thread through later.

Now, cut two pieces of closed cell pad 3 inches wide by 16 inches long. Insert into the tubes. Stitch tubes shut at the top to hold the padding in place.

Measure down about 7 inches from the top of the pack and sew the straps on the back. Place them about two inches apart. Shoulder straps should be lying flat, going downwards, right sides facing up.

Make the lid for the pack by cutting a rectangle 17 inches wide by 38 inches long. You will use this extra length to form a front lid pocket and corresponding flap.

To form a pocket the width of the lid, hem one 17-inch end of the rectangle. Then, fold the hemmed end up 10 inches, and stitch the sides together. Just above the pocket opening, fold down 2 inches of fabric over the pocket opening, the entire width of the lid to form a flap. Pin in place. This flap protects the contents of the pocket.

Sew down part of the top edge of the flap, stitching through the pocket top at the same time. Sew from each side towards the center about 5 inches. Then add a Velcro closure to the remaining pocket opening.

Along each long edge of the lid, make a draw cord casing, by double rolling the fabric and stitching close to the inner edge. This casing will run the entire length of the lid, including the sides of the pocket you just made.

Thread cord through so that the lid can be tightened, and prevent rain from getting in while you are hiking. Stitch down cord at the end to be attached to the pack. Put cord locks and clips on the opposite ends of the cords, which were threaded out at the bottom corners of the pocket. These cord locks will allow you to cinch up the lid, and secure with the clips that were added previously, so that it will stay that way while you are hiking.

Sew the lid onto the pack ½ inch below the seam that attaches the shoulder straps to the pack. You will have the top, right side of the lid facing the outside of the pack and lying over the shoulder straps. The pocket will be downwards, touching the shoulder straps, and not be visible. As you stitch the lid on, you will be sewing through the shoulder straps also, serving to reinforce them.

Next, fold the lid up over the top of the pack. Pin a 13-inch piece of web strap over the lid seam, beginning where the shoulder straps start. You will have excess strap, which will serve as a lift loop right at the center. This lift loop really comes in handy when you need to grab your pack, or hang it on a hook. The easiest way to center this web is to begin at the farthest side of one shoulder strap, and stitch toward the middle. When you get to the middle, reinforce with an x stitch pattern, then sew back to where you started and reinforce with another x pattern. Then stop, turn the pack around to the other shoulder strap and sew the web strap on there, working your way to the middle. You should end up with a loop right in the center.

To make your hip belt, cut a rectangle of silnylon measuring about 8 inches wide and as long as your waist. You will carry this pack lower, but you want to have some guideline. Once the seams are taken in, and it is attached, the padding will be shorter than your waist. This is important because on a long hike, your waist and hips will shrink, and if the padding is too long, you won't be able to tighten your belt enough.

Cut two web straps, one about 6 inches, the other about 15 inches. These will be inserted on each end of your belt. Fold the silnylon in half lengthwise, stitch the long seam, inserting one end of the shorter web strap as you did previously for the shoulder straps. Turn right side out.

Cut closed cell pad 3 inches wide by the length of your tube. Cut this into three sections, one for the back, about 14-16 inches long, and two for each side, about 5 inches each. Insert into tube, one side first. Stitch fabric together to hold in place. Do not include the pad in this seam. Insert the back pad section. Stitch fabric together to hold this in place. Then add the last piece of padding, fold fabric to the inside, and stitch this closed while also inserting the web strap for your other side of the belt.

Put the pack on, and mark where the hip belt is to be sewn on, so that it will ride on your hips, just below your belly button. There will be some adjustment with the shoulder straps, so it is just necessary to be close. It should be near the bottom of the pack itself.

Sew belt onto pack at the same places you stitched the fabric together to hold the padding in the hip belt tube.

The bottom sections of your shoulder straps will be two short pieces of web strap about 15 inches long. They will thread through the two plastic non-slip buckles that were sewn onto the shoulder straps previously, and at the same time serve to reinforce the hip belt.

To do this, lay the bottom section of shoulder strap over the vertical seam that attached the hip belt to the pack. The bottom end of each strap will be at a bottom edge of a vertical seam of the hip belt. Sew the straps over the vertical seams. Sew close to the edges, reinforcing with x stitching patterns.

Thread a ¼ inch diameter cord for the draw cord on your pack. When the pack is full, you need a cord thick enough for the cord lock to grasp securely. Add the belt buckle.

Your pack can have a mesh ditty bag sewn onto the front, centering it over the other silnylon gear pockets. This will add about one ounce of weight to your pack.

Seam seal every seam with 100% silicone. Apply to one area at a time, and allow each to dry between steps.

Congratulations! You are now a bona fide gram weenie.

The Ultralight Resupply

Many long distance hikers at some point will mail a drop box to themselves. This box may be sent parcel post or priority, at least 2 weeks in advance of the projected arrival time. A common practice is to obtain a medium size box, and start adding things to it. Food, vitamins, maps, insect repellent, shampoo, toilet paper, shoelaces, new socks, new zip lock bags, reading material, tape, hexamine tablets (fuel source), toothpaste, laundry powder, and batteries are typical supplies. Sometimes a few extra clothes are included if weather or terrain is changing.

Hiker boxes are filled with the extras mailed in this way. I have learned to weigh the box at home before sealing it up. If the box weighs more than 10-12 pounds, I know I will not carry its contents out of my resupply town. The best time to discard the extra weight is at home. Are my non-food items in the smallest plastic containers possible? Snack size zip lock bags are perfect for vitamins and hexamine fuel tablets. An .85-ounce tube of toothpaste will last several weeks. Only ¼ cup of dry laundry detergent is needed for that town's laundry. An ounce of shampoo is all that can be used in town. Shampoo isn't used in the backcountry, and so it will not be hauled out of town. If I am picking up new socks, I discard the old ones.

Some folks will carry extra weight for many miles to save money in the next town. Would you carry one pound of weight for 10 cents per mile? Using that rate for a reference, it would mean being paid, or saving $10 to carry one pound for a hundred miles. Take a one-pound can in your hand, and wonder if you would carry that for 100 miles, if someone gave you $10. Usually, when you get to town, you find you have carried several pounds of extra fuel, shampoo, food or paper, and saved just a few dollars. When the hills are really steep, the weight adds up to misery, and the money seems inconsequential.

When packing food for a drop box, divide the food into each day's allotment, and keep it as close to your minimal comfort level as possible. If packing several boxes at once, variety of food will be important. Weigh those bags of Gorp, and vary the recipes. Seriously. I like to put each day's worth in a zip lock bag, keeping it to 10 ounces. If this bag of Gorp is to be used as breakfast as well (high mileage or cold days) my Gorp for the day may weigh up to 14 ounces. In camp that evening, I will have a cup of soup with crackers, then my supper of ramen, rice or oatmeal. Any Gorp left from that day's allotment would be dessert. I drink instant coffee before and after supper, but will seldom carry hot cocoa, pudding mixes or Jell-O because its weight is mostly sugar. As a small woman, I need less food than a larger male would need. Twice this amount would probably be adequate for a man.

Try to leave town with your stomach full of good, healthy, high protein food. It's okay to pull into the next town hungry. Keep in mind, though, that sufficient fat and calories are needed on trail to keep energy levels up. In cold weather more calories are needed, especially before bedtime in order to sleep warm. It isn't bad to have a lot of food weight, because you can always just stop and eat it. Picking up your pack will get easier each morning. It's those first days that are rough. Some hikers will carry an extra day of food in case of emergency. Some hikers pack scantily, especially in hot months when appetites lessen, making big days easier. Food weight is definitely a variable that needs much practice and individual consideration.

Using a Convenience Store/Grocery Store

Using the same principles discussed above, a resupply is almost always possible at a food mart, convenience store, and certainly at any large grocery store. If the store has any deli food available, be sure to enjoy a meal there as well.

An easy fuel source for the soda can stove is 70% rubbing alcohol. There will be some water when the flame goes out, which is drained by turning the stove upside down. Rubbing alcohol (which can be used for personal hygiene as well), requires one ounce to cook most simple meals, and can be found nearly everywhere. It does burn a bit sooty, and if it gets cold it should be warmed in its bottle next to your body. ISO-Heet, a gas line additive, can be found at almost any convenience store and it makes great soda-can stove fuel. Be ready to dump or stash in a hiker box any extra fuel you don't need. Eight ounces should last 8 meals; many times it is sold in 16-ounce containers.

When buying food for a resupply, shop with a hand basket instead of pushing a cart. This way, you get a feel for how much weight you have picked up. Some weight will be lost in repackaging, but not enough to consider at this point. I keep a mental estimate of weight, knowing that 4 bags of Gorp ingredients, each weighing 12-14 ounces each, will give me 48-56 ounces, or enough for about 5 days.

If the store is very small with limited food, walk down the aisles to get an overall picture of what is available. At this point, variety is not that important, but quantity and calories are. Almost any gas station, convenience store, or small town shop will have candy, candy bars and chips. These can be combined into Gorp mixes, or repackaged separately. Look for candy bars that have nuts in them. This will see you through to supper. Some small stores sell boxes of cold breakfast cereal, which make fine finger food. Check for bread, hamburger or hot dog buns or bakery items. If there is something to go on that bread, great! Peanut butter, cheese, cream cheese, beef sticks or jerky on the side will all make a fine supper. Something hot to drink is really nice. Look for instant soups, coffee, or tea. It's not important to get all the four food groups now. All you are after is enough reasonably tasty food to see you through to the next resupply. If you see something that takes longer to cook, like white rice or pasta, keep any extra fuel and spend a little more time cooking. Buy between one and two pounds of food for each day, regardless of the vitamin content. This junk food will provide enough energy until your next

Applying the Techniques

resupply, and will save hitch hiking into the next town, which is sometimes an impossible or dangerous endeavor. I never go shopping when I'm hungry unless I plan to buy my town lunch at the store. If one has had a bad or scanty resupply in the last section, the normal reaction is to overcompensate in the next town. To avoid overbuying, sit down to a satisfying meal first. At the very least, buy a quart of ice cream, drink some chocolate milk, or eat a large deli sandwich. Taco chips and soda also take the edge off hunger before resupplying.

Rainmaker taught me to break down the extra packaging, discarding jars, plastics and cardboards. Using the best zip lock bags possible, repackage oatmeal, pasta, cookies, cereal, coffee, and chips. This definitely saves on the amount of trash that must be carried later. Taco chips, pretzels, Fritos, cookies, and candy all come in their own plastic bags, which can rip down the side later on and spill. It is much easier to put them in zip lock bags while you're in town.

Gear list/ Winter and Summer Checklist
The following list is intended to be very complete. Its main purpose is to help you not to forget anything. For complete discussion on each category, see Chapter Seven.

The Big Three, and Their Components
- Sleeping Bag with stuff sack
- Sleeping Pad
- Shelter with stakes, and guy lines, in stuff sack
- Ground cloth, if desired
- Pack, pack liner or garbage bag liner
- Pack cover

Clothing
- Rain jacket, rain pants
- Warm layer (fleece top, pants, hat, gloves, socks)
- Mid weight layer (silk or polyester blend top, mid weight bottom, socks)
- Hiking layer (shorts, top, socks, hat)
- Sandals
- Stuff sack for clothing
- Sleep wear
- Town wear (optional)

Hygiene/ Medical/Murphy
- ❑ Tooth brush, tooth paste, dental floss
- ❑ Comb
- ❑ Ultralight mirror
- ❑ Tweezers for tick and splinter removal
- ❑ Disposable razor
- ❑ Rubbing alcohol, cotton balls
- ❑ Toilet paper
- ❑ Trowel
- ❑ Hand sanitizer, or use rubbing alcohol
- ❑ Body lotion or Vaseline, traveler's size
- ❑ Camp towel/ bandana
- ❑ Pain reliever
- ❑ Imodium
- ❑ Multi-Vitamins
- ❑ Sun block
- ❑ Insect repellent
- ❑ Electrical or duct tape
- ❑ Needle and thread
- ❑ Safety pins
- ❑ Free flowing super glue
- ❑ Any prescriptions you are taking
- ❑ Eye glasses, sun glasses
- ❑ Two or three ditty bags for all this

Cook System
- ❑ Stove
- ❑ Fuel
- ❑ Matches, lighter
- ❑ Windscreen, pot support, pot lifter
- ❑ Cooking pot
- ❑ Cup, spoon
- ❑ Pot scrubber, if wanted
- ❑ Plastic bags for repackaging food
- ❑ Zip lock bag for trash
- ❑ Ditty bag for pot and stove
- ❑ Stuff sack for food

Water Treatment and Capacity
- ❑ Chemical treatment (always bring)
- ❑ Filter, if wanted
- ❑ Water bottles
- ❑ Water bag/Platypus

Applying the Techniques

- ❑ Water bottle carriers, or use pockets on pack

Other Items and Tools
- ❑ Paper and Pencil/Pen
- ❑ Driver's license, and /or photo ID
- ❑ Non-debit credit card
- ❑ Emergency telephone numbers, insurance card
- ❑ Flashlight/ LED /Photon light
- ❑ Knife
- ❑ GI-style can opener
- ❑ Watch
- ❑ Trail guide, maps, data sheet
- ❑ Compass, if needed or wanted
- ❑ Cash
- ❑ Ditty bag as wallet
- ❑ Quality zip lock bags for all paper products
- ❑ Rope for hanging shelters, guy lines, or food bags

Luxury Items
- ❑ Cell phone
- ❑ Radio, batteries
- ❑ Pocket E-mail
- ❑ Camera (digital, disposable or regular)
- ❑ CD player, discs
- ❑ Quality zip lock bag and ditty bag for any luxury item
- ❑ Knee braces, if needed or wanted
- ❑ Reading material, books
- ❑ Mace/ bear spray
- ❑ Bear canister

My Gear List for January Bartram Trail Hike 2003

The Big Three, and their Components
- ❑ Sleeping Bag, Hydrogen Marmot 800 fill, rated at 30 degrees, with stuff sack: 24 ounces
- ❑ Fleece Bag liner: 8 ounces
- ❑ Sleeping Pad, closed cell, 48 inches long by 19 inches wide, corners trimmed: 8 ounces
- ❑ Reflective ground sheet, for inside tent: 4 ounces
- ❑ Shelter, my Tacoma Solo, with 6-skewer type stakes, and guy lines, in stuff sack: 18 ounces
- ❑ Pack and garbage bag liner: 9 ounces

- Pack cover, same as used on the AT thru-hike: 1.5 ounces

Clothing
- Silnylon rain jacket, rain pants: 6 ounces
- Warm layer (fleece jacket with hood and mittens attached, socks) 15 ounces
- Mid weight layer (thermal top, nylon tights): 9 ounces
- Hiking layer (polyester pants: 13 ounces, long sleeve shirt: 6 ounces; sports top: 3 ounces; socks: 3 ounces; gloves: 2 ounce): 27 ounces total
- Stuff sack for clothing: 1 ounce
- Sleep wear (balaclava 1 ounce, fleece tights 7.5 ounces, wool socks 4 ounces, polyester top 5.5 ounces)

Hygiene/ Medical/Murphy
- Toothbrush, toothpaste, dental floss:
- Comb, ultralight mirror
- Rubbing alcohol, cotton balls
- Toilet paper, trowel, bandana
- Vaseline, traveler's size
- Pain reliever, Imodium
- Electrical tape, wound around water bottles
- Needle
- Sunglasses
- One ditty bag for all this: 8 ounces total

Cook System
- Soda can stove, windscreen, pot support: 1 ounce
- Fuel, 4 ounces alcohol, and 9 hexamine tablets
- Stick matches, lighter: 20 grams
- Minimalist pot, cup, spoon 1.5 ounces
- Zip-loc bag for trash: 2 grams
- Stuff sack for pot and stove: 12 grams
- Stuff sack for food: 14 grams

Water Treatment and Capacity
- Chlorine chemical treatment: 14 grams
- Water bottles: 2.2 ounces
- Platypus: 1 ounce
- 2-water bottle carriers: 1 ounce

Other Items and Tools
- Paper and Pencil/Pen: 1 ounce
- Driver's license, non-debit credit card, emergency telephone numbers: 14 grams

- ❑ LED Photon lights: 12 grams
- ❑ Box cutter-knife: 5 grams
- ❑ GI-style can opener, watch: 20 grams
- ❑ Trail guide, maps: 2.7 ounces
- ❑ Cash: 6 grams
- ❑ Ditty bag as wallet: 6 grams
- ❑ Zip-loc bag for papers: 4 grams

Luxury Items
- ❑ Cell Phone, in zip-loc bag: 6 ounces

Ultralighting in Winter

My base weight here was 11.3 ounces. In the Big Three category I decided not to bring a ground cloth because my tent already had a good, leak-proof floor. However, with temperatures predicted to be in the low teens, I decided to include a fleece liner and reflective ground sheet, adding 12 ounces for both.

I had a good hood on my fleece jacket, and a hood on the silnylon rain jacket. The wind was gusting between 10-20 mph, so the silnylon jacket hood was very useful. I didn't bother to bring any sandals because it would be too cold to use them, and no town stops were planned. My clothing included an extra long-sleeve shirt, and long hiking pants instead of shorts.

In the hygiene/medical category, I didn't need insect repellent or tweezers. I brought a bandana and a camp towel to help insulate my food when cooked, dry condensation in my tent, and use for stuffing in my pillow. I didn't use any sun block, but the sunglasses came in handy with bright winter glare. I brought dental floss, which can double as thread for repairs. The trail is only 117 miles, so I didn't need a razor, extra lotion or vitamins.

I carried my mini pot, because of the additional clothing weight. In retrospect, I think the larger pot would have been worth the extra 5 ounces. I never carry a pot lifter, but instead use fleece mittens as potholders. I don't bring a pot scrubber and instead use water and a finger to clean my pot. If you don't burn food, and wash the pot immediately, this is usually adequate. A pot scrubber can harbor bacteria and food smells. The food smells can attract animals.

I have never carried or used a water filter, but rely on chemical treatment. For winter backpacking I bring a Platypus instead of a water bag because frozen water can be carried in a Platypus, but not in a water bag. I put water in my pot and cup at night. Before bed, I dumped all the water from my water bottles and Platypus. I knew it would all be frozen in the morning.

The liquid fuel was difficult to light in the evening, as the temperature dipped below freezing. The next morning, a companion reported that the temperature had dropped to 12 degrees. I used 4 hexamine tablets to thaw my water on the soda can stove. When water came to a boil, I poured some over the ice in the cup, thawing it this way. As planned, all my water was used at breakfast, and I didn't carry any worthless ice. Within half a mile after leaving camp I came to good water, and filled a bottle for the morning's hiking. Because of the possibility of leaks, I never take the chance of sleeping with my water to prevent it from freezing. A person's perception of thirst is less in cold weather. However, it is very important to be well hydrated in winter.

When winter hiking, bring plenty of high calorie food, and eat well before going to bed. Eating salty peanuts or beef jerky can cause incredible thirst, so when it's this cold that can cause some problems. During the night it will be hard to drink a lot as your water becomes frozen, and if you do drink a lot it's hard to get up to pee. It's a good idea to plan on having a midnight snack, which will help you to stay warm. Do not eat or drink anything that could upset your stomach, and do not eat a lot of fiber, or quantities of chocolate, which can act as a laxative. It's very hard to dig a cat hole in frozen ground in the middle of the night.

There is a lot of darkness in the winter. Unless you night hike, plan on spending nearly 14 hours inside your tent in your sleeping bag and out of the wind, where body heat can be trapped. Wear all your clothing, if necessary. Use your pack under your feet for insulation. The coldest hours are just before dawn.

In the morning, any condensation in your shelter may be frozen. It's hard to get up in such cold conditions, but once you get moving, the blood will circulate and you will warm up. So, pack up quickly, but carefully, so you do not loose any gear. Get out of your tent, turn it inside out, and shake out the frost. Place the tent in its stuff sack while wearing a spare pair of gloves. They will get wet and cold and you will want to replace them with dry gloves or mittens. Winter backpacking requires an oversized stuff sack for your shelter. You want to quickly stuff this frozen mass, and get hiking. Stakes may be frozen to the ground, so use a stake to remove each one by lifting upwards through the hooked end. Do not bring gutter nails on winter backpacking trips because they can be very hard to get out of frozen ground, having little or nothing to grasp. We ultralighters can backpack all year long with proper gear and preparation. The biggest concern is staying warm. Generally while hiking this is not a problem. In camp, use all you have, and stay out of the wind. Don't have your water bottles full if you expect them to freeze. They are of no value then. A water system that has a thin hose, or inline filter, can become frozen, even if the water in the sack doesn't freeze. The water is inaccessible then, yet must be carried. There is a lot of darkness, so be prepared with enough lighting, even if it means bringing a small tea candle. And, one last tip, eat well, and eat often. Some of the best views can be enjoyed in the winter, and the trails are less crowded. When cabin fever is getting to you, an overnight trip, even in the dead of winter, can do a person good.

The Future

I think we will see a counter movement to ultralight backpacking, a backlash to the fascination of ultralight packs. It is human nature. Some will purposely carry heavy loads just to prove they are stronger, unconcerned with pack weight, and defiantly independent of all ultralight innovations. There will always be those who question the motives of ultralighters, suspicious of ulterior motives, wondering how we can see or enjoy anything while hiking long days and doing big miles. My reply is that our enjoyment comes with walking in the woods, without feeling like a pack mule. Feeling light and unburdened, we appreciate our adventure, having come primarily to hike and not to camp.

The ultralight movement will continue to grow. New fabrics, plastics, and metals will make the low weights of our present gear seem heavy. Paging through The Complete Walker, written by Colin Fletcher in 1971, 33 years ago, one can see remarkable differences just in cooking systems. He lists his two nesting cook pots at 1 pound, 4 ounces, and the spoon at 2 ounces. His Svea 123 stove weighed 1 pound, 2 ounces, with a windscreen listed as 3 ounces. Today we have whole cook systems that weigh less than 8 ounces.

The "gram weenie" extremism should continue; I hope to promote it myself. I realize it is, and should only be, for experienced backpackers. But every sport has its extremists. Extremism got us to the moon, to Mt. Everest, and to the North Pole. Someone had to believe it could be done, and then went out to prove it.

And then, thankfully the moderating effects of mainstream America will keep us all reasonable. Given the best information, these mainstream backpackers will choose what works for them. And, with more people enjoying the trails, new ones will be built and promoted and maintained. Our national lands, forests, and waterways will be protected from exploitation so that future generations can enjoy their majesty. That's my hope, anyway.

As long as I can walk, I plan to hike America's trails. In the next couple of years, I hope to gain the Triple Crown, the backpacking "world title" for completion of the Pacific Crest Trail, Appalachian Trail, and Continental Divide Trail. I expect to continue designing backpacking gear, using it on long hikes as well as overnight adventures. This is presently a field dominated by men, so it represents pressing limits on my part, and breaking down barriers. There is a real need for custom tailored gear, and it is fascinating to work with individuals who want to achieve an ultralight system that is uniquely theirs.

Many times I am embarrassed by my lack of cultural awareness resulting from what I call "The Lost 25 Years". I am catching up, though, on films, literature, music and art that were created while I was "gone". It's pretty exciting. However, Rainmaker often has to remind me that some of graphic special effects in the movies are only simulation, and no matter how vivid it appears, it's not real. That's a relief!

Visit me on the web at
http://www.trailquest.net
Or e-mail me at brawny03@yahoo.com

Ordering Information:

To get additional, autographed copies of this book, return this order form and your check or money order to:
Carol Wellman
PO Box 198
Clayton, GA 30525

Please send _____ copies of "My Journey To Freedom and Ultralight Backpacking" at $14.95 per copy and $2 for shipping. Enclosed is my check or money order for $_____

Mail Books To:
Name_____
Address_____
City_____
State_____Zip_____
E-Mail_____(optional)